Strategic Management
of
Professional Service Firms

Strategic Management
of
Professional Service Firms

Bente R. Løwendahl

Copenhagen Business School Press

Strategic Management of Professional Service Firms

© *Copenhagen Business School Press, 2005*
Illustration: Sven Sønsteby
Cover designed by Morten Højmark
Cover illustration: Scanpix, Copenhagen
Set in Plantin by ABK-SATS ApS, Denmark
Printed in Denmark 2005 by Narayana Press
3. edition, 1. impression

ISBN 87-630-0127-6

Distribution

Scandinavia:
DJØF/DBK, Mimersvej 4
DK-4600 Køge, Denmark,
phone: +45 3269 7788, fax: +45 3269 7789

North America:
Copenhagen Business School Press
Books International Inc.
P.O. Box 605
Hendon, VA 20172-0605, USA
phone: +1 703 661 1500, fax: +1 703 661 1 1501

Rest of the World:
Marston Book Services, P.O. Box 269,
Abingdon, Oxfordshire, OX14 4YN, UK
phone: +44 (0) 1235 465500, fax: +44 (0) 1235 465555
E-mail Direct Customers: direct.order@marston.co.uk
E-mail Booksellers: trade.order@marston.co.uk

Contents

Preface to the third edition

It is now eight years since this book first appeared, and close to twenty years since I started my journey into understanding the dynamics of professional service firms. I have been very pleased to hear from practitioners and academics alike that the book is helpful, and that it makes sense in terms of offering some useful concepts and discussion points which actually do belong in partner meetings, board rooms, or academic conference discussions about what are the key challenges and opportunities for professional service firms. What has been even more rewarding, has been to see that positive feedback comes from not only all over the world (Australia, Belgium, Netherlands, Germany, Canada, USA, United Kingdom, Denmark and my own country Norway), but also from managers in a lot of different professional industries (consulting, auditing, law, engineering design, communications advisory firms, etc.).

Personally, I am convinced that we are moving from a largely industrial economy dominated by manufacturing firms and the managerial and economic logic of industry production, to an economy more and more dominated by knowledge intensive firms, driven by knowledge, innovation, ideas, rapid adaptations to new customer requirements, global competition in more and more areas, and so on. In this complex and fluid economic context, I think it is imperative that we turn our research and theory development to extreme knowledge based organizations (see e.g. Løwendahl & Revang, 1998; 2000; 2004). In my view, professional service firms offer excellent examples of such firms and the managerial challenges they highlight. Their impact on the economy is growing, they are trying to hire the best of the graduates within their areas of expertise, they pay higher salaries and demand more of their employees than most other organizations, they are frequently seen as role models for other firms, in particular when it comes to knowledge management, and some of them have even become a potential threat to the traditional institutions of knowledge creation and dissemination, such as the Universities. Hence, there is no reason to believe that their impact is going to decrease in the years to come; on the contrary.

I am currently involved in several research projects related to professional services, in personal interaction with companies as well as through doctoral students (currently two, one with a focus on competence development, the other with a focus on client relationships and how clients perceive the value creation of professional service firms). Since this is a topic I am very interested in and enthousiastic about, I very much appreciate feedback, questions, and comments from readers. Please do not hesitate to contact me on bente.lowendahl@bi.no, if you have any comments, questions or suggestions!

About the third edition of the book

The third edition is fundamentally the same as the two previous editions, but with substantial expansions on several subchapters, to make the book more up-to-date on current developments. The reference list has also been substantially updated and expanded. Please see the subsection below for an overview of the structure of the book and the different chapters.

Background about the original study

The original book was based on close to a decade's interest in the work of professionals. It started out as research for a Ph.D. dissertation when I was a student at the Wharton School of the University of Pennsylvania. Professor Peter Lorange, now at IMD, and I were discussing interesting research topics with some executives of his advisory board on multinational management. We then decided we wanted to look into strategies for "brain driven" firms; firms where value creation was based purely on people and their expertise as opposed to machines and other tangible resources. Two of these executives, Derish Wolff, president of Louis Berger International and Dennis Moran, President of the international division of Camp, Dresser & McKee (CDM), were particularly encouraging. They were both experienced senior managers from large and highly reputable engineering consulting firms, and yet they expressed frustration with the support they could get from management training or publications. They claimed that their firms, like other professional service firms, were to such an extent different from the traditional text book (read: manufacturing) firms that they needed new and different approaches to strategic management as well.

A research project was then designed (including my Ph.D. dissertation) in order to explore the main dimensions that made these firms so different and challenging to manage, as well as the key success factors for the successful strategic management of such firms. The dissertation research focussed on three industries: management consulting, engineering consulting, and insurance brokerage.

Since that period (late 1980s), the interest in professional services has increased substantially, and several books and articles have taken up the challenges of particular types of professional service firms. See Appendix 1 on current research in this area for some references to other publications. I have followed this development with great interest, conducted additional studies, given classes and seminars for top management of a number of professional service firms in Norway, and interviewed and discussed key issues with a large number of managers over the last years. Together, these insights have contributed to a process in which the results from my dissertation study have matured and broadened.

At this point, one conclusion seems clear: professional service firms are different to such an extent that a direct application of traditional strategic management assumptions and tools is at best misleading and at worst disasterous. Such concepts as economies of scale, profit maximization, incorporation and external ownership, human resource allocation, quality control procedures, and hierarchical authority may take on an entirely different meaning in professional service firms, and such fundamental strategic goals as market share, growth, and internationalization must be seen as possible strategic options rather than obvious virtues. Still, it is not true that the professional service firm has to be small and inefficient, and that ex ante strategies are impossible to develop. On the contrary, strategic management is crucial for the long term viability of the firm, even if the content and the emphasis may be different from that of the traditional manufacturing firm.

This book will spell out the critical success factors of professional service firms, with a particular emphasis on the, in many ways paradoxical, importance of strategic management. In fact, where the processes are not stable and driven by production machinery or established routines, the strategic choices seem to have more impact on the firm's viability, not less! Yet the average professional service firm manager has less interest, time, and incentives for managerial issues than managers in firms with more routine operations.

Structure of the book

In Chapter I, the fundamental issues of the role of professional services in society, the definition of what distinguishes professional services from other services, and the role of the professions are discussed. Emphasis here is on the practical implications of these issues, rather than the complex debate about how to define services and separate them from tangible goods. Then, in Chapter II, the challenges making professional service firms particularly interesting but also difficult to manage are discussed, as well as the reasons for these challenges. In Chapter III, the resulting managerial challenges are discussed in detail, with particular emphasis on the need to find talented managers with professional authority and respect, who are both willing to spend time and energy on internal matters of the firm, and able to maintain their professional prestige vis-a-vis internal as well as external peers.

Chapter IV introduces the resource based perspective on strategic management and spells out how this perspective may help in the dynamic management of professional service firms. The focus here is on how to direct the efforts of the professionals towards targetted areas both in terms of new clients and projects and in terms of competences added through recruiting and learning. In Chapter V, the strategic issues are further discussed, extending the resource based discussion to a discussion of why very different types of professional service firms coexist and remain profitable even within the same industries. Three different strategic modes are suggested, as well as the fundamental reasons why firms need to consciously maintain one of the modes in order to counter the severe tensions pulling them in opposite directions.

Chapter VI goes on to discuss implications for further development of professional service firms, including the pros and cons of growing large and going international. Chapter VII, which is a slightly abridged version of a chapter I published in Aharoni, Y. & Nachum, L. (Eds). 2000. The Globalization of services: Some Implications for Theory and Practice, published by Routledge, discusses opportunities as well as challenges related to internationalization or globalization of professional service firms. We thank the publishers for the right to republish this chapter here. In the final chapter, the conclusions and implications are summed up, once again highlighting the particular challenges of professional service firms and why a number of the traditional goals and measures of performance may not be applicable to all such firms. At the end of the book, there is also an appendix outlining some of the research I personally find particularly relevant to professional service firms, as well as a brief description of my own research background.

Primary focus

This book is written about professional service firms or, even more specifically, professional business service firms. The underlying research has focussed on key dimensions and processes of firms selling professional services to other firms or institutions and hence contributing to the quality of their clients' value creation processes. However, even though the professional-client interaction will be different for firms primarily delivering to individual buyers, the internal processes of the firms will be very much the same. Similarly, professional service organizations which are not organized as firms, such as hospitals and schools, will also have many of the same characteristics as the firms described here. Even a large number of public service offices such as embassies and tax authorities at least in part deliver professional services to firms as well as to individuals.

The book is primarily written for professionals with managerial responsibilities, whether they be partners in small partnerships or employed by large firms. For this reason, the number of academic references is kept to a minimum. With a professional audience in mind, references are still included, so that the original source of concepts and models will be possible to trace for those who are particularly interested, and each chapter ends with some suggested additional readings.

The book should also be of interest to graduate students and academics focussing on strategic or managerial issues relevant to knowledge intensive firms. Professional service firms are, in my opinion, the most extreme type of knowledge intensive firms, as they rely primarily, and in many cases exclusively, on professional expertise in their value creating activities. Hence, it should also be possible to extend these insights to firms with a combination of professional competence and more traditional production processes.

Acknowledgements

This book is the end result of years of curiosity as well as hard work aimed at understanding the inner workings of professional service firms. These are complex firms and sometimes very difficult to understand. Professionals, including academics, know well that time is their most precious resource. For that reason, I acknowledge first of all that this book would not have been possible without the extremely positive response from the professionals involved. Perhaps the fact that we share some of the same curiosity and desire to understand and explain complex phenomena contributed to their willingness to spend their scarce "non-billable" hours exploring these issues with me. At any rate, the support has been remarkable!

I would not have been able to gather an extensive insight without the contribution of each and every one of the professionals I have talked to over these many years. However, some of these professionals have showed an exceptional willingness to spend time and contribute personally to this process of knowledge generation, and they deserve special thanks: From my dissertation study: Partner[1] Stephen B. Oresman of The Canaan Group; President and CEO Richard M. Page and Vice President Frank J. Huffman of Sedgwick James Ltd; Chairman and CEO Robert C. Marini of Camp Dresser & McKee (CDM) Inc, Vice-Chairman (and previous President, Chairman and CEO) Joseph E. Heney of CDM Inc, and President W. Dennis Moran of CDM International; President and CEO Henry Michel of Parsons Brinckerhoff; President and CEO Derish Wolff of Louis Berger International; Managing Director Halvard Lesteberg and Marketing Director Morten Tarøy of Norconsult; Managing Director Reiar Ness of the IKO Group, Chairman Jørgen Grønneberg of Partners International, Managing Director Tore Gulli of IKO Strategy, Co-founder and previous senior partner Johan Sagen of the IKO Group, and previous Managing Director and CEO Per Hatling of The IKO Group; Senior Partner Heinrich Steffen of Experteam; Senior Partner Robert McLean of H. Whitehead and partners; and President and CEO Kjeld Rimberg of Asplan AS. Following the completion of my dissertation, a large number of professionals contributed to my understanding of these issues. In particular, President and CEO Per Chr. Gomnæs of Berdahl-Strømme AS; Vice President Asle Berger of Gemini consulting; President and CEO Bjørn Myklatun of Grøner AS and Director of Business Development Olav Holtestaul of Grøner AS; Partner Maja Arnestad of Pharos ANS; President Anne Grete Stykket of Alpha & Omega AS; Personnel Manager Ellen Gjerde of Selmer Advokatfirma DA; Margrethe Geelmuyden of Geelmuyden.Kise AS; senior manager Patrick Tepfers of several advertising companies (between jobs); and CEO/Country Manager Morten Thorkildsen of IBM Norway. In addition, I wish to thank all the professionals, students, and friends I have discussed these issues with.

Academically, I owe special thanks in particular to my advisor and mentor Professor (and now President of IMD) Peter Lorange. I would also like to thank Professor John Kimberly and Associate Professor Kenwyn K. Smith for their support as committee members, not to mention as teachers during my early years as a doctoral student. Associate Professor Harbir Singh and Professors Edward H. Bowman, William E. Evan and

[1] Titles as well as names of firms are cited as they were at the time of the interviews, despite the fact that many of these professionals have changed jobs and some of the firms have merged and changed names. The original firm name and titles have been kept in order to give an indication of their affiliation at the time of their inputs.

Howard V. Perlmutter – all of the University of Pennsylvania, and Professor Torger Reve of the Norwegian School of Economics and Business Administration also deserve special thanks for their support. For special support during my early years, I would also like to thank Professors Royston Greenwood, Yair Aharoni, Raffi Amit, J.-C. Spender, and Jay Barney for their support in multiple discussions and seminars. Later, I have also taken great pleasure in multiple discussions with academic colleagues such as (in alphabetical order) Mats Alvesson, John Brown, Laura Empson, Bob Hinings, Namrata Malhotra, Chris McKenna, Tim Morris, Andrew Pettigrew, and Jacky Swan. Finally, my good friends and colleagues professors Øystein Fjeldstad, Odd Nordhaug, and Øivind Revang (also in alphabetical order) have been wonderful peer professionals, contributing to both the learning and enjoyment of a professional experience. In addition, I would like to give special thanks to my doctoral students within this and related areas, Knut Haanæs, Ragnhild Kvålshaugen, Fred Strønen, Thorvald Hærem, Siw Fosstenløkken, and Tale Skjølsvik (in the sequence of year of graduation – or anticipated graduation). It has been said many times before, but it is amazing how much learning, fun, and motivation you get from discussions with bright, young students!

Financially, a number of institutions and grants have supported my research: the Norwegian School of Economics and Business Administration, the Wharton School of the University of Pennsylvania through the Dean's Fellowship for Doctoral Students, the ARCO Chemicals Company/the Huntsman Center for Global Competition and Leadership dissertation award, the Fishman-Davidson Center for the Study of the Service-Sector dissertation grant, and, after my employment in late fall 1991, the Norwegian School of Management. In addition, the William H. Wurster Center for Multinational Management Studies at the Wharton School provided the forum where the first professional service firm managers lit the spark for the study and gave me the first insights into the complexity of these industries and firms. In the more recent years, the Norwegian Research Council ("KUV-programme") provided a major grant for the study of competence development in professional service firms.

Finally, a number of people have helped me in the process of writing this book, and I owe Lauge Stetting, senior editor of Copenhagen Business School Press, particular thanks both for his encouragement and for his thoughtful advice on the text itself. Many thanks also to Stephanie Wold Hadler for helping me reduce the Scandinavian flavor of the original English text. I would also like to thank Associate Professor Heather Hazard of Copenhagen Business School for putting me in touch with Mr.

Stetting, and Professor Peter Lorange for both advice and encouragement. Special thanks also to those who have reviewed and commented on previous versions of the manuscript. And last, but certainly not least, thanks to Ola, my best support in every respect! Thanks to your patience, encouragement, and excellent dinners, the writing process was mostly fun!

I. Professionals and professional service firms

Introduction

In this first chapter, the fundamental issues of what professional service firms are and which role they play in society today will be discussed in detail. The emphasis here will be on a pragmatic and practical approach to what delivering professional services means in reality, and where the boundary between professional and non-professional services may be found. The complex and possibly futile debate of where to draw the boundaries between services and goods has been consciously omitted as, in my opinion, the primary challenges result from the delivery of services that are tailored to client needs, regardless of the tangibility of the actual delivery.

The first section of this chapter discusses the current role of professional services. The following section delves into the issue of what constitutes a professional service and ends with a pragmatic definition of professional services. Finally, the role of professions and their influence on the firms is discussed in the last section. The resulting managerial challenges will be discussed at length in Chapter III.

Why are professional service firms interesting?

It is now widely acknowledged that services account for a very large part of economic activity and that the service sector constantly increases its share of GDP, employment, and international trade. About ten years ago, services accounted for roughly two-thirds of GDP in developed countries and almost one-half of GDP in developing countries (Aharoni, 1993). This share is increasing rapidly. In addition, services are crucial to quality even in traditional manufacturing industries, e.g. through product development, transportation, and after-sale service. Transactions are recorded by accountants, annual reports are prepared by PR and information specialists, employee training is provided by the Human Resource staff, and janitors and security staff look after the production plant. Even though there seems to be an increasing trend towards the externalization of many such services to specialized firms, thus transferring the activities from the manufacturing to the service sector and making their contribution visible as services in the GNP calculations, the figures calculated for manufacturing firms still include a large part of value creation from services.

Services are highly heterogeneous and extremely difficult to define in general terms. Even the three fundamental characteristics of services typically discussed in the literature, namely that they are intangible, instantaneous and produced in close interaction with the buyer(s), are problematic. Services such as restaurant meals, hotel accommodation, and air transportation have highly tangible components but are clearly perishable. On the other hand, engineering design services typically result in drawings, calculations and plans, which are tangible, storable, and reusable. Auditing services require close cooperation between the auditor and the accounting department of the client firm, whereas the patient cannot assist the surgeon in his/her service delivery process once the diagnosis has been made and the appendectomy is in progress.

The wide variety of services makes it difficult to generalize about service management as if services are one thing and goods something quite different. On the other hand, the important and increasing impact of services means we cannot continue to focus on manufacturing firms as if they were the only sources of value creation in today's society. Rather than continue to discuss the difference between services and goods, we may learn more from an in-depth segment-by-segment analysis of different types of services and from limiting our discussions and theories to the types of firms and industries included in the particular segment discussed in each study.

This book emphasizes one such set of service firms and industries, namely those which involve the delivery of professional services from one firm to another. Professional services rely to a large extent on the interaction between knowledgeable buyers and highly educated service providers who engage in some form of joint problem solving activity. The actual content of the services delivered by the hired professionals may range from help in defining the problem to be solved, to a complete process of problem definition, solution development and implementation, result control and follow-up.

In some "service encounters" (Czepiel et al, 1985), the client knows exactly what is required and which professional firm is likely to be the best supplier, whereas in other situations the client only has a vague idea of which problem may need to be solved and what kind of expertise would be appropriate. Services may be delivered from one supplier firm representative to one client firm representative or involve large teams in either or both firms. The process of service delivery may be very brief, such as when a computer soft-ware hotline representative answers the client's question over the telephone, or of a long duration, such as when the management consulting firm is involved in the fundamental restructuring of a major company.

The number, diversity, and quality of professional service firms has increased substantially in developed countries over the last decades. For instance, Aharoni (1993:11) stated that the employment in professional business services had grown much faster than in other sectors of the economy; a staggering 53.8% growth in the United States between 1979 and 1986 compared with 13.1% growth across all sectors, or 25.4% in France compared with 0.1% growth in total employment in the same period. Later studies confirm these results: In 2002, Lorsch and Tierney report that revenues in key professional service industries in the US have grown from 107 to 911 billion USD between 1980 and 2000, representing a compound annual growth rate (CAGR) of about 11%. Despite a recession in 2000 and 2001, the companies are now back to an annual growth rate of about 4% (Byrnes, 2005). These figures should not surprise us, as both the number and percentage of employees with a higher level of education increase, and the firms increase their expertise in "procurement" (Porter, 1985) such that more and more segments of operations may be outsourced to a specialist firm rather than included in firm "infrastructure".

Outsourced business services lead to the development of highly specialized service firms delivering such services to an increasing number of buying firms, and hence their impact on the economic activity goes beyond the direct effects on employment and GNP. Since these services are inputs in the value creation processes of other firms, they also have an indirect effect on the quality and efficiency of these firms' outputs. As the expertise and service quality of the business service firms become well known, service outsourcing may become critical to competitiveness in an increasing number of areas.

This trend seems to be deeply rooted in the fundamental restructuring processes taking place in many industries today, where the emphasis is on "lean production", flexible organizations, and "just-in-time delivery", combined with the extreme requirements for cost-efficient solutions. In addition, the increasing level of specialization and expertise required within a large number of areas such as legal contracts, tax regulations, accounting practices, environmental protection, advanced technology development, consumer market trends, etc. suggest that only very large firms will have the capacity to develop and utilize all the necessary expertise in-house. Therefore, we are likely to see a continued growth in professional business service industries in the years to come, and their impact is expected to increase beyond today's high level.

In the following section, a pragmatic definition of professional services is provided, before the discussion turns to the challenges involved in the provision of such services at maximum quality and with minimum efficiency loss.

Professional services – a pragmatic definition

Despite the variety of services, clients, and suppliers, a number of characteristics appear to be common across firms involved in the delivery of professional services to other firms. The notion of a "professional service", as opposed to just any service, may be interpreted two ways: services delivered by "professionals", or services delivered according to "professional norms or rules of conduct". The first interpretation is frequently used but causes a number of problems because it requires a further definition of who is and who is not a professional. The identification of professionals further requires the identification of professions, which involves the classification of occupations, many of which strive to be recognized as professions in order to gain higher status and esteem. In the literature (see e.g. Blau & Scott, 1962, Hughes, 1958 and Vollmer & Mills, 1966), a profession is defined as:

1) a vocation founded in a body of knowledge, typically a higher (academic) education
2) a vocation concentrated on the application of this knowledge, combined with experience, to problems of vital importance in society and in a way which involves the altruistic service to clients, rather than self-seeking motives such as profits or status
3) a vocational organization based on a common code of ethics, where self control is supported by peer reviews, such that members who break the code of ethics may be excluded.

Members of obvious professions, such as the medical profession, are easily classified as professionals. However, a number of highly educated groups of people have attempted to have their vocational organizations recognized as professions. Some have been more lucky than others. National and international associations of lawyers, architects, and auditors, to name but a few, serve as professional organizations, even to the extent that an exclusion from the association may prevent the individual from selling his/her services to clients.

Other vocational groups, such as MBAs and management consultants, have sought to establish such professional organizations, but with limited success. For instance, some of the most prominent management consulting firms in the United States established the Association of Consulting Management Engineers (ACME) as early as 1933, with the explicit purpose of distinguishing themselves from "the number of charlatans in their ranks" (Higdon, 1969:22). The association requires adherence by all its members to its professional code of ethics, and thus satisfies the third of the criteria mentioned above. However, it would not be appropriate to say that the existence of ACME substitutes for a professional organization for consultants employed by member firms. There is no established body of knowledge for consultants as such, and in fact many management consultants are members of other established professions — in particular engineering — in addition to being consultants. There is no licencing of management consultants, and there is no professional organization with the right to supervise and potentially exclude consultants from the management consulting ranks. As a result, for individual professionals there is no established system of peer review beyond the firms, and there is no set of sanctions to enforce ethical behavior other than what is imposed by the firms.

The fact that there is no established profession does not, however, mean that highly educated individuals cannot deliver professional services and abide by the general professional rules of conduct. Management consultants may behave just as professionally as lawyers and medical doctors, and there may be charlatans in the ranks of all vocational groups. I therefore find it more meaningful to talk about professional services as a type of service rather than to attempt to classify the people delivering the services. People classified as professionals may behave unprofessionally, just as people who are not classified as members of a profession may behave professionally. The characteristics of the behavior required in order to deliver the service drive the challenges involved in these firms to a much greater extent than the (lack of) professional affiliation of the individuals involved. This is not to say that the relationship between the firm, its employees, and a profession (if it exists) is irrelevant. The profession may have a significant influence on the firm, especially through the norms or code of conduct which is considered acceptable both by the surrounding society and by the employees. The implications of this relationship between a firm and a profession, multiple professions, or rather a broad variety of vocational groups will be discussed in further detail in the following section.

As indicated above, a primary characteristic of a professional service is "the altruistic service to clients", meaning that in cases of conflict of interest between what is profitable for the supplier and what will be the best solution for the client, the latter alternative must be chosen. This is a difficult constraint to impose on a firm, but it is critical to the long-term reputation of the company. In addition, professional knowledge involves a rather limited sphere of expertise, and professionals must recognize that they have no expert authority outside the scope of that sphere. This is also a difficult constraint for many firms, especially when they are in need of new projects in order to keep their professionals fully employed. However, in order to maintain a high quality professional reputation, it is critical that the firm limits its engagements to projects within its area of expertise. To sum up, then, a professional service has the following characteristics:

1) It is highly knowledge intensive, delivered by people with higher education, and frequently closely linked to scientific knowledge development within the relevant area of expertise.
2) It involves a high degree of customization.
3) It involves a high degree of discretionary effort and personal judgment by the expert(s) delivering the service.
4) It typically requires substantial interaction with the client firm representatives involved.
5) It is delivered within the constraints of professional norms of conduct, including setting client needs higher than profits and respecting the limits of professional expertise.

A list of professional business service industries based on discussions with industry executives included the following[2]:

- law-firms/attorneys,
- accounting firms/auditors,
- management consultants,
- technology consultants,
- engineering consultants,
- insurance brokers,
- investment bankers,

[2] The list is meant to illustrate the breadth of the industries involved – not to provide a complete list of all possible industries delivering professional services.

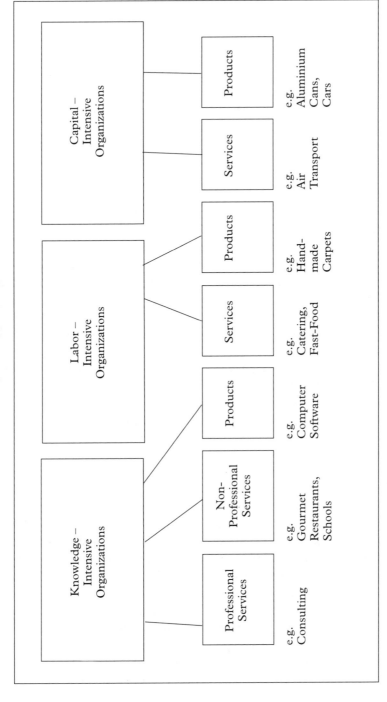

Figure 1. Types of Organizations.

- marketing and PR services,
- advertising agencies,
- architects,
- personnel and actuarial services,
- suppliers/sub-contractors delivering computer designs and software to the large computer manufacturers,
- management information systems and computer science consultants
- economists and development planners,
- specialized designers delivering firm specific design of all kinds – e.g. computer systems, graphic and industrial designs.

Professional service firms are knowledge intensive firms; however, as the above discussion indicates, not all knowledge-intensive firms deliver professional services. The previous figure indicates the relationship between professional service firms and other knowledge intensive firms.

In this figure, professional service organizations are seen as a sub-category of knowledge-intensive organizations. The distinction between organizations and firms is not critical here; in my opinion, firms are a sub-segment of all organizations. Organizations that are not firms include non-profit organizations, municipal or governmental agencies, foundations, and most schools and hospitals.

This figure, like all figures, involves fundamental simplifications in terms of categorizing organizations that obviously do not map perfectly on reality: First, it assumes that organizations are unique in their resource intensity. Clearly there are many industries and organizations which can belong to more than one category, such as a hotel, which is both labor and capital intensive and also has certain knowledge-intensive sections such as its gourmet restaurant. Secondly, it assumes a clear cut boundary between services and products, which, as discussed above, in many cases is inappropriate. However, for the present purposes, the figure illustrates the manner in which professional service organizations are both similar to and different from other knowledge intensive organizations. As indicated above, the difference between professional and non-professional organizations in this figure lies in the characteristics of the service delivered, rather than in the characteristics of the people employed. Professionals employed in firms developing products, such as soft-ware engineers developing computer soft-ware for consumer markets, work in knowledge intensive firms although they do not deliver professional business services. Similarly, many service organizations are knowledge intensive and employ professionals without delivering professional services. A classic example is schools.

It is important to bear in mind that the present emphasis on professional services is in no way meant to indicate a superior type of firm, employee, or output. Knowledge intensity is on the increase in a number of industries, product or service oriented alike, as both higher levels of education and modern information technology lead to a higher degree of customization even in such traditional products as automobiles. This results in superior products and services, better adapted to individual needs at an acceptable price, precisely because of the input of highly knowledgeable people. Many of the challenges involved in balancing the needs of highly educated people with the requirements for efficiency are likely to be at least as complex in firms where capital equipment and stream-lined production processes constitute the foundation for most of the value creation. Nevertheless, the delivery of professional services involves extreme challenges which make these organizations different from manufacturing firms in several respects. These differences will be discussed in detail in the following chapter.

The firms delivering professional services may be more or less specialized, as even more traditional service firms may give professional advice to clients. In the following, the discussion will be limited to firms designed to deliver professional services as a rule, rather than as an exception. However, many of the challenges involved in professional service delivery will presumably also apply to firms delivering such services on a small scale or on an ad hoc basis. Similarly, these challenges exist in sub-sections of traditional corporations as well, such as their R&D departments.

What is the role of professions?

Professional service firms employ highly educated individuals who in many, if not most, cases are also members of professional organizations. The relationship between professions and organizations was a topic of great interest in management and sociology in the 1950's and 60's but has received surprisingly little attention in the last decades. One notable exception is Professor Joseph Raelin, who brought the topic back in focus again with his 1986 book: A clash of cultures. The book was immediately so popular, especially among managers and practicing professionals, that a second edition was published the year after. The topic of most interest was the effect on employee loyalty to the organization when his/her primary reference group was his/her professional peers rather than the superiors and colleagues of the employing organization. Gouldner (1958, 1959) found that some people were "cosmopolitans" with their primary loyalty to their profession and peers, whereas others were "locals" with their primary loyalty to the employing organization. Cosmopolitans are highly mobile, even though they may choose to stay with the same employer for the entire span of their careers, whereas locals invest a great deal of energy in one specific organization and attempt to improve their situation internally rather than looking externally for alternative employers.

In my studies of professional service organizations, I have found that cosmopolitans and locals exist in all types of organizations, regardless of the existence of a profession or not. Hence, it is not the existence of a strong profession that develops cosmopolitans, but rather the characteristics of the individual experts as well as firms. Kjeld Rimberg, then-CEO of the Norwegian engineering design firm ASPLAN, claimed that engineers are typically loyal to projects rather than to firms. "Take an engineer employed by firm X," says Rimberg, "and hire him into a project managed by firm Y. On Monday morning he finds his new desk, is given the new company's sports equipment, and in the evening he is out jogging with his new colleagues and with the new company logo on his back. He has already shifted his loyalty to the new employer, but it will last only as long as his project engagement lasts." This is clearly a cosmopolitan moving from one firm to the next. On the other hand, in the two U.S.-based engineering design firms of my dissertation study, I found that the average tenure of senior engineers was extremely high: twenty years or more. Henry Michel, then-CEO of Parsons Brinckerhoff in New York, agreed that engineers primarily seek interesting and challenging projects, but chose to view the situation as follows: "Many people say that all our resources go down the lift in the evening after a day of work, and that the firm is then empty. That is why I see it as my primary concern to make sure that they want to come back tomorrow." The long tenure of highly qualified engineers indicates that he succeeds at making fundamentally cosmopolitan engineers act like locals. In the following chapter on managerial challenges (Chapter III), this issue will be discussed in further detail.

The assumed conflict of interest between individual professionals with a cosmopolitan orientation and the firm's desire to lock in and control the competence on which it is dependent, seems to be reduced substantially when the employing organization engages exclusively in professional activities, as is true of most professional service firms. There need not be a conflict between the professional and the firm, when the firm primarily employs professionals, if the firm goals include the altruistic service to meet client needs, and if the firm code of conduct incorporates the norms and values of the profession. Rather, they have common interests in the same professional goals and standards. Table 1 summarizes these dimensions for both individuals, firms, and vocational groups.

Rather than focus on the problematic role of professions in terms of creating mobile cosmopolitans with little need for loyalty to specific firms, I will highlight two positive implications of the existence of a profession. First, the professional membership of employees may allow the firm to build a quality reputation more rapidly and with less effort than in situations where such professions do not exist. For instance, when auditors employed by an auditing firm are members of a highly recognized professional organization with the right to licence, supervise, and sanction members, this membership serves as a service quality guarantee to clients, even if the firm is new and thus an unknown entity. Without such professional membership, the firm itself must build a reputation for service quality, supervision, and sanctioning, before the client can feel reassured. It is much easier for a small client firm to hire an unknown chartered accountant from a newly established partnership than to hire a management consultant from a new firm. The existence of a profession guarantees both a minimum of qualifications and a commitment (at least formally) to the professional code of ethics of that particular professional organization. If there is no profession, the firm must develop this reputation itself. For example, when a client firm hires a team of McKinsey consultants, they expect the McKinsey "way of doing things" (Bower, 1966) to guarantee the quality performance of the consultants. They do not, in most cases, ask for the professional affiliation of each team member. This quality image is the result of decades of careful investment in company culture and codes of conduct, as well as the reputation resulting from thousands of assignments over more than fifty years. Firm reputation may substitute for professional affiliation, but it takes years to establish.

Secondly, the profession has a set of common norms which may be directly applicable inside the firm. When all or most of the employees of the firm are members of the same profession, they share the same internalized norms and code of conduct, and hence communication and coordination within the firm is facilitated. The firm can simply adopt the same code of conduct, and does not need to spend time and effort to teach it to employees. Where multiple professions and educational backgrounds co-exist, as is the case in most management consulting firms, the firm must invest substantial time and effort to develop shared norms and a common code of conduct.

In some firms, such common norms are imported from other sources than the profession, such as in the small information technology consult-

Table 1. Characteristics of Professions, Professionals, and Professional Firms

---

Characteristics of professions
The "profession" is seen as an ideal, but occupational groups may be more or less "professionalized" along each of the following dimensions:

- Degree to which members are required to have a high level of education
- Number of years of education
- Extent of cooperation with or tightness of link to academic institution

- Extent of emphasis on altruistic problem solving for the client
- Extent of emphasis on affective neutrality vis a vis clients
- Extent of emphasis on problems of vital interest in society

- Extent of professional norms guiding member behavior
- Extent of peer reviews
- Extent to which peer sanctions are enforced against members not respecting norms

- Extent of limitations on expert authority

Characteristics of professionals (individuals)
- Members of a highly professionalized occupational group
- Higher education
- Emphasis on application and improvement of knowledge
- Respect for professional norms of behavior, including altruistic problem solving for the client, affective neutrality, and the limitations of professional expertise
- Respect for and willingness to participate in peer reviews and sanctions

Characteristics of professional organizations (firms)
- Majority of professional employees[3]
- High priority for professional goals; including altruistic problem solving for the client
- High degree of respect for professional norms, including the limitation of expertise
- Emphasis on creation as well as application of knowledge
- Professionals in charge of key decisions and activities

Figure 2. Influence of Profession on Firm and Individuals.

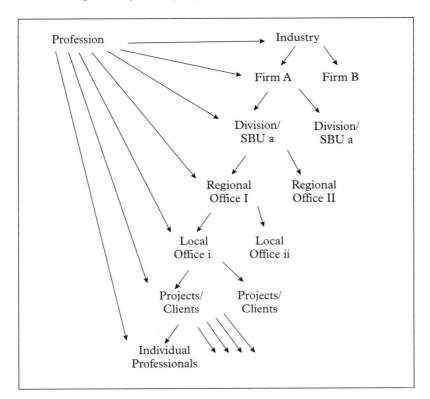

ing firm Pharos, located in Oslo, where all the establishing partners knew one another before they founded the firm and had worked together for the same employer. They imported the norms from their previous employer, but they also developed new norms as the result of their shared frustration with the firm they left. A similar effect is achieved by firms which recruit (almost) exclusively from a single or a small number of schools and even establish close ties with their alma mater. Combined with a profession, norms are reinforced even more firmly when the majority of the employ-

---

[3] Interestingly, some large consulting/law firms may have more than 50% of non-professional staff, and the number of such firms seems to be growing. The reason is that highly paid professionals who are extremely conscious of maximizing their number of billable hours, prefer to have more reasonably paid support staff to help them with non-professional matters. Many such firms have late working hours, and therefore keep double shifts of support staff, including secretaries, cantina food deliveries, etc. However, when it comes to strategic decisions, the professionals – and especially the partners – are those who decide, even if the majority of the employees are staff. In a sense, the partners see themselves as both employers and employees, other professionals are respected as potential partners, whereas staff are "only" employees and have no say in decisions regarding business development.

ees are educated in the same tradition and share the same student experiences. Where there is no profession, a common educational background facilitates the establishment of shared norms and allows the firm to establish a cohesive culture more rapidly.[4]

Figure 2 illustrates the way in which a profession may influence the firm directly and indirectly. Not only does the profession, if it exists, influence the education and norms of the professionals hired into the firm, but it also affects the external environment of the firm, such as industry norms and standards and in many cases the expectations of clients.

Professional organizations and codes of conduct often span national boundaries and cultures, in such a way that a common professional training may facilitate internationalization as well. As pointed out by Dr. Asle Berger, a senior engineer with substantial international experience from his years with Norconsult and CapGemini, it is extremely important in an international context not to forget that although the body of professional knowledge is shared, the cultural differences should not be underestimated. The issues related to internationalization will be discussed in further length in Chapter VII.

Suggested Readings

Aharoni, Y. (Ed.) 1993. Coalitions and competition. The globalization of Profesional Business Services. London and New York: Routledge.

Aharoni, R. & Nachum, L. (Eds) 2000. Globalization of Services – Some implications for theory and practice. London and New York: Routledge.

Alvesson, M. 1989. Ledning av kunskapsföretag. Stockholm: Norstedts. English version 1995: Management of Knowledge Intensive Companies. Berlin/New York: de Gruyter.

Alvesson, M. 1994. Med känslan som ledstjärna. Stockholm: Norstedts.

Blau, P.M. & Scott, W.R. 1962. Formal organizations: A comparative approach. San Francisco, CA: Chandler.

Bower, M. 1966. The will to manage. New York: McGraw Hill.

Etzioni, A. 1961. A comparative analysis of complex organizations. New York: Free Press.

---

[4] The effects of such cohesive cultures are obviously not all positive. Research has shown that heterogeneous groups are much more likely to see environmental threats early, as well as to develop creative solutions. Negative implications of cohesive cultures will be discussed at further length in chapter III.

Gouldner, A. 1957-58. "Cosmopolitans and Locals: Towards an analysis of latent social roles I and II", Administrative Science Quarterly, Vol 2, No 3 and 4.

Higdon, H. 1969. The business healers. New York: Random House.

Newell, S; Robertson, M; Scarbrough, H & Swan, J. 2002. Managing Knowledge Work. New York: Palgrave.

Maister, D.H. 1993. Managing the professional service firm. New York: Free Press.

Raelin, J.A. 1986/1991. The clash of cultures – Managers managing professionals. Harvard Business School Press.

II. What's unique about professional service firms?

Why are they so special... or are they?

Introduction

The present chapter will analyze in detail the underlying characteristics that make professional service firms particularly interesting but also challenging to manage. Whereas managers of professional service firms would not be likely to question the assumption that their firms are very different and more complex than traditional manufacturing firms (or other types of service firms for that matter), for our purpose it is critical to determine the extent to which such an assumption is true. Also, in order to discuss available strategic options, it is important to have an understanding of the underlying dynamics that need to be taken into account.

This chapter begins with a bit of background about the uniqueness of professional service firms; my starting point is the beginning of my first study. The next three sections analyze the characteristics of what is delivered, the inputs to the delivery process, and the interaction between the client and the service provider. When combined, these characteristics lead to a number of managerial challenges to be discussed in the following chapter. The final section of this chapter discusses some of the differences between professional service firms and the traditional manufacturing firms that are often taken as the starting point for the models and theories applied in strategic management.

Are professional service firms different?

My first interest in studying professional service firms was sparked by a discussion with senior managers of two large U.S. based engineering design firms, namely Derish L Wolff, President and CEO of Louis Berger International Inc, and W. Dennis Moran, President of the international division of Camp Dresser & McKee (CDM) Inc. They made a strong and clear statement about the professional service firm being fundamentally different from the more traditional firms taken as an explicit or implicit model in most strategic management textbooks. Only a few years earlier,

Mr Moran had completed the executive MBA program at The Wharton School, and he had hoped that this program would teach him how to be a better strategic manager at CDM International. His engineering background gave him the technical and professional expertise he needed, his international experience gave him substantial market and organizational knowledge, and what he wanted was additional knowledge about how effective strategic management is achieved. Despite the many excellent qualities of the program and the many interesting contacts he made with alumni, he was frustrated with what the program didn't teach him: the reality of his own firm and others like it.

For the reader who is familiar with traditional strategic management models and techniques, Mr. Moran's frustration is probably no surprise. A couple of examples may illustrate the challenges involved: One of the most popular and widely applied models, the value chain (Porter, 1985), is difficult, if not impossible, to adapt to a firm where no linear production process with input, transformation, and output exists. Similarly, a portfolio analysis with emphasis on market shares and market growth seems meaningless for a firm which is used to changing in size and competitor ranking with every large project added or completed. Neither the market, the market growth, nor the market share can be measured in the same way as in traditional product markets.[1] To give one illustration, in 1989 the Norwegian engineering design firm Norconsult AS was ranked as number 39 on ENR's annual list of the largest international engineering consulting firms classified by overseas billings. In 1990 they had dropped to 64th place, despite the fact that 1990 was a better year for the firm than 1989 (ENR 1989, 1990). When their largest project of all times, a telecommunications project in Saudi Arabia, was at its peak, Norconsult was ranked among the top ten firms. The market for large engineering projects is largely global, and the best firms have a global reputation and keep track of their main competitors world wide. However, their competitive intelligence cannot be limited to industry statistics, as it is normal for even the most reputable firms to shift abruptly in terms of size or "market share" with the portfolio of projects. The shifts, naturally, may be both upwards and downwards in industry statistics.

[1] It is a fact that industry boundaries are difficult to define even in traditional manufacturing industries and product markets. However, if one is willing to make certain assumptions, such an analysis may add significant insights to management of multidivisional manufacturing corporations. For further insights into portfolio analysis, see e.g. Hax, A.C. & Majluf, N.S.: The strategy concept and process: A pragmatic approach, Prentice Hall, 1991.

International comparisons are also difficult to make due to the fact that major differences exist in the organization of engineering services across countries. For instance, in the U.S. and Norway the engineering design firms are separate from the construction firms, and the design contract is subject to a separate bidding process from that of the construction itself. Those in favor of this system claim that such independent processes increase the likelihood of developing the best design for the client, rather than developing the design that best incorporates the construction capabilities of one specific firm. In many European countries, the entire contract is awarded to a construction firm, which may or may not hire external design engineers to support the in-house design team. One obvious result of these differences is that statistics on firm size and market share are very difficult to compare, as the design component is not clearly accounted for when it takes place within the construction firm.

From the discussions with Mr. Wolff and Mr. Moran, it seemed clear that the management of engineering design firms was facing challenges that were substantially different from those of traditional manufacturing firms. Additional discussions with Stephen B. Oresman, who was partner of a small and relatively new management consulting firm and had previously worked for one of the largest international consulting companies, served to reinforce this impression. In fact, none of the professionals I have interviewed have found models developed for manufacturing firms which were applicable to their reality. Only one person, a management consultant, thought that a value chain analysis could be applicable, "with minor modifications," but even he admitted that adapting the model required so much conceptual thinking that he might be better off with a different model. (Incidentally, value chain analyses were part of the core services delivered by his consulting firm, so he may have felt the need to be positively inclined.)[2]

However, being convinced that professional service firms are "different" is not enough. In order to determine which theoretical concepts are

---

[2] Since the publication of my first edition – and the second was unaltered in this respect – there has been a major development in terms of alternatives to the value chain. E.g. In 1998 Stabell & Fjeldstad published their article: *Configuring Value for Competitive Advantage: On chains, shops and networks.* **Strategic Management Journal** 19 (5): 413-437, where the value chain is explained to be the appropriate model for firms transforming inputs into outputs, what Thompson (1967) called "long-linked technologies", i.e. where value creation takes place in a sequential manner, and planning is excellent for coordination. Value networks, on the other hand, create value through linking different nodes together by transferring people (e.g. airlines), goods (e.g. UPS or the Royal Mail), bits and bytes (telephone companies and others, or money (banks and other financial institutions). Value networks represent what Thompson (1967) called "the mediating technology," where standardization – for interconnectivity – is key to coordination. The third value configuration is the value shop, where diagnosis and problem solving are key to value creation. Value shops apply what Thompson (1967) called "intensive technology", where coordination requires mutual adjustment. This is the configuration which best fits the reality of the professional service firms.

applicable and which are not, it is important also to identify these differences. Which are the key dimensions driving these challenges? Maister published his book on the management of professional service firms in 1993 (two years after the end of my interviews)[3]. He concludes that there are two fundamental dimensions driving the "special managerial challenges" of professional service firms: First, the high degree of customization, making traditional management principles such as standardization, routinization, and supervision difficult to apply. Secondly, the "strong component of face-to-face interaction with the client," which leads to major challenges in quality assurance, and requires "very special skills" of "top performers" (Maister, 1993:xv).

These two dimensions provide a useful starting point and highlight three of the fundamental characteristics of professional service firms:

- *Highly qualified individuals,*
- *Idiosyncratic client services, and*
- *Subjective quality assessment.*

Implicit in this set of characteristics is also the substantial requirement for individual judgment involved in each "service encounter" (Czepiel & al, 1985), such that services are to a large extent centered around named individuals rather than the more objective firm. Professionals are in many cases not substitutable in the service delivery process, and this fact leads to a number of managerial challenges which will be discussed in further detail in Chapter III.

In the following, these three dimensions are discussed in further detail, in addition to one more critical dimension, namely that of *information asymmetry*. Professional service firms primarily create value through processes that require them to know more than their clients, either in terms of expertise or in terms of experience in similar problem-solving situations. This information asymmetry adds to the quality assurance difficulties involved due to the idiosyncrasy of the services, and it is one of the areas

---

[3] Maister has, since 1993, published another three books:
1997: True Professionalism – The Courage to Care About Your People, Your Clients, and Your Career. New York: Simon and Schuster (Touchstone).
2000: The Trusted Advisor. With Charles H. Green & Robert M. Galford. New York: Free Press.
2001. Practice What You Preach! – What Managers Must Do to Create a High Achievement Culture. New York: Free Press.
In my opinion, the later books offer more in depth insights on some of the topics also covered in the 1993 book, but "Managing the Professional Service Firm" remains the "classic". I still use it in several classes, and the students – especially excecutives – like it a lot. It has been reprinted as a paperback, and I still recommend this as a fundamental source to understanding the functioning of professional service firms. In addition to the book you are reading now, of course.

where the existence of professions supervising their members may support the reputation of the service firm. None of these dimensions are absolute in the sense that all professional services are extreme in all characteristics. Similarly, these dimensions are not unique in the sense that only professional service firms have these characteristics. However, what does make the professional service firms unique is the fact that all of these characteristics apply simultaneously and are extreme most of the time.

Challenges resulting from characteristics of the output: Intangible, idiosyncratic, innovative

As discussed in the previous chapter, services are largely intangible and developed in interaction with the client. For the professional service firm, the intangibility of the service leads to two major challenges: service quality is difficult to guarantee, as it is impossible to "test-drive" a service, and operations management is highly complex, as the services cannot be stored. "Production" can only occur when the contract is signed, and hence production capacity should ideally fit the (partially unpredictable) volume and timing of contracts. The ideal professional service organization is thus a highly flexible organization, both in terms of size and type of expertise available. However, when selling the service in terms of a project proposal, the professional service firm must also be able to guarantee that the required types of expertise, or even named experts, are available. This is one of the managerial dilemmas which will be discussed at further length in Chapter III.

In terms of the service quality, the more idiosyncratic the service required is, the more difficult it will be for the service firm to guarantee the quality ex ante. What is perceived to be a high quality service depends very much on the expectations of the client, and the less clear the client is about what is expected of the supplier, the more difficult it is to deliver what is expected.

In the 1960's, several articles in FORTUNE magazine attacked the poor performance of management consulting firms, criticizing consultants for delivering quasi-solutions that would require further involvement by the same consulting team in additional projects. They claimed the consultants were more concerned about securing their own future than about improving the operations of the client firms, as illustrated by the title of one of the articles: "The men who came to dinner" (Fortune, February

1965). Tilles (1961), on the other hand, questioned the abilities of the buyers, and made the important point that high quality consulting services require substantial inputs from the client firm. Not only should the client firm know what kind of service is required and which problem needs to be solved, but it must also know enough about potential service suppliers to choose the most appropriate service firm.

Since the 1960's, the competence of both the clients and the supplying firms has improved substantially, and the frequency of clients getting something very different from what they thought they were buying seems to have been reduced. From the point of view of the professional service firm, it is crucial to manage the early stages of the service definition process proactively such that client expectations are known to those who are going to deliver the service, and client expectations are realistic relative to what the service firm is capable of delivering. Many firms may be tempted to promise services they may not be in the position to deliver, only to find that such projects typically end with losses both financially (additional services are added to compensate for the reduced quality) and reputationally. With intangible deliverables and unclear client demands, the quality of the expectations management process steered by the professional service firm becomes absolutely crucial to the perceived quality of the final output.

The process of quality management becomes further complicated by the fact that in most situations professional business services involve more than one representative within the client firm. It is not enough to satisfy the manager assigned as the primary client contact, as the perceptions of other key stakeholders are also crucial to the final evaluation of quality. In management consulting this challenge is particularly salient, as the manager deciding to undertake the project is frequently not a member of the stakeholder group that will have to suffer the negative effects of a change process. There are even projects where the satisfaction of all parties involved is impossible, where the service provider must have a very clear agreement ex ante as to the quality criteria to be used in assessing the service. Some projects are so controversial or intertwined with intra-firm politics and manoeuvering that the professional service firm is better off refusing to enter into the contract, as there is no way they can help the client firm within the constraints set on which problems are to be solved and by what means. (See e.g. Koppang & Løwendahl in Høivik & Føllesdal, 1995, for an in depth discussion of how both clients and consultants may deceive each other in a professional service definition and delivery process).

In addition to the multidimensional nature of service quality, the degree of innovation required complicates the service quality assessment both ex ante and ex post. When the service required is well defined and similar to previous services delivered by the same firm, the client may have a relatively clear idea of what to expect and the likelihood of the service firm delivering the same quality again. The more that is known prior to the project being undertaken, the better. For auditing firms, many client contracts are of this nature, in particular when they audit the same firm on an ongoing basis. Most of the problems encountered are known in advance, most of the solutions are known and have been tested in interaction with the client, and both parties know what to expect. However, when the client firm changes operations, such as when it enters a new international market, when new managers are hired, or when the auditing firm assigns a new auditor to the client, uncertainty increases. In the extreme case, when a problem is completely new to both the client and the auditor and they have no established relationship, the uncertainty is also likely to be extreme on both sides. A pertinent example is firms from previously closed economies such as the Soviet Union establishing new subsidiaries in Western countries and hiring local auditors with no previous knowledge of either the parent company, their traditional accounting practices and laws, or their expectations from a local auditor.

Challenges resulting from the interaction: Simultaneity, information asymmetry, double moral hazard

Services cannot be delivered without a close cooperation between the service supplier and the client. The client participates in both the problem definition, the choice of solution, and very often also the process of developing and implementing the solution. Once again the heterogeneity of services makes it difficult to generalize, as it is important to have a clear picture of what type of service is implicitly assumed. For the engineering design firm, the interaction with the client is most intense in the early definition stages, whereas after the project proposal has been accepted, the design process takes place largely within the engineering firm. The auditing firm, on the other hand, needs a close cooperation with the client throughout the entire process of spot checks and detailed control of the books and is totally dependent on the commitment of the client in order to deliver a high quality service. In management consulting projects involving organizational change, the interaction is also crucial, to such an extent that in many cases it is difficult to separate the inputs of consultants from those of client firm representatives. Typically, the more process oriented the service is, the higher the degree of interaction required.

Selling professional services to potential clients is very different from the mass-marketing of consumer goods or services, as it involves both interaction with the client (often, but not always, face-to-face) and a high degree of uncertainty in terms of what is actually going to be delivered. The more similar the service is to previous projects undertaken by the same supplier, the easier it is for both parties to determine the quality criteria involved. However, when the service involves a high degree of innovation, it is not the capacity to deliver a given service that is required, but rather the ability to solve an under-specified problem. How do you know ex ante that the advertising agency can develop the first-rate new campaign you need, when what you need is something new and different, based on creative ideas that your own employees are unable to provide? And how do you know that the engineering firm will be able to develop the oil platform required, when it must be designed for far deeper waters than ever before attempted? A large number of professional services require the development of completely new concepts and solutions, and the more distant these solutions are from already existing versions, the more difficult it is for both the service firm and the client to evaluate the likely service quality ex ante.

In addition to the degree of innovation, the information asymmetry or knowledge gap between the service provider and the client also creates challenges for both parties. Professional service firms are typically hired because they have some expertise that the client firm does not possess, and the more specialized this expertise, the more difficult it is for the client firm to evaluate the quality of what is, or is to be, delivered. When you hire an expert tax lawyer to help the firm with a specific problem, you may only discover that his advice was inadequate when you run into a colleague who has found a better solution for the same problem. In many cases, the quality of what is delivered can only be assessed by other professionals within the same area of expertise, which is precisely the reason why society accepts professional associations taking charge of peer reviews, licencing, and sanctioning of inappropriate behavior.

In a well known case in Norway, the ceiling of a newly constructed center city subway station in Oslo was leaking so badly that the station had to be closed for major repairs. Needless to say, the disputes between the engineering firm, the construction firm, and the municipality as client were substantial and difficult to resolve. The construction firm claimed that it had observed all contractual agreements, and said they were not responsible. The engineering design firm claimed that the weaknesses resulted from the unwillingness of the client to utilize materials of sufficient dimension and quality, and that they had warned the client of the risks involved, but that the client had insisted that the quality was sufficient. The client claimed that they would never constrain the quality beyond what the experts advised, since they obviously did not have the necessary expertise to counter the advice of the specialists of the engineering firm. After substantial press coverage and tough negotiations, a compromise was reached in which all parties had to cover some of the costs involved in solving the problem. However, the greatest loss of all may have been to the engineering firm's reputation, regardless of whether or not they were to blame for the problems. Whenever an expert is called in to solve a problem, the client cannot be trusted to behave like an equal partner in the expert assessment of what is required for an adequate solution. However, as the client is in charge of setting the budget constraints, the dilemma may be difficult for the expert in charge to solve, as the cost difference between the very best solution and what will probably be adequate may be substantial.

The challenges of the knowledge gap between the professional service provider and the client representative(s) lie at the very core of the management of professional service firms, and contain both a fundamental and a strategic dimension. In general, it seems that the wider the knowledge gap, the more pedagogical the service provider must be. Hence, the delivery of professional services to people with very little knowledge of the necessary services requires a different set of skills in order to first define the appropriate service together with the client and later assure the client of the quality involved. In many industries, the client may be unable to see the difference between the promises of "charlatans" and serious professionals, and where there is a profession, membership in such a highly reputable association is likely to be a minimum requirement for most clients. Personal trust is another important criterion, and here both the reputation of the firm and the personal relationship with a specific professional are important factors for the client.

The fundamental problem lies in the fact that professional service firms sell the expertise of their professional employees, and hence cannot resell the same expertise to the same client if the client is involved in the learning process. The larger the knowledge gap and the less freqently the expertise is needed, the less likely the client firm is to invest in the internalization of the expertise either through learning processes or recruiting. However, when the person ordering assistance in the development of a brochure has both the necessary skills and the software required to complete the next similar assignment in-house, the learning process may erode the knowledge gap that constituted the market opportunity for the advertising firm in the first place. Professional service firms need to manage their knowledge transfer processes consciously and make certain they remain one step ahead of their clients with the necessary competence to continue to deliver value added. On the other hand, holding back on the knowledge transfer can easily backfire, if the client expects to be educated in the process.

Another and different challenge results from the fact that professional services may be bought by highly qualified professionals, and this is particularly true of professional business services, as firms often develop their own in-house expertise as buyers to match the expertise of the suppliers. In the extreme cases, the client firm may be a competitor in the market for professional employees, and many professionals are hired from their professional service firm employer to a client after establishing a successful relationship. Management consultants are hired into client firm management, experienced auditors are hired as chief financial officers, and contract lawyers are hired as in-house counsel in firms where the demand for their particular expertise recurs relatively frequently.

The strategic aspect of the knowledge gap involves the positioning of the firm relative to different types of clients. Some professional service firms specialize in the delivery of services to clients with little or no complementary expertise in-house, whereas other firms specialize in the delivery of advanced services to highly sophisticated clients. Both types of services may require high levels of expertise, but the first type involves high pedagogical skills in order to help the client define the problems as well as understand the possible solutions available. The second type involves a direct interaction between experts with a close connection to their scientific community and an ability to interact with the client in a joint problem solving effort at a high level. The types of skills required of the professionals involved in the service encounters in each of these situations are fundamentally different, and this affects both the recruiting and the organization of the firm.

An excellent illustration of these differences was found when majority ownership of the Norwegian engineering design firm Norconsult was shifted from a number of similar engineering firms to Norwegian Petroleum Consultants (NPC). The engineers of Norconsult were experienced in conducting infra-structure design projects in third world countries, in which the client would be a local municipality teamed with international lending agencies providing the funding. The engineers were heavily involved in the processes of explaining techniques and teaching local engineers how to continue the work and do repairs after project completion. Each Norconsult engineer working in a third world country needed, and was granted, substantial autonomy in terms of choosing the solution most appropriate to local needs. They frequently had to make important decisions without referring to headquarters, as it might take a week or more to get a telephoneline established to a senior manager in Norway. The contrast was stark to the engineers of NPC, who were used to senior managers interacting with extremely sophisticated engineers as representatives of the large oil companies. Their services typically involved complex designs such as that of a new oil drilling platform for the North Sea. Here, the client firm engineers would specify every single detail of their terms of contract, and each NPC engineer would be given "a complete bookshelf full of manuals" detailing the specifications of his or her specific design task. The roles of both management and individual judgment were fundamentally different in these two firms, and the resulting differences in their "ways of doing things" led to a number of misunderstandings and conflicts when the two firms were trying to integrate parts of their operations.[4]

The challenges involved in the interactive delivery of services in a process in which both the client and the supplier have to be involved are not limited to the challenges resulting from the actual simultaneous interaction required and the knowledge gap resulting from the supplier having more expertise than the client. In addition, there is a challenge involved in the interdependence between the client and the supplier in terms of the inputs required for a high quality service. It is not only a challenge for the client firm to spell out their demand and manage the process of delivery in order to get what they contracted. For the professional service firm the problem is reversed, as opportunism may also occur on the client side. In the finance literature, this challenge is identified as the "double moral hazard" problem, indicating that there is a hazard involved for the client in terms of the supplier cheating, and a similar hazard involved for the supplier in terms of the client cheating. A good illustration is offered by the problems of auditors, who are responsible not only to the client firm's board of directors but also to the authorities and, if the shares are publicly traded, to present and potential owners. The auditing firms apply a number of procedures and criteria in order to secure that they get all relevant

---

[4] The integration turned out to be more difficult and costly than the expected benefits from such an integration, and in the end the majority ownership of Norconsult was sold out. Later, Norconsult was integrated into the operations of another of their previous owners, Berdahl Strømme AS, and the new firm operates under the Norconsult name.

information from the client. Some of these procedures are specific to the auditing firm and developed in-house, whereas a large number of them are imported from the profession. Many procedures are also dictated by laws and other regulations. Norms result both from the training of the professionals prior to their recruitment and from the joint efforts of members of the profession to develop improved procedures that may enable all members to provide even higher quality services to clients. Despite this continuous process, however, we have seen a number of court cases where auditors have been sued because owners or other stakeholders claim they have been misled by information provided by the firm and authorized by the auditor. In some cases, auditors have been fired from their firms and even excluded from their professional association, due to the poor quality of their work. But in other cases, the auditors have been found innocent as they had completed all the required tests according to the established code of conduct, but had been misled by the client representatives deliberately holding back relevant information. It is obvious that the auditor cannot oversee every transaction within the firm, and that unless (s)he is lucky enough to find leads within the spot-checks performed, (s)he cannot deliver a high quality auditor's report without the honest cooperation of the client firm management. However, the effect on the reputation of the professional service firm may be devastating.

A recent case in the US illustrates this situation very well, namely the case of Enron and Arthur Andersen. After a period of unwillingness/inability among the auditors in charge to spot the moral hazard involved in the client company, as some members of top management "cooked the books" for their own personal benefit, client company "whistle blowers" brought the matter out in the open. As a final consequence of this, the well-renowned auditing company Arthur Andersen, known to have the strictest and most explicit codes of ethics and some of the best trained auditors in the world, disappeared completely, world wide. Experts in the area also suggest that a combination of auditing and consulting assignments for the same client may have contributed to the problems. Whereas auditors report to the board and society, consultants are hired by and report to management. If the auditors "blow the whistle" on management, vis-à-vis the board, the consultants (from the same firm) risk losing their assignment to a competitor. Frequently, the consulting assignments involve much larger fees than the auditing ones. Hence, for the auditors the choice may have been perceived to be between ethical behavior and major loss. In the long run, it turned out that this choice was fictional – the loss came anyway, in a disastrous way, only a few months later!

Challenges resulting from characteristics of the inputs: invisible assets and individual professionals

Professional service firms face a set of managerial challenges resulting from the combination of service characteristics, client characteristics, characteristics of the interaction between client and supplier firm representatives, and specific characteristics of the "resources" involved in the value creation processes. Manufacturing firms rely to a large extent on technology, machines, and highly routinized and standardized operations. Their efficiency is based on their ability to produce a large number of similar products in a repetitive process involving more capital and labor than ad hoc problem solving capabilities. Managerial supervision is appropriate, and the number of exceptions which need to be handled by management is sufficiently low for a hierarchical structure to function relatively smoothly. For capital-intensive or labor intensive services, the situation is quite similar to that of the manufacturing firm.

The well-known example of McDonald's restaurants offers an excellent illustration of how successful a service firm may be at translating principles of standardization, routinization, and managerial supervision into a service industry where quality is largely dependent on the repetitive application of rigid procedures to given inputs in order to provide the same predictable output every time. There is very little room for individual discretion in performing the service, and customers know exactly what to expect. You may order your hamburger with or without a certain prespecified set of ingredients, such as ketchup, salad, and mayonnaise, but you cannot order it "on the rare side of medium rare" with some finely chopped echalottes and french mustard added to the hamburger prior to cooking. Even the modifications required due to differences in local culture and eating habits have been resisted by management and only very reluctantly did they allow their German franchisees to sell "Bier" and their French counterparts to call the globally known "quarterpounder with cheese" a "Cheese Royale".

The routinized organization is very efficient at replicating procedures in a predictable way, but it is not designed for exceptions. If you have needs other than those specified in the repertoire of the routine-based firm, you have to go elsewhere to get your service. This type of strategic positioning and perfectioning of services fit for a certain set of needs allows for cost efficiency and gives even the gourmet the choice between an inexpensive but prespecified meal or a more expensive and time consuming meal with more customization.

The professional service firm is, by definition, placed in the niches where a high degree of customization is required. The definition of professional services in the previous chapter involved the critical dimension of "altruistic service to client needs," which requires non-routine adaptation to whatever the client may require in order to solve the problem. As a result, by definition the professional service firm must rely on non-routine problem-solving based on a high degree of professional expertise and individual judgment. The core of the resource base of the professional service firm thus resides in the professionals employed and their ability to solve whatever problems the clients may want them to solve. The professionals bring to the firm their expertise, their experience, their skills in relationship building and maintenance, their professional reputation, their network of professional peer contacts, and their established relationships with past, present, and potential clients. These strategic resources are critical to the success of the professional service firm, but they are to a very large extent owned and controlled by the individual professionals rather than by the firm itself. The early history of most professional service firms highlights such strong individuals with competence, ideas, and the necessary contacts to establish the first project. See e.g. Bobrick's (1985) history of Parsons Brinckerhoff for a very interesting description of how the founder, William Barclay Parsons, was absolutely critical not only to the establishment of the firm but even to the development of the first New York subway. He had competence and ideas, as well as the energy and staying power required to learn enough about this idea to persuade decision makers to develop the project he wanted.

Why professional service firms are not like manufacturing firms

The discussion of the previous section supports the fundamental idea behind this book: Professional service firms are different from the firms we have learned to take for granted in strategic management and organization theory, and these firms cannot be aided in improving their strategic management practices through the application of traditional concepts, models, and techniques. Mr. Moran and Mr. Wolff were not exceptional in finding that the traditional theories were difficult to apply. They were representative. Their conclusion that we need a set of different theories and concepts applicable to the extreme challenges involved in the management of professional service firms was quite appropriate. In the following chapters, the managerial and strategic implications will be discussed in detail, together with a number of illustrations of more appropriate ways of dealing with the critical challenges involved.

The value creation processes of professional service firms may be summarized by three critical processes, as illustrated in Figure 3.

Figure 3. Value Creating Processes.

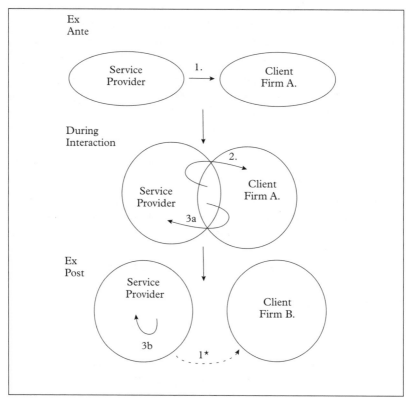

The first process concerns the ability of the firm to sell a credible promise. The more innovative and idiosyncratic the service, and the larger the knowledge gap, the more complex this first process is likely to be. The credibility of the promise depends on firm reputation, on their ability to document success from previous projects, and on the professionals the firm says it will assign to the project. This first process also includes the negotiation of the terms of contract, including efforts to develop the appropriate level of expectations in the client firm and the assurance that the service supplier only promises what the firm can keep.

The second process involves the set of activities required in order to deliver what has been promised and involves both the client firm and the professionals assigned. In this process, the firm is concerned with both the actual quality of what is delivered, the perceptions of quality by all relevant client firm representatives, and the efficiency of the delivery. Many excellent projects have turned into nightmares for the professional service supplier, not because the quality was insufficient but, on the contrary, because the professionals delivered a quality requiring twice the effort stipulated in the contract. One important aspect of this service delivery process concerns the investment in methods, procedures, and modular solutions which allow for a more efficient service delivery the next time a similar problem arises with a client. The challenges involved in the management of such processes will be discussed at further length in the following chapter. Suffice it to say, the development of more efficient approaches carries with it two difficult dilemmas: first, the dilemma of how to apply standard procedures to unique problems and still deliver the customized and idiosyncratic solution that is appropriate for the client, and secondly, the dilemma of how the processes can be organized for efficiency without transferring too much of the project to juniors who have not had a chance to participate in the interaction with the client.

The third process illustrated in the figure is one that is even more readily neglected in professional service firms than the second process directed at making operations more efficient, and that is the process of learning from the project and institutionalizing this learning to the extent that it can be utilized for both improved service quality and improved efficiency with future clients. Again, this process involves dilemmas that are difficult to solve and that require managerial attention: First, how to keep the best professionals happy and working on the most challenging problems while at the same time persuading them to invest in the development of procedures and approaches to be utilized by others in the future. Secondly, how to convince the clients that the learning is utilized ethically, rather than sold to client firm competitors at a high price, supporting the new client's competitive intelligence. Says one management consulting client about a large and highly reputable consulting firm they decided to terminate after ten years of cooperation: "we paid enormous sums to educate their consultants about our industry, only to find that at the time the consultant became a true expert, he was transferred to a different team within the firm and thereby won a contract with our toughest competitor. It is true that we learned a lot from them, in particular in the early years, but in the long run, I think they gained more new knowledge from the contract than we did, and still we were paying them (horrendous amounts). From this perspective I wonder if they should have been paying us instead for the education of their consultants!"

Whereas these three processes exist in all service sectors, the complexity of the processes increases substantially in professional service firms, precisely because of the key dimensions discussed above: the idiosyncracy of the service, the interaction with the client, the information asymmetry which makes the credibility of the promise so hard for the client to evaluate, and the extreme dependence on individual and non-interchangeable professionals in all three processes.

In the last years, I have been working with my colleagues Professor Øivind Revang and Doctoral candidate Siw M. Fosstenløkken in an attempt to develop a more comprehensive model of how value is created in professional service firms. We ended up defining value creation at two levels: first, value creation for and with the client, in the services delivered. That process hopefully also provides enough financial value for the service provider, that salaries and bonuses can be paid out, and even some surplus profits be retained for further firm development. This is the most well known process of value creation, what we view as the short-term orientation. However, given the fact that professional service firms create most of their new knowledge or competence through their interactions with the clients (see e.g. Fosstenløkken, S.M. Ph.D. dissertation on the topic of competence development in professional service firms, forthcoming BI Norwegian School of Management, fall 2005.), these investments in knowledge development must also be looked at as part of the value creation in these companies. Strategic investments in future capabilities are largely made through the choice of projects and clients to work for, and these elements also need to be included in an analysis of professional service firms' short-term and long-term value creation. Our model, called the VCPs for PSFs (VCP=Value Creation Process, PSF=Professional Service Firm), was published in Human Relations 54 (7), july 2001, pp. 911-931. I will revert to the complete model in chapter IV.

Finally, before going deeper into the challenges of managing such firms, I would like to highlight some of the dimensions where professional service firms encounter problems if they try to force-fit traditional theoretical models: they may not want to give first priority to profitability, they may not want to grow, they may refuse to produce a formal organization chart and do their utmost to avoid hierarchy, they may refuse the authority of managers as well as to see managerial positions as promotions, and they may refuse wealthy capital owners the right to invest in their firms. All of these "provocations" are consistent with the characteristics outlined above and underscore the fundamental differences between traditional firms and professional service firms.

First, professional service firms are typically established by one, or a few, founding professionals who have some expertise or experience that is of value to others. They sell their professional insight and thus help clients solve problems they could not have solved otherwise. Many of these firms are established as part-time engagements of professors and researchers who find that their valuable knowledge may more adequately benefit clients if they set up a distribution channel allowing them to involve junior partners, and in so doing reach more clients than would otherwise have been the case. Whereas some such firms are established because the founders see a profitable niche and want to capitalize on their expertise, most firms seem to be established either to help clients or to establish a forum where challenging client problems can be attacked and hopefully solved. For professors and researchers, an additional motivational factor lies in the possibilities of applying new insights in future research and teaching. When I asked the professionals participating in my dissertation study, surprisingly many of them (including co-owners and managers) replied that their primary goal was to help clients and have fun, rather than to make profits. This was particularly true of the engineers in the engineering design firms. They said they needed enough profits to continue to have fun, meaning that they could afford to buy whatever support technology and assistance they needed and to take sufficient time for non-billable activities to remain updated on the latest developments in their field of expertise, but they would not be willing to prioritize the most profitable project over one with more professional challenges and only satisfactory profits. Profit maximization is thus not the rule in professional service firms, although there are firms where this is the first priority. This alternative primary goal is not a problem as long as the owners of the firm accept this set of priorities, but it does challenge the traditional way of thinking about why firms exist.

The emphasis on professional challenges over maximum profits creates a number of challenges if the firm decides to have external owners. External ownership should not be automatic in professional service firms, as such ownership involves a shift in the right to the "residual claims" (see e.g. Fama & Jensen, 1983 for a discussion of this concept) from the professionals to the financial capital owners. External ownership involves investors who are willing to place some of their capital at the disposal of the firm, with the expectation that the profits generated through the firm will give more compensation for these "residual claims" (relative to the risk involved) than what the investor could obtain elsewhere. Professional service firms provide a major challenge to this notion of capital owners having the right to the residual claims, as the role of the capital invested in the value creation process may be minimal, whereas the role of individual discretionary efforts may be critical. In many cases, then, it is more natural that the right to the residual claims resides in the professionals providing the critical assets, and as a result it is not surprising to see so many partnerships and internally owned firms among professional service firms. Many professionals with whom I discussed this issue were envious of firms with wealthy owners and capital to spare for international investments, etc. However, most professionals who were in this situation found that the freedom lost from first having to satisfy the capital owners outweighed the benefits from extra capital available, as they were no longer free to make independent choices in cases where they had to choose between the most interesting and the most profitable projects. However, in most industries we see partnerships, employee owned firms, and incorporated firms with external owners side by side (except, of course, in industries where the partnership form is required by law). The variety of ownership forms indicates that even this dimension may be one of strategic choice, rather than a dimension with an optimal solution for all firms. Chapter V will discuss these issues further.

Similar to the debate over which projects to prioritize in terms of professional challenges versus profits, many firms engage in a fundamental debate over growth and optimal size. In the following chapter on strategic implications (Chapter VI), this issue will be discussed in further detail, but from the above discussion it is obvious that not all firms will be more profitable, more able to attract talented professionals, nor more able to win interesting projects if they grow. There may be benefits to scale and growth, but there are also substantial diseconomies of scale in terms of organization and coordination, and for many professionals the smaller firm is more attractive than the large firm. The small and large firms exist side by side in the same industries and have different strengths and weaknesses that match different needs of clients and professionals. Hence, growth is neither necessary nor an appropriate criterion for judging the success of a professional service firm.

Finally, and fully in line with the above, professional service firms frequently resist the tendencies to establish hierarchical organizations where career success involves promotion to ever higher managerial positions. Most professionals came into their professions through higher education because they were driven by an intellectual curiosity and an interest in the topics of their area of expertise. The best technical experts rarely want to spend their time supervising others, and only exceptionally do they have the necessary talents and skills to become good managers. On the other hand, professionals like to be independent and rely on their own judgment and tend only to respect managers with proven professional expertise. They take advice and seek support from peers and senior experts, but they do not take orders from managers who are "simply bureaucrats." As a result, a major dilemma results for most firms, as even small and flat professional service firms need managers who supervise and take charge in matters of strategic or overall interest. This challenge will be discussed at further length in the following chapter.[5]

In Table 2, the critical dimensions of professional services are summarized, together with a reference to original sources discussing the dimensions where appropriate. Complete references to these works are found in the bibliography at the end of the book.

Table 2. Characteristics of Professional Business Services

Characteristics of "market entities" (what is delivered)
- Degree of tangibility: Typically "intangible dominant" (Shostack, 1984)
- Degree of customization to client needs: High (Lovelock, 1983)
- Simultaneity of production and consumption: not defined (Grön-roos, 1985)

Characteristics of service supplier
- Resource base: people dependent, highly trained people (Thomas, 1978)
- Number of professionals involved: varies
- Single profession versus ecclectic teams: varies
- Degree of capital intensity: Typically low
- Capacity: relatively unconstrained beyond short term (Lovelock, 1983)

Cont'd

---

[5] Over the last decade or so, a stream of research has emerged in which researchers explore the transformations of traditional professional partnerships (wat Greenwood, Hinings & Brown called P2-companies) towards what they now call "Managed Professional Businesses" (MPBs). Some key participants in this stream of research are professor Royston Greenwood and a group of researchers with him at University of Alberta, Canada, and lecturer Laura Empson and some of her colleagues at the Saïd Business School of the University of Oxford. I will revert to a more in-depth description of their work in the following chapter.

Table 2 continued:

- Demand: fluctuating or stable depending on niche (Lovelock, 1983)
- Number of service outlets: strategic decision (Lovelock, 1983)
- Degree of innovation: typically high, partly strategic decision
- Degree of individual (professional) judgment involved: high (Lovelock, 1983)

Characteristics of client
- Client: a firm or another institution/organization
- Degree of certainty of service needs: varies substantially (Mills, 1986)
- Service recipient: mainly an organization, partly strategic decision (Lovelock, 1983)

Characteristics of interaction
- Degree of information asymmetry: high
- S-factor (degree of simultaneity of demand and supply processes): typically high, but varies – even over time (Hirsch, 1993)
- Place of interaction: typically client site (Lovelock, 1983)
- Nature of interaction: may be both formal and informal (Lovelock, 1983)
- Length of interaction: varies
- Continuous vs discrete interaction: varies, but typically discrete (project to project) (Lovelock, 1983)

Suggested Readings

Ahrnell, B.-M. & Nicou, M. 1989. Kunnskapsföretagets marknadsföring: Att utveckla förtroende, relationer och kompetens. Liber.

Czepiel, J.A.; Solomon, M.R. & Surprenant, C. F. 1985. The service encounter: Managing Employee/Customer Interaction in Service Businesses. Lexington Books.

Edvardsson, B. & Gummesson, E. E. 1988. Management i tjänstesamhället. Stockholm, Sweden: Liber.

Eiglier, P. & Langeard, E. 1987. Servuction: Le marketing des services. Paris, France: McGraw Hill.

Greenwood, R. & Empson, L. 2003. "The Professional Partnership: Relic or Exemplary Form of Governance?" Organization Studies, 24(6), pp. 909-933.

Greenwood, R.; Hinings, C.R. (Bob) & Brown, J. 1990. ""P2-form" strategic management: Corporate practice in professional partnerships." Academy of Management Journal, 33(4), pp. 725-755.

Greiner, L. E. & Metzger, R. O. 1983. Consulting to Management. Englewood Cliffs, NJ: Prentice Hall.

Grönroos, C. 1985. Strategic Management and Marketing in the Service Sector. Lund, Sweden: Studentlitteratur.

Heskett, J. L. 1986. Managing in the Service Economy. Boston, MA: Harvard Business School Press.

Koppang, H. & Løwendahl, B. R. 1995. "Advise us what to do; decide for us." In: Høivik, H. v. W. & Føllesdal, A. (Eds.) The ethics of consultancy. Kluwer.

Kotler, P. & R. A. Jr. Connor. 1977. "Marketing professional services." Journal of Marketing (January) pp. 71-76.

Kubr, M. Ed. 3rd revised edition 1996. Management consulting: A guide to the profession. Geneva, Switzerland: ILO.

Levitt, T. 1981. "Marketing intangible products and product intangibles." Harvard Business Review :MAY-JUN.

Lovelock, C. H. Ed. 1988. Managing Services: Marketing, Operations, and Human Resources. London, UK: Prentice Hall Int.

Løwendahl, B.R.; Revang, Ø. & Fosstenløkken, S.M. 2001. "Knowledge and value creation in PSFs: A Framework for Analysis". Human Relations 54 (7), pp. 911-931.

Maister, D.H. 1993. Managing the professional service firm. Free Press.

Maister, D.H. 1997. True Professionalism. – The courage to care about your people, your clients, and your career. New York: Simon & Schuster.

Maister, D.H. 2001. Practice what you Preach – What managers must do to create a high achievement culture. New York: Simon & Schuster/Free Press.

Maister, D.H.; Green, C.H. & Galford, Robert M. 2000. The Trusted Advisor. New York: Simon & Schuster/Free Press.

Mills, Peter K. 1986. Managing service industries. Ballinger.

Sveiby, K. E. & Risling, A. 1987. Kunnskapsbedriften. Oslo, Norway: Cappelen.

Thomas, D. R. E. 1978. "Strategy is Different in Service Businesses." Harvard Business Review, JUL-AUG, pp. 158-165.

Zeithaml, V. A. ; Parasuraman, A. & Berry, L. L. 1990. Delivering quality service; Balancing customer perceptions and expectations. New York, NY: Free Press.

III. Managerial Challenges

Why don't strict procedures and hierarchy work?

Introduction

In the previous chapter, a number of characteristics of the service as well as the individual professionals were highlighted, and some of the resulting challenges briefly discussed. At the heart of professional service firm operations lies the management of the processes whereby the professionals with the appropriate expertise are matched with client problems in need of a solution. If humans were like machines or money that could be allocated to the optimal application by managers knowing both the needs of the clients and the skills of their employees, this match would be relatively simple to achieve. However, as pointed out in the previous chapter, this is absolutely not the case. Client needs are typically only discernable through active participation in the interaction, and even then the needs are frequently not fully apparent. Hence, no manager can supervise all service encounters and know precisely what is going to be needed in each interaction.

In this chapter, a number of the managerial challenges involved in attracting, motivating, controlling, developing, keeping, and "allocating" professionals are discussed. The following two sections discuss why management is a critical process for professional service firms. Two sections then follow discussing some of the reasons why it is so difficult to find, develop, and retain excellent managers in professional service firms, in particular due to their desire to remain active professionals rather than to become immersed in internal affairs. The remaining six sections of the chapter highlight different aspects of managerial challenges that are particularly salient in professional service firms. These challenges need to be taken into account for the development of a viable strategy for a professional service firm, as will be discussed further in the following chapters.

Managing "resources" that make their own decisions

Professionals are not like machines or money and cannot be allocated to a project unless they themselves see that project as the most interesting option available to them at that moment and appropriate for their exper-

Figure 4. Management as playing chess.

tise. The following illustration by Sønsteby, taken from an article I published in Norway in late 1994, shows, humourously, what may happen if a traditional top manager tries to treat highly educated expert employees as deployable resources similar to chessmen that can be moved from one position to another if the game requires it. Chessmen stand still and wait for the players' next move. Professionals do not. The player has more information about the overall game than the chessmen. The opposite is typically true of professionals and managers in professional service firms.

In deciding whether or not to accept an assignment, professionals typically consider both intra-firm and external alternatives, and they assess both available and potential but probable alternatives. They also assess both the short term implications and the effect on their future assignments, such that they may be willing to take on a trivial project occasionally, if they think they will earn goodwill from which they will benefit next time around. As a result, strategic changes in professional service firms require negotiations and persuasion. The professionals who fundamentally disagree are likely to leave the firm, and the examples of such exits and resulting spinoffs are many. A now classic story of such a split due to disagreements on strategic issues was the one in which the firm A.T. Kearney was formed as a spinoff from McKinsey in the early years of the firm (Higdon, 1968). Similarly, in the history of the Norwegian management consulting company IKO (which was merged into Gemini Consulting, which later became Cap Gemini Ernst & Young, currently Cap Gemini), several spinoffs have resulted from such disagreements, and in many of these cases the professionals who walk out end up establishing a new and tough competitor in the market.

The two primary processes in professional service firms are highlighted here: recruiting and keeping the best professionals and winning the most interesting clients and projects. Needless to say, the two processes are not independent. If you have the best experts in the world, you have a very strong position vis à vis competitors and are likely to win the challenging projects. On the other hand, if you are able to win the most interesting contracts, it is easy to attract the best professionals and if the probability of winning new interesting projects seems high, the professionals will remain with the firm. Still, the professionals also consider the internal processes they have to live with, and if these are bad, the cost-benefit analysis done by each professional may tip to the "too costly" side. Says Mr. Steffen, senior partner at the German management consulting firm ExperTeam:

> "Consultants just don't have – and don't want to take – the time for detailed reports and formal procedures. Controls have to be simple, make sense to the individual, and enhance interpersonal communication. You must never forget that a good consultant can always find another job..."

Monetary rewards do play a significant role in the calculation of whether to stay with the firm or look elsewhere for better options, but in my interviews the economic side of the calculation was emphasized much less than what might have been expected. A salary which is perceived to be unreasonable compared to the value created as the result of a professional's input, is likely to lead to an exit. But as long as the remuneration is reasonable, the professional "glue" seems to be much more connected to the professional challenges available. On the other hand, staying with the most interesting projects where the learning and reputation effects are greater obviously adds to the value of the professional in the market, so that an individual may be willing to accept lower salaries in the short run in order to build professional capital and gain more in later assignments. Discussions with junior level auditors or lawyers in large international firms underscore this analysis; the workload is extreme and the salaries relatively low, but the early years in such a company with so many challenging clients and highly qualified colleagues add so much to their learning and reputation that the investment is seen to be worth the high cost.

To most firms, however, this may be a risky strategy which needs to be closely monitored, as the best juniors are also those who may more easily find alternative jobs. The balance needs to be carefully managed, and open channels of communication must be available so that frustrations among the juniors are known early.

There are many factors that affect the attractiveness of a firm, as seen from the point of view of a junior professional. Some firms try to market themselves as "the best schools in the profession," thereby indicating that juniors who choose their firm as first employer both improve their professional competence more rapidly and increase the value of their CV faster than in competitor firms. Firms that succeed with such a strategy can choose among the very best applicants of the year, every year, because both the juniors and the market are convinced that they are making a good investment, regardless of whether they stay in the firm to the partner level or not. Good "schools" for junior applicants often also apply the "up-or-out"-principle quite strictly, whereby only a small number of juniors make it through each level of promotion, and a very small percentage – maybe 5% – make it to the partner level. Such firms typically also make a point of maintaining good relations and staying in touch with juniors who have left the firm, the so-called "alumni". McKinsey & Co. may be one of the best known examples of such a recruiting and retention strategy, but the model is used by many firms, and it is particularly common among law firms.

The role of management in professional service firms

Management is critical to success for professional service firms and maybe more so than for traditional manufacturing firms. There are two reasons for this: First, that the critical strategic resource is individual human beings with strong opinions as to both what they want to do and what is most appropriate for the clients. Secondly, operations consist of a very large percentage of exceptions rather than routine replications of earlier procedures. As pointed out by Stacey (1993), managers and in particular middle managers are primarily employed to deal with exceptions. The organization is designed and the routines and procedures developed in order to maximize the efficiency with which any recurring task can be undertaken, and as long as the firm is involved in "business as usual," these established procedures allow employees to carry out their tasks without needing the judgment of a manager. It is in the situation where the tasks required are so different from those prescribed in the procedures that the manager is called in. The same is true for delegation of authority. The authority granted to an employee is limited by certain rules, and whatever issues go beyond this limited authority need to be referred to higher level management. But if this logic is transferred to professional services, where, by definition, a large part of operations involve exceptions, managerial decisions are required continually. The very flexibility of the resources makes it easy to take on tasks that are fundamentally different from earlier projects, and in order to maintain some strategic focus, managerial judgment is required both in terms of types of new projects, types of new solutions offered, and in particular new people hired even on a temporary basis. Hence, the managerial tasks may be both more challenging and more important in professional service firms than in firms with more routinized operations.

A major challenge in these firms is therefore to find, encourage, and develop good managers, i.e. good coaches for other professionals. Says one senior professional in a large law firm: "*A big problem with the "stars" is that they do not want to share the applause, even when there was a team behind the achievement.*" How do you get the best individual professionals to share in the pride of a strong team? Most likely that is only possible if you insist on recruiting team oriented professionals, even among the senior "stars". It may be very tempting to hire extremely good individualists, but it is dangerous, if the goal of the firm is to develop and/or maintain a team-based culture. I will get back to this issue, in particular in chapter V.

Why waste a good professional in management?

Although management is critical to professional service firm success, the paradoxical fact is that professionals generally do not want others to have the authority to supervise and interfere in their own decisions. The fundamental reason for this lies in the reversed power structure of professional firms, as the control over the most critical resources for value creation resides with the professionals rather than with owners of firm equity. I will revert to this issue in the following chapter, but only highlight the implications for management at this stage.

An organization is typically established to create and deliver value, e.g. through the solution of some critical problems for a group of people. The decision makers may be owners of firm equity or, as in the case of most public organizations, an elected authority. A hierarchy is set up, whereby these stakeholders (Freeman, 1984) can control the operations of the organization, in particular through a board of directors or its equivalent. The board employs top management, and top management reports back to the board. As a result, employees at all levels are responsible vis à vis the management, which again is responsible vis à vis the board of directors. The hierarchy has a natural logic, since firm operations are put in place to achieve the goals defined by the stakeholders represented by the board of directors. The top manager is given authority by the board and, as their primary link to the organization, also has to be accepted by the employees as the top authority figure.

Traditional hierarchies also build on another principle: The most knowledgeable people are promoted to higher level positions with the task of overseeing the work of others (Weber, 1947). If this mechanism works, the hierarchy functions well, as all lower level employees naturally refer to higher level managers for advice and help to solve new problems. At the top level all critical decisions are made by highly knowledgeable managers. The balance between organizational priorities and those of the external stakeholders is achieved through the interactions between top management and the board of directors (see e.g. Fama & Jensen, 1983 for a broader discussion of agency theory and how these mechanisms work when markets are efficient).

When professionals who are employed by the firm also individually hold the critical resource for value creation, the goals are typically developed through an interaction between the senior professionals. These goals are not set by outsiders, and operations are developed jointly by the professionals over time, not designed in order to fulfil the needs of external stakeholders. Goals of the organization are compatible with those of the individuals, and as long as the firm is small, the professionals oversee each other's work. In the extreme case, all professionals are equal partners, and all decisions concerning the firm and their joint efforts are made in partner meetings with everyone present. In this situation, the managerial tasks of division of labor and supervision are reduced to a minimum, yet even in this situation exceptions arise frequently, and hence partner meetings take place at least every week.

The moment the firm employs juniors who are not equal partners, a hierarchical structure emerges. However, it does not take on the same natural structure of referral to top management as in the case of managers who are appointed by external stakeholders through the board of directors. Rather, the partners mutually agree on a delegation of authority to one of their peers, who takes on the responsibility for handling issues that require managerial judgment but do not need to be referred to the partner meeting. In many cases, managerial responsibility for different types of professional matters is referred to different professionals, such that e.g. one partner is in charge of business development or new projects, another is responsible for the development of improved methods, and yet another is responsible for public relations and printed matter.

The managing partner, if the firm decides to elect one, is a "primus inter pares" (first among equals), not a supervisor appointed by external stakeholders who determine the future of the firm. (S)he is only allowed to keep the top position as long as the other professionals find that (s)he does a good job, and hence is responsible to those (s)he supervises. As the CEO of one of the engineering firms of my study (Inc but employee owned) put it: "I am their boss, and they are my bosses. It is sometimes very hard to know when they see themselves as reporting to me and when they are evaluating and supervising my performance!"

The main difference between the CEO responsible to external owners and the managing partner responsible to his or her peers lies in the criteria for both the choice of this person and the evaluation of him/her. Since the managing partner is in charge of professional affairs on behalf of other professionals, the Weberian hierarchy returns, where priority is given to promoting the most competent person. Authority is granted on the basis of professional expertise and experience. On the other hand, in firms with external owners, authority requires special skills and experience in the management of operations for the generation of maximum return on capital invested, as well as the management of the reporting relationship to the representatives of capital owners. CEOs of externally owned firms are judged on their ability to generate high returns on equity and their ability to convince the owners of the quality of management and operations. Managing partners are judged on their professional wisdom and the quality of their managerial decisions in terms of securing the quality and direction of the professional development and reputation of the firm, and they are judged by peers who evaluate their decisions on a day to day basis.

As a result, excellent professional service firm managers are difficult to find, and this problem is exacerbated by the fact that most professionals do not seek managerial responsibilities. Whereas the traditional hierarchy offers higher status and pay and more challenging and flexible tasks at a higher managerial level, the professionals typically see hands-on problem solving as the most challenging and are perceived to be generating more money when they are directly involved in selling and delivering services to clients. As a result, managerial responsibilities are seen as an unwanted burden by individual professionals, and internally focussed activities are typically low status activities among peers. Whereas traditional hierarchies reward people who develop managerial skills by giving them higher level managerial positions with more status and higher salaries, professionals who spend most of their time in management typically are prevented from maintaining their professional development and, as a result, their expertise may become obsolete. Status resides with professional expertise, and payment is linked to the income generated for the firm through the number of billable hours worked and the price charged per hour. When managerial tasks drive out the number of billable hours and the expertise loses its relative value because other professionals are improving their knowledge base and taking the lead as experts, the professional manager loses on both fronts. No wonder so many excellent professionals refuse to take on managerial tasks!

A quote from a senior vice president of one of the engineering firms illustrates this situation:

> *"The result is that we end up being only second-rate professionals, as we do not have the time to keep up-to-date on new developments, and at the same time we are only half-good managers!"*

However, the problem of finding excellent managers in professional service firms has two natural sides: one is to persuade good professionals to take on managerial responsibilities; the other is to find and develop good professionals into good managers. The paradox is that in order to be respected as a manager, the manager must have an excellent professional reputation. If not, the other professionals do not accept him/her as a primus inter pares. The examples of organizations where administrators have neither authority nor respect are many, and anyone who has worked in a professionally driven organization seems to relate the same experiences: "The administrators don't understand us", "the directors only care about rules and red tape", "when we need support, what we get are more instructions and forms to fill out." In order to maintain an excellent professional reputation, the professional is required to spend all or most of his/her time on professional, rather than managerial, affairs. The solution for many firms seems to be temporary managerial roles.

According to Greenwood and Empson (2003), among others, many large professional service firms are currently turning from the professional partnership (P2)-form to a more hierarchical and formalized form called the "managed professional business" (MPB). They have particularly studied this phenomenon in auditing and law firms. The managed professional business hires full time managers, and the owners/partners delegate substantial authority over day-to-day operations to the hired manager. In Norway, we have over the last few years seen a growing interest among major law firms in investing in personnel management, Human Resource (HR) management, organization development, etc., through hiring such experts into the management of the law firms. One firm has even gone so far as to hire a CEO with a business administration background, even though the firm remains a partnership. Since these hired managers have no background in the legal profession, the big question remains how they will get the legitimate authority to achieve their goals. Presumably the only possible way to achieve this, is if they manage to convince the majority of the legal professionals – at least the partners – of the value of the suggested efforts. In other words, the authority of such managers is valid only until the partners say otherwise. One might say that the same is true for the relationship between the CEO and owners as stockholders, yet it is rather different when all the owners both report to the manager in his/her managerial role and at the same time control the manager, from the partnership/board perspective, on a day-to-day basis!

Part time management

Many professional service firms have solved the managerial dilemma by rotating managerial responsibilities, as is common practice in the universities where most professionals are trained. If everyone is required to take on managerial responsibilities and knows these only last for a limited period of time, the chore is more acceptable. For many professionals, the best compensation for such a service to the firm is a guaranteed time off after the period in management; a so-called "sabattical", where the professional can concentrate on recovering his/her pre-managerial "state-of-the-art" professional knowledge. Other professional service firms accept that professional managers will be professionals most of the time and managers only a very small part of the time. In this way the professionals maintain their professional activities in a parallel with their managerial responsibilities.

However, as a result, managerial challenges tend to be crowded out by more pressing issues, in particular where prioritizing involves the choice between internal issues and client related issues. In most professional service firms, professionals describe the situation as one in which management tasks are taken care of late at night and over the week-end, after client related issues have been dealt with. Even managerial issues that are handled under severe time pressure are prioritized in such a way that the most pressing short term concerns take priority over long term strategic decisions. Personnel problems are handled if they are salient and urgent, and hence professionals demanding attention and urgent recruiting needs are the two most highly prioritized tasks. Issues requiring the joint attention of a large number of professionals typically tend to be crowded out by more pressing needs, and as a result, the firm needs a very strong willed manager to force major strategic debates to take place.

Three major problems result from the wide use of part-time management: The crowding out of strategic issues, the inability to develop excellent managers, and the challenges of attracting and keeping good junior professionals without having the necessary time to solve their problems when they need support. The first issue has already been discussed. The second one, of managerial competence, is absolutely critical. Professional expertise is developed over time and through its application to complex problems. The same is true for managerial competence. Managerial competence requires talent as well as training, and when management is a low priority part time activity, it is clear that this training is rather limited. Finally, the ability to recruit, motivate, and develop talented managers who also are able to maintain their professional reputation through their work directly with clients and indirectly through juniors is absolutely critical to a professional service firm's success. In most firms this is an underdeveloped source of value added. The paradox lies in the eternal "chicken-or-the-egg" problem: It takes excellent managers to develop new managers. If the firm does not have an excellent managing partner, it is also unlikely to be able to select and motivate other partners with the ability to develop their managerial skills towards excellence. The dual focus on both billable activities and managerial investments in future quality can only be sufficiently handled if the senior managers signal the importance of prioritizing managerial responsibilities both through stated sets of prioritized tasks and through setting an example.

In addition, it is very important that all senior professionals recognize the importance of their role as coaches to juniors. As one senior partner in a law firm said: "This is almost like "back to the future"; in our profession, training of juniors has been very much like the master and the guild training the apprentices in the different crafts. As a result, juniors are to a large extent dependent on the ability of their closest seniors to be good coaches. Some are lucky and get a true "mentor", others are to a large extent left to themselves."

The underdelegation problem

In addition to the problems resulting from the lack of priority given to internal affairs, the professional service firms face substantial challenges from the fact that for most such firms a large part of their billable hours in service delivery processes take the professionals out of the office space of the firm. When most of the professionals spend very little time in their offices, they meet substantial problems in terms of coordinating with people who are not with them on a given assignment. Since plans and procedures cannot account for unexpected changes, coordination must take place through interaction and mutual adjustment (see e.g Thompson, 1967 and Mintzberg, 1983 for a review of different types of coordination), and such interaction is by definition difficult to achieve between people who are not present simultaneously. A large number of meetings are scheduled in order to achieve the necessary coordination, and support staff such as secretaries and switch board operators provide a crucial and frequently undervalued service in terms of keeping track of who can be reached where and to what extent they can be disturbed at any given moment. Needless to say, modern equipment such as cellular phones with answering machines, portable computers, and e-mail services, have contributed substantially to the increased efficiency of communication and coordination across multiple locations. Yet despite all this helpful equipment, the experience and judgment of a senior secretary cannot be replaced by any kind of technology, when it comes to weighing the urgency of the communication need against the priority of protecting the client-professional interaction from interruptions.

The complexity of such coordination and interaction makes the costs of coordinating very high, especially in terms of the time required by all parties involved. As a result, in many situations professionals prefer not to attempt such coordination and rather become extremely independent. They type and print their own letters, type reports (possibly with assistance for layout and graphics) if they are in a hurry, make photocopies themselves and spend hours in the evening getting their presentation materials ready before important meetings with clients. The situation has been described by Maister (1993) as "the under-delegation problem", and it is evident that in most professional service firms the potential for efficiency enhancement is substantial, if only the professionals were able to allocate more such tasks to assistants and free up more of their own time for managerial or professional tasks. On the other hand, many firms experience problems in terms of fully utilizing the time of an assistant or a secretary, as the unpredictability of when the assistance is needed makes it difficult to plan the capacity in advance. Again, the professional service firm requires attention to managerial issues, but typically ends up with the default solution, namely that of adding more late night hours to the working hours of professionals doing the work themselves, as they did not have the time to delegate the tasks to others.

However, to the extent that the firm manages to develop a sophisticated support structure, it also develops another of the typical professional service firm challenges, namely that of the "dual hierarchies". Since status and authority typically is granted in a bottom-up fashion on the basis of professional achievements, excellent assistants face the same status and remuneration problems as full time managers, as described above. Assistants who are recruited as junior professionals focus primarily on professional tasks and assisting the professional work of the seniors supporting them, in order to learn as much as possible and be promoted to independent professionals or partners. Assistants employed as secretaries or other support personnel typically "belong" to a different career hierarchy and can never cross over to the professional hierarchy, as they do not have the necessary educational background. The administrative hierarchy normally has much lower status, and as professionals with managerial responsibilities do not prioritize administrative tasks and personnel, the administrative assistants often find professional firms to be frustrating employers. One example may illustrate this challenge:

In an earlier study of an engineering design firm, conducted with peers when I was a Ph.D. student in the U.S., three types of careers were identified: professional, pure assistant, and quasi-professional. The pure assistants were people hired to be secretaries, take care of archives and photocopying, etc. They were comfortable with living a different life from the professionals and were happy to have stable working hours and the right to go home every day at 5 p.m. But some senior assistants were college graduates with career ambitions of their own. By doing a good job they were given increasingly challenging office tasks, and the top of their career track in this small office was the single position of office manager. At this stage, the person employed was so experienced in the business of the firm, that she very often could do a better job than the engineering interns coming in from local universities. Everyone from the president to the switchboard operator agreed that she was indispensable as a coordinator of all the different tasks taking place in the office, and yet she was terribly frustrated. There was no way her practical experience with supporting engineering work could possibly qualify her for any further advancement in the firm. In addition, her excellent qualifications as coordinator and support for the engineers led to a situation in which the engineers tried to "protect her" from further learning, as they were afraid they might lose this excellent assistant. Her qualities and popularity actually got her stuck in her present job. Said one of the senior managers: "Taking Ms X out of her present job in order for her to learn new tasks means, in the short run, that we are losing on two fronts. On the one hand, we get an inefficient assistant in her previous place. And on the other hand, we get a beginner in the new job she is hired to learn. Of course we recognize the dilemma, as we are afraid she may get so bored that she seeks new challenges with one of our competitors. We are trying to find alternatives that keep her happy, but I must admit that it is extremely difficult not to load all the coordination tasks onto her as usual. She knows everyone around, both in our office here and in the other offices. She knows how to get hold of the right person, and she always manages to get them to deliver on time. I don't know what we would do without her!"

Despite the challenges, some excellent assistants are attracted to this kind of work and stay with these firms. It may be because they like the excitement which results from the ever changing characteristics of the tasks, such as when an engineering design firm employs every available resource in the development of a bid for a new contract before a deadline. The excitement of the fight against time, the exhilaration of being part of such a hectic joint effort, the satisfaction of making it on time, the pride of the high quality product ... – these are all elements of professional work that many people find attractive, whether they be professionals or not. However, as one of the assistants in a U.S. based international engineering design firm said: "It is great when we finally hear that we actually won the bid that we all worked day and night for, but why don't they congratulate me as well? Why am I not invited to join in on the champagne? Why do I only know about the success through overhearing the excitement in the corridors? After all, I spent day and night for the last weeks working on getting the layout and graphics right. At that time, they brought me coffee and kept telling me how important my work was to the quality of the proposal. Now that the contract has been won, I am back to being "just assistant", and all the credit goes to the engineers who provided the numbers. I know I couldn't do my job without them, but it would still be nice if at least they said "thank you"!"

The danger of being too successful

One of the major problems of professional service firms is the need to develop new project or client proposals continuously. The portfolio of clients and projects shifts with every project completed or new client added, and one of the main managerial challenges is to keep all employees busy but not too overworked. This is no small challenge, as in most firms the development of a new contract takes months or even years. In engineering design the situation may be most dramatic, as most contracts are won on the basis of long bidding processes where a large number of competing firms participate. No firm can afford to bid only on the number of contracts which would fit perfectly with its own capacity. Hence, they need to bid on more projects than they can actually complete while maintaining a flexible work force. The latter is achieved both in terms of people who may be asked to leave (employed on limited contracts) and people who may be called in on short notice. But excellent professionals typically find alternative jobs very quickly, and by the time a new project is in place, the temporary people may no longer be available. In Norconsult, the Norwegian engineering design firm, it was not unusual to pay an excellent project manager a full salary for as much as three to six months after the completion of a project, just to stay in the Bahamas, relax, and not search for new jobs with competitors. The best project managers for developing country projects were so important for the projects and so difficult to find, that the price of keeping a manager waiting for a few months was considered a

cheap insurance compared to the cost of finding and possibly training a
new person after the new project was won.

Even though this may be perceived to be a luxury problem, the problem
of being too successful or winning more bids than the firm can complete is
very real in professional service firms. The problem is exacerbated by the
fact that many bids or clients require the firm to name each individual professional who is going to be assigned to the project, at least at the most
critical positions. In many cases, the firm may win projects that are not
sufficient to fully employ all their professionals and still be forced to give
up one or two projects because the key people have been "overextended."
If the client is unwilling to accept a renegotiation of the staffing of the project, the job may be turned over to a competitor. This extreme situation of
scarce resources is probably the most painful to professional service firm
managers, in particular in periods where supply is abundant and demand
is rather scarce.

Management as "herding cats"

In the above discussion, emphasis has been placed on challenges involved
when the firm is fully employed and has to prioritize its allocation of scarce
resources. However, another major problem resides in the possibility of
not being fully employed. The strategic implications of taking on tasks
which do not fit with the desired firm profile will be discussed at further
length in Chapter IV, but some of the managerial challenges need to be
highlighted here.

If the firm is temporarily unable to utilize all employees on projects, in
the beginning most professionals who receive a salary (and are not partners) find it very attractive to spend time updating their professional
knowledge. For a couple of weeks, they see it as a luxury to be allowed to
read through the piles of material they have accumulated on their desks
and floors during periods of extremely hard work. But very soon they
become restless, and their sense of value as professionals is threatened. If a
professional is "stuck in the office", this can soon lead to reduced status
among peers. When all your colleagues (or so it seems) run out of the
office in their newly pressed suits and ties, it becomes difficult to fight an
inferiority complex.

Most professionals in this situation generate new ideas. If there is more
than one professional "stuck in the office," as a group they will soon start
developing these ideas, and unless there is a senior manager around with

the ability to spend time and energy, very often these ideas extend beyond the strategy of the firm. Said Johan Sagen, founding partner of the management consulting firm IKO (founded in 1945): "Whenever you have two or more professionals in the office with idle time, you risk major problems." When the ideas deviate substantially from firm strategy, either the creative professionals convince a majority of the others to buy into the new strategy, and hence more or less commit to mutiny, or they find that they are alone. If they still strongly believe in their new ideas, they often decide to leave the firm and start a competing company. To keep the creative professionals in line with firm policy, thus, is a crucial but far from easy task, especially with part time management and employee (partner) ownership. No wonder many managers have suggested that managing a professional service firm is like "herding wild cats." Mr Sagen likened it to "making ten or twenty racing horses pull a cart together."

The problem of "free riding," on the other hand, was not seen as a big issue in the firms I have studied. For example, in the small Norwegian IT-consulting firm Pharos, where all thirteen professionals were partners with equal say but allowed to take out all income they brought in after paying their share of accepted common costs, the partners had agreed to support each other (up to a limit, defined as a specified sum) if one partner had a bad year. This, they say, was important as an ex ante insurance to professionals who were not quite sure they could generate enough billable hours on their own and hence were afraid of leaving a safe job in a larger consulting firm or in the public sector. Ex post, as a payment to a partner with insufficient income, the agreement is unlikely to be used for more than a very short period of time. A partnership with equal partners does not offer the individual many opportunities to hide or "free ride" and contribute less than his/her fair share. In fact, the agreement had only been utilized once, at the time of my interviews (1996). The unfortunate partner received about NOK 20 000,- in the interim, before he decided to leave the firm and return to a larger and more traditional consulting firm. As the incidence illustrates, for most professionals the idea of being a burden on friends and colleagues is barely tolerable and, if necessary, accepted only for a very limited period of time.

Another challenge is that if partners are sharing profits equally, or scaled up or down according to some seniority criteria, the challenge in terms of choosing the right partners who will contribute to increasing the average partner bonus, as opposed to reducing it, becomes extreme. How can you know, when people are in the late thirties or early fourties, whether or not they will perform at an excellent level when they reach the age of sixty? Can you demote seniors from partnership? In principle it should be possible, but very few firms practice such rules. There are, however, firms where partners have been asked to "voluntarily" move quietly to a less demanding work environment.

The pros and cons of a cohesive culture

If it is true that managing a professional service firm is similar to herding cats, it is also critical to find the kinds of professionals that are able to pull together and develop a strong and competitive culture to retain the best experts and outcompete other groups. They may be strong-willed and individualistic, like cats, but they are not unable to form a cohesive culture. In fact, since the two key managerial challenges of the professional service firm involve keeping the best people and winning the best projects, the culture and the support structure surrounding the professionals are absolutely critical both to maximizing the probability of their staying with the firm and to helping them complete the projects with minimum time lost in coordination and communication.

If we stick to the metaphor of herding cats, however, one important thing to remember is that cats do come when you want them to, if only you have the right incentive – for cats, even a dead herring might work! In other words, incentives are important, even to professionals.[1]

In many firms this problem has been quasi-solved through recruiting people with a very similar background, as they bring comparable norms and communication patterns when they enter the firm. In its most extreme, the professionals are the same age, come from the same educational and vocational background, are the same race and gender, and have the same cultural background. This is a comfortable situation for the professionals, as communication is facilitated in every way possible, and it may also enhance the ability of the firm to develop a coherent image in the market. The extremely cohesive culture is very often the result of the similarity of backgrounds at the founding stage, and as the firm grows through recruiting peers and friends who are well known to the existing partners, there is a natural tendency to reinforce this profile.

However, such a culture can also create major problems for the firm, as it soon becomes difficult to recruit new professionals with different back-

---

[1] Thanks to Øivind Revang, professor and dear colleague at BI Norwegian School of Management, for the image of the herring.

grounds. As pointed out by economists decades ago, labor market discrimination reduces the pool from which the firm is able to choose new employees, and hence the firm is not sure to get the best candidates. This discrimination does not need to be deliberate, but as the profile of the firm is based on one type of background, potential candidates with different backgrounds are less likely to apply. The problem frequently becomes apparent after ten or twenty years, when the founding partners are no longer in their thirties but rather in their late fifties. They feel better than ever and know each other extremely well, but find that the client representatives with whom they need to negotiate are no longer their peers. Whereas, in the past, they finished a meeting as equals, albeit employed by different firms, over a beer at the local bar, they now find themselves with a client representative who could be a son or – even worse – a daughter.

Firms in this situation often fail at recruiting new professionals with the background matching that of these new client representatives, as their cohesive cultures make it almost impossible for a new and different partner to come in and alter the traditional ways of doing things in the firm. If they do succeed in recruiting the right kind of different partner, it is often not the best professionals who apply, as the best have many options and see no need to go into a firm where the coordination and communication challenges are going to be substantial from the beginning. Two Swedish authors, Sveiby and Risling (1987) have discussed what they call the importance of "managing the age pyramid." This is absolutely crucial, but age is clearly not the only factor. Professional experience and educational background, as well as race, gender, and cultural diversity are issues that need to be managed at an early stage. Even though there may be substantial benefits to the development of a cohesive culture, the culture should ideally be able to accomodate multiple backgrounds such that the professional firm is able to match the representatives of the client firms as these also evolve over time. If not, either it will live and die (or retire) with its present professionals, or it will have to start all over again with new partners after a major transformation process.

The tyranny of tangibles

Another managerial challenge of professional service firms, partnerships in particular, lies in what one of the management consultants called "the tyranny of tangibles." Despite the fact that the professional service firm by definition generates most of its value on the basis of intangible resources such as professional competence, it is typically very difficult for professional firms to invest partnership money in intangibles. Strategic resource deployment and development will be discussed in further detail in Chapter IV. Here the emphasis is on the challenge of developing resources that to a large extent involve individual learning and thus are appropriable by single professionals who may walk out to capitalize on the investment. "The tyranny of tangibles" means that it seems to be much easier for a partner meeting to agree on the acquisition of a set of new computers, for instance, than to set aside money for the development of new project management procedures or freeing a partner from some billable hours and paying him/her to invest in the training of juniors.

Many professional service firms have also been trapped in their desire to invest in tangibles that symbolically indicate to the outside world how successful they are. Norconsult, the Norwegian engineering design firm referred to previously, invested substantial amounts of capital and committed firm cash flow to very high interest and debt payments after designing and building a particularly impressive office building. The professionals were extremely proud of this symbol of success, but the fixed costs incurred did not match well with the flexibility of the cash flow required as the portfolio of projects kept shifting. The expensive building was one of the reasons for the crisis the firm experienced in the mid-1980's, as the firm had no slack cash to meet the problems resulting from a couple of projects with substantial losses. As a result, several of the previous owners decided to sell out, and the majority ownership of Norconsult was transferred to NPC (Norwegian Petroleum Consultants). One of the first decisions of the new majority owner after taking over was to sell the office building and rent less expensive and more flexible office space.

Managing development spirals

Professional service firms, then, can be characterized by a successful blend of projects won, projects completed, and people recruited. At the heart of all professional service firm operations lie the people employed and the clients or projects they work on. When the slack professional time available is adequate to accomodate work on new proposals or potential clients, the firm may be able to develop and maintain positive spirals of value creation (Normann, 1984), whereby excellent professionals are able to attract excellent projects that contribute to profitability, professional development, and improved procedures.

On the other hand, if the process goes awry, the spirals may rapidly turn negative. As described above, professionals without interesting work quickly search elsewhere for new challenges. When some of the most mobile and often most visible experts leave the firm, the probability of winning new challenging clients or projects is reduced, and the perceived attraction of the firm to both present and potentially employed professionals is reduced. Hence, the probability of winning new projects is reduced even further, and the firm very often relaxes its strategic priorities and takes on projects that are peripheral and possibly barely profitable. The motivation is reduced and the ability to enhance both procedures and reputation is also reduced. Negative spirals may rapidly destroy professional service firms, as the most critical professional resources are so flexible and mobile that the firm may be reduced to a shell within a few weeks. The story of the rise and fall of Arthur Andersen, mentioned earlier, in chapter II, offers an excellent illustration of how fast a professional service firm can disappear. When reputation is lost, client faith in the integrity of the professionals is also lost. Law suits follow, and clients world wide prefer to choose one of the competitors.

Conclusions

In this chapter, the challenges involved in the management of professional service firms have been highlighted, along with the importance of paying attention to these challenges. Even if it may be difficult to employ professionals as full time managers to deal with these issues on behalf of their colleagues, it is absolutely critical that the issues are discussed and dealt with. Without attention, the firm easily loses its clear and strong reputation, as it takes on too many differing tasks and employs too many different types of professionals. Focus may be implicitly or explicitly agreed upon, but without attention paid to any deviation, the firm is likely to be in trouble. In the following chapter, the possibilities of developing and maintaining strategic focus without reducing flexibility and client responsiveness will be discussed at further length, with particular emphasis on the resource based perspective on strategy which has been developed in strategic management research over the last two decades.

Suggested Readings

Alvesson, M. 1989. Ledning av kunskapsföretag. Stockholm: Norstedts. English version 1995: Managing Knowledge Intensive Companies. Berling/New York: de Gruyter.

Fama, E. F. & M. C. Jensen. 1983. "Separation of Ownership and Control." Journal of Law and Economics 26: pp. 301-325.

Greenwood, R. & Empson, L. 2003. "The Professional Partnership: Relic or Exemplary Form of Governance?" Organization Studies, 24(6), pp. 909-933.

Maister, D.H. 1993. Managing the professional service firm. New York, NY: Free Press.

Mintzberg, H. 1983. Structure in fives; Designing effective organizations. Englewood Cliffs, NJ: Prentice Hall.

Ogilvy, D. 1988. Confessions of an Advertising Man, 2nd ed. New York. NY: Atheneum.

Normann, R. 1983. Service Management: Ledelse og strategi i produksjon av tjenester. Oslo, Norway: Bedriftsøkonomens forlag.

Sveiby, K. E. & Risling, A. 1987. Kunnskapsbedriften. Oslo, Norway: Cappelen.

Thompson, J. D. 1967. Organizations in action. New York, NY: Mc Graw-Hill.

IV. Strategic management

Why bother with strategy when opportunities arise anyway?

Introduction

More than any other type of firm, professional service firms are driven by opportunities created in the interaction between clients with problems to be solved and professionals with relevant expertise and experience. As a result, firms evolve through processes in which the flexibility of adding new clients, services, and competent professionals is absolutely crucial, and strategic planning may be seen to be unnecessarily constraining. In the previous chapter, the importance as well as the difficulties of managing these firms were discussed.

The present chapter presents a theoretical framework which may be productively applied to the strategic management of professional service firms, namely the resource based perspective. In the first section, the reasons that strategy has been underemphasized in professional service firms are explored in further detail. The next two sections present the resource based perspective and discuss how it may be applied to professional service firms. Next, the different types of resources of professional service firms are discussed, with particular emphasis on the role of different types of competences and other intangible resources. The following section discusses an expanded version of the resource based perspective, stressing the particular challenges involved in strategic management when the critical strategic resources have their own opinions and can leave the firm any time. Issues of who owns and controls the resources are discussed in further detail, before we turn to the dynamic processes of resource accumulation, resource leverage, and vulnerability to exits by key professionals. The next section briefly discusses the development of resources – and in particular competence, reputation, and relationships as byproducts of daily activities. Then follows a discussion of key issues in strategic management in professional service firms, with an emphasis on priorities as opposed to plans. Finally, the issue of how to organize the operations of professional service firms is highlighted. In the following chapter, the implications of differences between firms and industries will be discussed, and the strategic options and implications founded in a resource based perspective will be further developed.

Why strategy has been underemphasized

The evolution and growth of the professional service firms have typically been driven by the effort, competence, and personal relationships of individuals with the ability to convince potential clients of their problem solving capabilities in certain areas, rather than by a planned growth targeted to specific markets. In terms of "deliberate strategy" (Mintzberg & Waters, 1985), even the most basic strategic decisions seem to have been neglected in professional service firms, including the fundamental questions of choice of domain (Levine & White, 1961), i.e. what to deliver to whom and where, and a direction for growth. For example, in the business history of Parsons Brinckerhoff, Bobrick (1985) describes the evolution of the firm before the 1980's ("the years of the partnership") as resulting from a combination of highly qualified and compatible people and interesting projects. For example, with no specialist bridge engineers, projects within bridge design were not considered a target area for the firm. But when a highly skilled bridge designer suggested that he might join the firm and develop such a core service, the firm agreed and the "bridge design division" became highly successful. Bobrick (1985) quotes the president as saying:

> *"In the days of the partnership, there was very little cooperation or even communication across technical areas. Each partner ran his own discipline out of New York as if it were an independent firm."* (Bobrick, 1985, p.213)

Similarly, when projects happened to be located overseas, such as those involving the design of Air Force bases in Newfoundland and Iceland, the firm became involved in international operations. People- and opportunity-driven growth is not unique to this firm. Rather, an evolution without any explicit overall plan or strategy seems to be the rule in professional business service firms, rather than the exception.

In a sense, then, proactive strategic management is often more or less neglected in professional service firms, at least in the early years. One reason for this may be the fact that early strategy literature emphasized strategic planning whereas the service firms were doing their utmost to avoid routinization, rigid formal structures, and predesigned activities that might reduce responsiveness and innovation. Many professional service firm managers probably thought, as Mintzberg (1983), that the innovative firm (or "operating adhocracy" in Mintzberg's terminology) which develops a stable strategy will have "restructured itself as a bureaucracy," and hence will no longer be able to respond flexibly to changing client needs.

Not only did the managers of these firms see strategic planning as irrelevant or even detrimental to success for their firms, but as discussed in the previous chapter, managers of professional service firms are typically also handicapped in their efforts to focus on long term issues. Senior professionals of the firms have typically advanced to the senior level through their professional qualifications and their ability to handle clients and convince them of their trustworthiness and problem solving capabilities. As managers, they are expected to maintain this external focus and continue to generate revenues for the firm. The time allocated to managerial tasks is very limited. Not only are the managers of professional service firms not trained as managers, but they are typically only part-time managers as they remain part-time professionals.

Another factor which may contribute to the lack of focus on strategic management in many professional service firms is the nature of the professional norms guiding appropriate conduct within the firms. As discussed in the introductory chapter, professional norms have typically emphasized service to the client as the primary goal and have not only de-emphasized profit-seeking as a goal but even made profits an issue not to be discussed among "true" professionals (Higdon, 1969). As a corollary to this, many professional service firms do not participate in direct marketing activities, and when a firm presents itself in an advertisement, this is frequently seen as an indication of trouble. The norms generally advocate that if the quality of service is high enough, clients will come to the firm automatically. Advertising is seen as a sign of an insufficient flow of clients and projects and may easily be interpreted as a desperate search for new projects, which again is typically interpreted as an indication of insufficient quality. If the firm is excellent, it must have clients. If it advertises, it does not have enough clients, and hence it probably is not excellent. This is really a "catch 22" situation, in particular for the small and newly established firm, and is one reason why the establishment and growth of new professional service firms typically take a long time before the reputation is known throughout a broad market. Advertisements are typically used indirectly: to announce the entry of a new partner to the firm or to congratulate a high status client on an anniversary, their new profile, or their new office building.

An interesting and innocent story may illustrate these interpretations of advertising in professional services. The small Norwegian partnership in IT-consulting, Pharos, decided to place an advertisement in the largest

Norwegian newspaper, Aftenposten, seeking new partners. However, when it appeared, the advertisement did not conform to the order, and Aftenposten apologized and agreed to reinsert the advertisement in the next edition. The day after, the partners of Pharos, as well as their colleagues and competitors, were all surprised to find the advertisement extremely visible on the front page of the newspaper. This was a spot which cost much more than the price paid for the advertisement in the first place, and from Aftenposten's point of view, Pharos was given excellent compensation. In terms of attention, certainly; but the consequence was also that both competitors and clients began speculating about the contractual situation at Pharos: were they desperate, since they put an advertisement on the front page of the paper, or were they able to generate unprecedented amounts of money for their projects, since they could afford such an advertisement simply to attract one more partner? Luckily the resultant signal was not interpreted as a desperate search for projects; had the misplaced advertisement concerned moving to a new address, the final result might well have been negative!

Finally, the competitive situation may have allowed firms to evolve in an ad hoc fashion and to deemphasize issues of efficiency and effectiveness as manifested in proactive strategic management. The emphasis on the uniqueness of each problem and solution has made comparison of services and firms extremely difficult — especially ex ante. Consequently, the pricing of professional services has typically been a matter of negotiation between each client and supplier, rather than subject to open price-competition in a free market. To a large extent, competent professionals and their firms have been able to carve out a market niche for themselves and to expand by adding services rather than by competing head on with other firms in the industry. Competition within these industries to date has been relatively limited, but currently seems to be increasing, as illustrated by the situation of the auditing industry, where the leading firms (previously called the "Big-Eight") were traditionally able to grow rapidly and profitably without having to compete with each other head-on. Today, however, they spend substantial amounts of resources in the search for competitive advantages which may distinguish them from their competitors and often find that they have to compete for client contracts through competitive bids. (For a broader discussion of the evolution of the auditing industry, see e.g. Greenwood, Hinings and Brown, 1990 or Stevens, 1981 and 1985).

Resource based strategic management: Background

Strategic management is critical to the professional service firm's success, but from the previous chapter it should be clear that strategy must focus on other issues than long term planning and return on financial investments. The critical decisions in professional service firms concern the recruiting of new professionals and the portfolio of projects and clients served. If the firm has no strategy, the evolution of both the project and client portfolio and the types of competences available from the professionals employed is likely to be largely opportunity driven. The result is more often than not that the strengths built in terms of relationships and competences are ad hoc and not further leveraged after the specific project is completed. In figure 5 below, this evolution over time is illustrated in a simplified sketch.

Cumulative reputation building and learning requires focus and conscious choice of the direction for growth, and it is the development of this focus that is the core of strategic management for professional service firms. However, given the nature of these firms, including the individual interests of the professionals and the ad hoc nature of new projects emerging, the development and maintenance of such a focus is not trivial. It typically does not sustain itself without conscious managerial effort.

My dissertation study was undertaken with the specific purpose of developing theory and models for the strategic management of professional service firms, implicitly assuming that such theories and models would contribute to improved performance for these firms. At a point in time when I was in the middle of my interviews and trying to make sense of the unique characteristics of the firms in my study, I was lucky enough to be the Wharton School nominee to the 1989 Academy of Management Doctoral Consortium (Business Policy and Strategy division), which took place in San Francisco. Little did I know at that time of the future impact of one of the Academy of Management sessions, but I was excited to see that the presentations on an emerging perspective called "the resource based perspective" attracted a huge audience. In fact, the room was so packed that people were standing both along the walls and outside to hear a bit of the presentations and discussions. In the years that followed, we have seen a great deal of new research on the resource based perspective in strategic management, and this literature offers promising implications not only for manufacturing firms but also for professional service firms.

The essence of the resource based perspective lies in its emphasis on the

Figure 5. Competence accumulation in a given competence area.

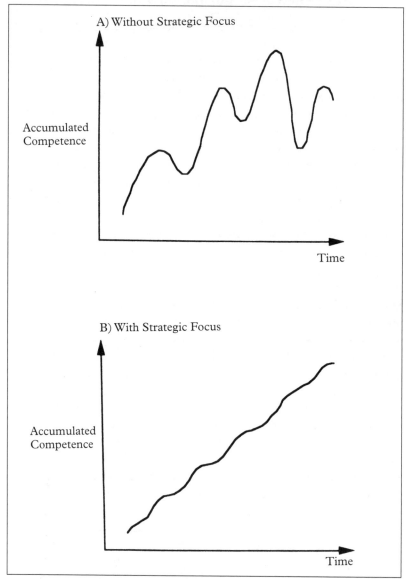

internal resources available to the firm, rather than on the external opportunities and threats dictated by industry conditions. Firms are considered
to be highly heterogeneous, and the "bundles of resources" (Penrose,
1959) available to each firm are different. This is both because firms have

different initial resource endowments and because managerial decisions affect resource accumulation and the direction of firm growth as well as resource utilization. Immersed as I was in my study of professional service firms, I found this to be extremely exciting. No more focus on discussions of generic strategies of cost efficiency versus quality, and no more emphasis on generic value chain activities and cost drivers in a linear sequence of input, transformation, and output. It was not that I wanted to discard the heritage from Porter (1980, 1985), nor that I believed that the new perspective could replace everything we knew. But I was so pleased to see a perspective which explicitly assumed firms to be fundamentally different and which focussed on idiosyncratic resources as sources of competitiveness. Firms that base a large part of their value creation on individual professionals are, in my view, by definition different. Professionals are extremely diverse both in terms of their competence, their experience, their interests and creative focus, and their networks of client and peer contacts. Assuming homogeneity of such firms would therefore be a rather unrealistic starting point.

In the following, I first present some of the core ideas of the resource based perspective on strategy, as it may be applied to strategic management in professional service firms. I then go on to discuss the different types of resources available to professional service firms and their management in further detail.

Resource based strategic management: Main principles

According to Itami (1987), strategic management should be centered around the management of firm resources such that the firm's resource base is improved over time. Figure 6 illustrates the key strategic processes within a resource based perspective.

In this figure three core processes are summarized. The first two are adapted from traditional strategic management texts and highlight the importance of viewing the earlier work by Porter, Ansoff, Williamson and others as complementary to the resource based perspective, rather than as competing views to be replaced. The third process is new. In the following, the three processes will be described in more detail.

The first strategic process concerns the *product/market strategy*, well defined by Ansoff (1967) and others following him: The firm must define which are to be the target markets to be served, in terms of types of clients as well as geographical reach, and also what types of products or services

Figure 6. Dynamic view of asset accumulation and strategy.

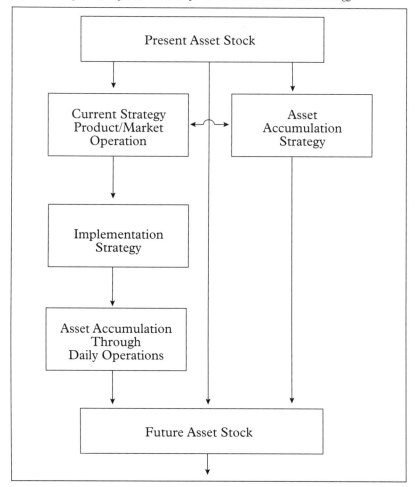

are going to be delivered to these markets. For professional service firms, this decision is important, as it sets boundaries for the types of expansions which are acceptable for professionals taking on new types of clients and offering different services from the traditional ones. As pointed out by Penrose (1959), one of the important roles of management is to take care of the entrepreneurial implications of the firm's activities, as the idiosyncratic bundle of resources available to the firm may be applied to multiple and differing activities. Neither the products nor the markets are given once and for all, and keeping an eye open for alternative and more valuable applications of the resources is a critical task of senior managers. For professional service firms this flexibility may be even higher than that of traditional manufacturing firms.

The second process, called *"operations strategy,"* involves setting limits for the activities that are to take place within the boundaries of the firm. This is also a critical process to manage for the professional service firm. The very moment independent professionals decide to hire a secretary, a switch board operator, an assistant to deal with graphics and photocopying, a part time cook to provide lunch, etc., the individuals incur joint responsibilities and need to make joint decisions. Should the person cleaning the offices be employed by the firm or contracted from a specialized company? For activities where such suppliers are common, this decision may be trivial, but in terms of graphics experts who may be needed on very short notice and expected to work day and night when a proposal or report needs to be completed, the answer is not that obvious. And when the firm needs an expert on contract law, not only for a single contract, but over and over again, should they then hire such a person or be dependent on an external service provider? Transaction cost theory and other literature on the internalization of different types of activities provide helpful insights to these decisions, and as the boundary-setting activities are not very different for professional service firms compared to more traditional firms, this literature is helpful. (See e.g. Williamson, 1975; 1985 for a detailed discussion).

The third and final process of the figure, namely that of *resource accumulation*, is the most interesting to explore here. This process consists of two different subprocesses: one – illustrated on the right hand side of the figure – characterized by specific activities undertaken in order to accumulate more assets (or resources, as I prefer to call them), and the other – illustrated on the left hand side of the figure – summarizing the indirect resource accumulation resulting from daily operations. After a more detailed review of the different types of resources, I will return to this critical process of resource accumulation.

Resource based strategic management:
Categories of resources

In order to make the resource based perspective more applicable, we need an in-depth understanding of what the relevant resources may be. Authors within the resource based perspective have contributed different definitions of resources, as well as analyses of how they may be combined to improve firm competitiveness. In the following, a brief review of these definitions and resource categories is presented, before I discuss a framework for resource analysis tailormade for professional service firms.

In a rather general definition, Wernerfelt (1984:7) defines resources as "anything that can be thought of as a strength or weakness of a given firm". Barney (1991:101) defines them as: "All assets, capabilities, organizational processes, firm attributes, information, knowledge, etc. controlled by a firm that enable the firm to conceive of and implement strategies that improve its efficiency and effectiveness." The resource based perspective has also brought back a renewed interest in the early work of Edith Penrose (1959) on the mechanisms underlying the growth of the firm. She classified resources into four categories: land, labor, capital and equipment. Labor here includes both skills and knowledge, and she thus makes the important distinction between physical and personal resources. Hofer and Schendel (1978) later identified five types of resources – financial, physical, human, organizational, and technological – arguing that, combined, they constitute a company's resource profile. Itami (1987) added intangibles, and this discussion has been further applied by Grant (1991). Research within what has now become a large stream of research with a lot of different theoretical as well as empirical starting-points has evolved out of the early days of the resource based view. The appendix on current research in related fields provides more updated references and suggestions for further reading.

The most frequently cited categories of resources today are probably those proposed by Barney (1991), which include three main types of resources: physical capital, organizational capital, and human capital resources.

Penrose (1959) also pointed out that the dynamics of these types of resources are different, i.e. that while the value of physical resources will tend to depreciate over time, human resources such as knowledge may be refined through experience. I would argue, with Penrose, that the different types of resources are driven by a different competitive logic both in terms of resource utilization and resource accumulation, and that for this reason it is important to look into the characteristics of the different resource types in order to analyze and improve our ways of managing them. Teece, Pisano, and Shuen (1989)[1], like Itami (1987) and Penrose (1959), also emphasize the dynamic aspect of strategic resource management, in what they call a "dynamic capabilities approach":

> "...*it is not only the bundle of resources that matter, but the mechanisms by which firms learn and accumulate new skills and capabilities, and the forces that limit the rate and direction of this process.*" (Teece, Pisano & Shuen, 1989:11)

The concept of dynamic capabilities has become a major area of research interest in the last close to a decade. That will also be discussed at further length in the appendix on current research.

Based on the underlying logics of accumulation, I suggest that there are four fundamentally different categories of resources:

(1) Financial assets
(2) Tangible resources, such as production equipment, plants, office buildings etc.
(3) Human resources, in terms of labor input
(4) Intangible or information based resources, including competence, reputation, and brand equity

In the following, each of these resource categories is explored in some more detail, with the main emphasis on the fourth and, in my view, most interesting category for the management of professional service firms, namely that of the intangible resources.

(1) The management of *financial assets* is a well established discipline, where research has given substantial insights into the interaction between firms and efficient markets for capital acquisiton, accumulation, and utilization. Much of the logic of resource accumulation and allocation has been borrowed from the financial management literature, and the sophistication of their tools and methods seems to fascinate resource based

---

[1] This article became famous all over the world as Teece, D.; Pisano, G. & Shuen, A.1989. "Firm capabilities, resources, and the concept of strategy". University of California at Berkeley, working paper. But in 1997 it was finally published in Strategic Management Journal. The title was slightly altered, and the content had to be updated to include at least some of the developments that had happened in the research area since their original contribution was made available. The new reference of the article is: "Dynamic capabilities and strategic management". Strategic Management Journal, 18, pp. 509-533.

authors today. The following quote from Prahalad and Hamel's 1994-book clearly indicates that models from finance may be seen as ideals for the management of other types of resources as well:

> "*Although human resource executives will proudly proclaim that*
> "*people are our most important asset," there is seldom any mecha-*
> *nism for allocating human capital that approaches, in its sophisti-*
> *cation and thoroughness the procedures for capital allocation.*"
> (Prahalad & Hamel, 1994: 232-233).

(2) Similar to the management of capital resources, we have a long and well developed tradition for the management of other *tangible resources*, such as production equipment, technology, and buildings. They may range from being highly flexible and general to being extremely in-flexible and specialized for only one particular production process. Typically there is a conflict between the need for flexibility and the need for efficiency in operations.

Most of the tangible resources are acquired in well functioning markets, although the more specific they need to be, the more complex the bidding process becomes. Investment theory as well as transaction cost theory and sophisticated analyses for procurement have given us substantial insights into how these resources may be acquired at minimum costs, how such investments may reduce flexibility and bind future investments, and how the benefit from such investments may be accounted for over a number of periods. Calculations of net present value based on risk-adjusted interest rates, etc. allow us to make highly sophisticated analyses of investments into tangible resources, both ex ante and ex post. Tangible resources depreciate over time, normally more so with use than if saved.

(3) *Human resources* have traditionally been viewed as sources of labor input, and from micro economic theory we have borrowed models defining the marginal benefits from adding one more hour of labor. We also have models developed to assess the relative benefits from adding more labor hours compared to other productive resources, such as tangible production equipment. Human resource productivity has been an issue of much interest over the past decades, and international statistics compare the labor hour productivity across countries and industries. Human resources are contracted from individuals but are generally seen to be obtainable in well functioning labor markets. When individual inputs are defined in terms of labor hours, individuals are typically seen as substitutable, and one hour of input is a fixed measure independent of who pro-

vides that input. As with tangible resources, there is a conflict between specialization and flexibility, and for human resources this conflict is further exacerbated by the different desires of employers and employees. The more firm specific the training and competence development, the more locked in the employee will be to one particular employer. On the other hand, human resources with general skills are typically abundant in labor markets, and can easily be replaced. The more a job can be deskilled, the less training the employer needs to provide, and the higher the flexibility. In its extreme, such highly repetitive and generalized jobs may be rejected on moral grounds, as the lack of development of employees will be unethical.

(4) Itami (1987), highlighted the fundamental distinction that human beings contribute not only labor but also competence and creativity, even in manufacturing firms. In professional service firms, the intangible aspects of human resource inputs are clearly the most important. Itami discusses the impact of these intangibles or rather *"invisible assets,"* which he further describes as information based. Information based assets are both inputs to the production process and outputs from the process, as they generate more information when in use. Information based assets are not used in the same sense as tangible resources, and they do not depreciate over time. Similarly, they cannot be saved to be utilized at a later point. On the contrary, their value improves with use, and this is particularly true of competences which are to a great extent accumulated through learning processes.

It is not enough to translate the ideal from financial management to resources with a completely different logic. Rather, we need to understand each of these logics in detail and develop relevant resource accumulation and utilization strategies on the basis of these logics and the relative importance of the different types of resources for each unique firm. In the following, I will go further into the different types of intangibles or "invisible assets" and discuss how these are attracted, accumulated, and utilized in professional service firms.

Intangible resources in professional service firms

The intangible or information based resources of the firm consist of a set of very different types of resources, all of which are frequently lumped together under the label "competences" or "capabilities." In my opinion, such a general category is likely to blur the critical dimensions of the dif-

ferent types of intangible resources, differences that are particularly crucial to the strategic management of professional service firms. Intangibles
include both elements of traditional good-will, such as firm reputation,
and competence or capabilities. In the following, the different characteristics of these two types of intangibles are explored in detail.

Competence may be seen as the overall concept covering all aspects
affecting the ability to perform a given task, and exists both at the individual level and at the collective or organizational level. The term "competence" has been used in a number of ways, both synonymous with "knowledge" and synonymous with "capabilities". Building on Nordhaug (1993)
I suggest that the term "competence" and hence also the now so popular
"core competence" (refer to Chapter VI for a further discussion of this
concept) is a broader term than either knowledge or capabilities and that
competence includes both *knowledge*, which is based on existing information, *skills*, which are predominantly acquired through apprenticeships
and "on-the-job training," and thirdly innate *aptitudes* or talents, which
allow people to perform certain tasks in a way superior to that of their
competitors.

There are at least four levels of competences which are crucial to study
in order to determine the competitiveness of a firm:

A) individual operative competences,
B) firm or organization level competences,
C) group level competences, and
D) intermediate competences in terms of managerial competence for the
    mobilization of the inputs from other members of the organization.

A. Individual operational competences.

Through their employees, firms have potential access to a wide array of
individual competences, in terms of strategically and operationally relevant knowledge, skills, and aptitudes. Individual competences may be task
or firm specific, and hence have little or no value outside the firm, or may
be general and easily transferrable to other employers (Nordhaug, 1993),
as is the case with most professional competences. To the extent that the
firm is able to mobilize these competence resources, it may have access
to a large portfolio of individual competences. However, one of the major
challenges for firms that are highly dependent on the competence
resources contracted from mobile individual professionals is the motivation of these professionals to stay with the firm and to utilize their competence for the benefit of firm value creation.

A major challenge for most organizations, and in particular knowledge-based organizations, is the fact that firms frequently do not know the competences potentially available for value creation. A number of relevant competences may be latent (Løwendahl & Nordhaug, 1994), both as the result of organizational ignorance and inadequate memory and because employees may choose not to reveal competences they do not want to utilize or develop further. The typical organization is likely to under-utilize its competence resources, as most employees have a number of relevant competences which they are unable to utilize, given the restraints of their present jobs. Even in the professional service firms of my dissertation study, where the management of individual competence resources was at the core of strategic and operational management, the professionals and managers alike were extremely concerned with finding ways of improving the utilization of these intangible resources.

Examples of individual competences include:
– Professional knowledge and experience
– Knowledge of client firms and industries
– Problem solving skills
– Project management experience and skills
– International experience and language abilities
– Knowledge of formal as well as informal organizational procedures
– Experience and skills in client relationship building and maintenance
– Knowledge of competitors and professional peers
– Experience in government lobbying, media handling, etc.
– Interpersonal competence, such as communication skills and abilities to cooperate in teams
– Meta-competences (Nordhaug, 1993) such as creativity, analytical abilities, and the ability to learn quickly from new situations (See Løwendahl & Nordhaug, 1994 for a further discussion of individual competences)

B. Organizational competences.

The collective or organizational competences manifest themselves in different forms, as do the individual competences. Figure 7 illustrates how collective competences may be classified as three different types similar to those of individual competences:

Firms possess knowledge, both in the form of data bases and other types of information about customers, competitors etc. In addition, firms possess skills which enable them to perform a given set of tasks at a certain

Figure 7. Individual and organizational competences.

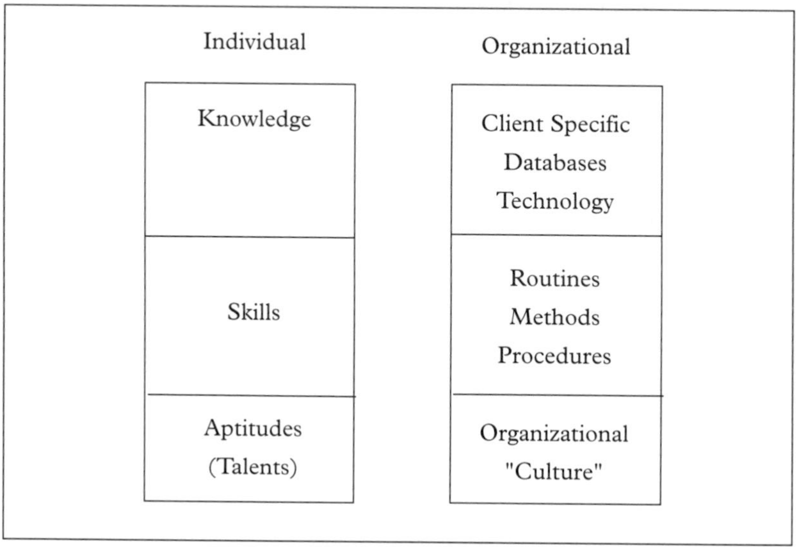

Individual	Organizational
Knowledge	Client Specific Databases Technology
Skills	Routines Methods Procedures
Aptitudes (Talents)	Organizational "Culture"

performance level, such as routines, standard operating procedures, etc. (Nelson & Winter, 1982). Finally, firms differ substantially in terms of their established "way of doing things" (Bower, 1966), including elements of corporate culture such as norms and shared values, and these may give some firms an edge over other firms in terms of creativity, flexibility, mobilization of unique problem solving skills, etc. This third part of collective competence may be seen as similar to individual aptitudes, although it may be a bit far fetched to talk about aptitudes for an entire company.

In addition to their contributions as individual professionals and as members of teams, the professionals also make substantial contributions to firm value creation through their role in the development of collective competences. Collective competences may depend on the individuals, such that they disappear if key individuals leave the organization, or may exist independently of the individuals, such as when routines are manifested in quality control manuals and hence can be transferred to new employees without the participation of senior colleagues. As stated by Itami (1987:14):

> "People are important resources, not just as participants in the labor force, but as accumulators and producers of invisible assets."

Similarly, Prahalad and Hamel (1990) highlight the role of individuals in the development — and potential deterioration — of core competences:

> *"When competencies become imprisoned, the people who carry the competencies do not get assigned to the most exciting opportunities, and their skills begin to atrophy."* (Prahalad & Hamel, 1990:87)

In other words, according to Prahalad and Hamel, part of a firm's core competence may be embodied in individuals who apply their competence to problems they attempt to solve.

C. Group level competences.

The firm may also have access to collective competences at a less aggregate level than the entire organization, such as when particular teams develop unique skills in creative problem solving. Such competences are not the same as individual competences, as they cannot be replicated in other teams just by transferring an individual. Very often the participants in such teams are unable to define why the team is so unusually effective, but they recognize that there is a synergy created by the team members which may completely disappear if one of the members is replaced. Frequently cited illustrations of such team-based competences include the complementary skills developed by some restaurant chefs and their assistants as well as the head waiter, or the art director of the advertising firm who always develops the most creative solutions when two or three particular colleagues work with him/her on an assignment. If one of these team members chooses to change employers, typically the entire team follows. As a result, the firm is particularly vulnerable to the loss of such teams of people with complementary skills, as they prefer to continue working in the rewarding atmosphere of the team and their loyalty may be much stronger to the other team members than to the firm itself.

D. Managerial competences.

The fourth and absolutely crucial dimension of competence has been discussed in Chapter III and concerns the managerial competences required in order to maximize the value creation from the competence resources available to the firm. This value creation depends on a number of aspects of competence management, which ultimately boil down to the managerial competences of the professionals in charge of these issues.

Managerial competences include, but are certainly not limited to, the following:

- Competence in terms of recruiting, motivating, and otherwise mobilizing other people's competences
- Competence in terms of putting together teams in order to achieve creativity and other key synergies
- Competence in terms of creating the necessary "glue" to keep key knowledgeable individuals loyal to the firm
- Competence in terms of how to share, develop, and create new/more competence, both at the individual and the firm level(s).

The dynamics of competence management

For the professional service firm it is critical to:

- have the necessary competences to solve the client's problem
- mobilize the competences and be able to apply them to the task at hand
- match competences and tasks for maximum value creation, including considerations of opportunity costs and comparative advantages in the appointment of professionals to given clients or projects
- put together teams for maximum synergies

These are complex managerial challenges, and the ability of the firm to utilize its total stock of resources for maximum value creation depends on both the competence of the individuals, the capabilities (skills as well as norms, etc.) of the firm, and the intermediate level of the competence of the managers in the management of the intangible resources of the firm. This final point is extremely important to professional service firms, so much so that in the two US-based engineering design firms of my dissertation study (CDM and Parsons Brinckerhoff) the professionals interviewed stated that the unique competence of the presidents of their firms was one of their firms' main sources of competitive advantage.

Management of competence resources includes several interrelated dimensions:

- Recruiting employees which enhance the competence available to the firm, at all four levels discussed above
- Keeping the employees with important value creating competence within the firm

- Increasing the transfer of competence from the most competent individuals to other colleagues within the firm, either on an individual basis, in teams, or by converting individual competence to organizational competence. For example, the best project managers of an engineering firm may be asked to spend time developing a project management hand-book which improves the competence of other project managers.
- Increasing the competence of employees through training programs, etc.
- Increasing the competence at all levels through prioritizing operational activities that enhance accumulated learning within the firm, both at the individual and the collective levels. Strategically, the task of management is to consider the learning potential when choosing between alternative sets of projects and clients, as well as to "allocate" people for maximum overall learning combined with efficiency and high quality service.

The management of competence streams within, into, and out of the firm, then, is crucial to its long term survival and success, as these competence resources have a direct effect on both the value creation and the recruiting potential (and competence addition) of their firms. In this sense, the managerial competences of the professionals taking charge of the overall strategic management of the firms, whether voluntarily or by default, are critical to the firms' competitiveness.

Relational resources. Not only competence, but also the reputation, client loyalty, etc. are fundamental to the performance of a professional service firm, and as with competence, these intangible resources may be collective and shared or highly idiosyncratic and individual. The reputation of the firm determines the probability of winning the most attractive client and project contracts, and hence the management of the evolution of this reputation is critical.

Resource ownership and control

Resources such as the competences of individual professionals, the routines and procedures of the firm, brand names and firm reputation are fundamentally different in terms of one critical dimension, namely that of who owns and controls the resource. Figure 8 illustrates the different types of resources, and classified in terms of ownership and control.

Figure 8. Strategic resources.

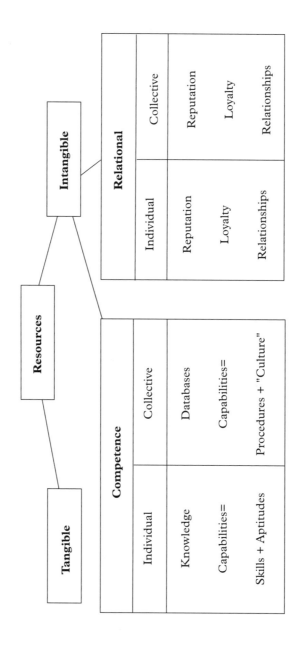

The individual competence resources are contracted or rented from individuals, whereas tangible resources are owned by the firm (Nordhaug, 1993). Resources such as reputation and client relations, the *relational* resources, are even "embodied in people who do not work for the firm. Brand name, for instance, is held by customers, not employees." (Itami, 1987:14). For professional business service firms, one of the most fundamental strategic management challenges involves the management of competences and other intangible resources which are only partially controlled by the firm. To the extent that the firm is highly dependent on competence resources that are controlled by the professionals and/or client loyalty and reputation linked to the individuals rather than to the firm, the organization is highly vulnerable to the exit of these professionals.

Figure 9 illustrates the different types of resources, and classifies them in terms of who ultimately controls their accumulation and utilization.

Figure 9. Controllability of firm resources.

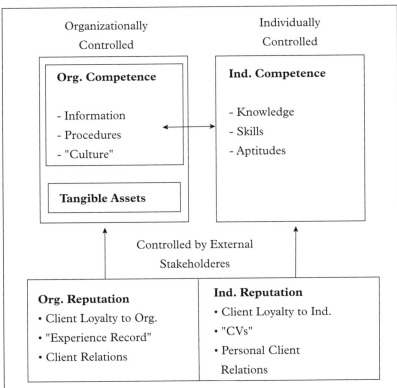

Professional service firms in general rely to a large extent on intangible resources controlled by individual professionals, even though these resources may also be complemented by capital investments, patents, organizational capabilities and databases, firm reputation, etc. These resources may increase as the result of activities aimed at the accumulation of resources, such as investments in the training of personnel, but the main source of intangible resource accumulation lies in the daily activities of the firm. It is important here to remember that information based resources do not automatically accumulate; they may improve or deteriorate as the result of the way in which these resources are utilized. This is particularly true of the intangible resources that are critical to professional service firms, namely competences and reputation.

Resource Leverage, Accumulation, and Vulnerability

In his general (resource based) framework, Itami (1987: 112) suggests that three fundamental questions need to be assessed as part of the strategic management of a firm's resources, which may be translated to professional service firms as follows:

1) Do we have the necessary resources?
2) Will the project or client contribute to efficient resource use (leverage)?
3 Will the project or client contribute to efficient and effective resource accumulation?

Whereas the first two questions relate to the short term performance of the firm, in terms of efficient utilization of existing resources, the third question involves long term competitive positioning. Professional business service firms seem happy to consider this third question if they have the luxury of choosing between multiple projects that are all viable and profitable. However, the investment in projects with a high degree of resource accumulation but which do not at the same time yield satisfactory profits, is harder to accept. This is because such trade-offs require a very high degree of consensus on strategic goals as well as the necessary financial reserves to allow the firm to choose such an investment in future competence. Both the consensus and the financial reserves seem to be very difficult to generate in professional service firms.

In addition to the three strategic questions emphasized by Itami, professional service firms face a fourth and fundamental strategic question, namely that of the effect on firm vulnerability. Different projects and clients have different effects on the dependence of the firm on intangible resources developed and controlled by individual professionals, and hence managers must also ask the following question:

4) Will the project or client increase, decrease, or stabilize the firm's degree of control over the resources accumulated?

In strategic management and organization theory, the importance for the firm of reducing uncertainty and its dependence on key resources that it cannot fully control has received much attention (see e.g. Pfeffer & Salancik, 1978; Thompson, 1967). If a large part of the resource accumulation takes place in terms of increased competences that key professionals could easily use for the benefit of other employers, the firm also needs to set priorities in terms of linking these individually controlled resources (i.e. the professionals) to the firm. The simplest strategy, which may be acceptable to some firms, involves minimizing the dependence on individual professionals and their personal competence. In this sense, the firm chooses to avoid the dependence on individual intangibles. However, this is not likely to be the first choice for most professional service firms. A strategy involving the reduction of the relative impact of individual competences on firm performance may reduce vulnerability but will normally also reduce the ability of the firm to deliver innovative and professional services. In the worst cases, the firm may reduce its expertise to such an extent that it moves from being a professional problem solver to being a knowledge based service selling firm offering standardized rather than professionally developed solutions. Naturally there is nothing "wrong" with a strategy leading to such an evolution, providing that this pattern is consistent with the goals and priorities of the firm.

For most firms with a high degree of dependence on individually controlled competence resources, there is no intention of becoming less innovative. Then, a second strategy is more likely to be chosen, namely that of linking the professionals more tightly to the firm and reducing the probability of losing them. These firms need to develop strategies for increased professional loyalty rather than strategies which reduce the reliance on key professionals and their creativitity. As a result, their ability to link the professionals tightly to the organization through incentives, the creation of loyalty, an alignment of individual and organizational goals, etc., is fundamental to the development and maintenance of a competitive advantage.

A third alternative strategy involves increasing the organizationally controlled competence resources without reducing the individually controlled resources. Such a strategy leads to a reduction in the relative impact of individual professionals on total performance, without reducing the absolute value of their contributions. Firms that have been able to develop a high degree of organizationally controlled resources, including relational resources that are linked to the firm rather than to individual employees, are likely to be less concerned about the exit and entry of individual professionals and more concerned about the development and maintenance of their organizational resource base. One example of a successful strategy for the development of organizational competence resources may be McKinsey & Co: The routines and procedures are institutionalized to such an extent that when a large number of senior consultants in Rome decided to leave the firm (sixteen in late 1989, another fifteen in early 1993), McKinsey & Co continued their operations with little delay. By bringing in consultants from other offices and employing new people, the firm was rapidly able to restore both production quality and capacity, although their reputation "suffered a few bruises" (Business Week, September 20 1993:39).

The strategic management of professional business service firms, then, involves not only leveraging resources for maximum performance and accumulating resources for the best possible future results, as discussed by Itami. In addition to these two aspects of resource management, the strategic management of professional business service firms includes the management of firm vulnerability through the balancing of the different types of resources available for firm value creation. As illustrated above, the importance of the management of this balance of resources only becomes clear when the resource based framework is extended through a more detailed analysis of the different types of intangible resources on which the firm is dependent for its strategic positioning and long term performance. The strategic implications of this balance will be discussed at further length in the following chapter.

Resource development through daily operations

As the previous sub-chapters clearly point out, in professional service firms resource development as a byproduct of daily operations is the most important in terms of people and firm development, by far. Some of these developments take place as a result of conscious investments, and sometimes they are included in budgets with specific funds allocated to them.

Other times, some hours are set aside for "internal development projects", sometimes with compensation, in the sense that the contributors get to account for these hours as billable, but more often simply as part of the general culture of knowledge sharing. Again, Itami's model, reproduced in figure 6 in this chapter, is very helpful. A couple of recent publications or streams of research may also be helpful in terms of understanding how such resource development takes place, in particular in terms of knowledge or competence development.

Hansen, Nohria, and Tierney (1999) argue that, with respect to management consulting, there are two different strategies for knowledge management; individually based "personalization strategies", and organizationally based "codification strategies". They relate "codification" to reuse economics, and "personalization" to expert economics. The first is typically linked to a low degree of customization, and involves (i) reuse of knowledge assets, (ii) large teams with a high ratio of associates to partners, and (iii) emphasis on scale and large overall revenues. Needless to say, information systems and databases are critical for the support of this knowledge management strategy. Expert economics, on the other hand, involves (i) high fees for highly customized solutions to unique problems, (ii) small teams with a low ratio of associates to partners, and (iii) emphasis on high profit margins. These categories are quite similar to those of March (1991), where he distinguished between "exploration" – i.e. knowledge creation, and "exploitation" – i.e. knowledge application and reuse.

Nonaka and his co-authors (e.g. Hedlund and Nonaka (1993), Nonaka and Takeuchi (1995), and Nonaka, Toyama & Konno (2000)), argue that knowledge is created through dynamic interactions and combinations of explicit and tacit knowledge. These interactions take place in a shared context termed "ba", where knowledge assets serve as inputs, outputs, and moderators in the knowledge-creating processes. In their so-called SECI-model (e.g. Nonaka & Takeuchi, 1995), knowledge is seen as incorporating processes of (i) "Socialization", which means developing tacit knowledge through shared experience, (ii) "Externalization", which involves transforming tacit knowledge into explicit knowledge, i.e. much the same as the "codification"-processes described above, (iii) "Combination", which means converting explicit knowledge into more complex and systematic sets of explicit knowledge, and (iv) "Internalization", which involves converting explicit knowledge into tacit knowledge. As you may have discovered, the four first letters of the key words together form the acronym SECI.

A major difference between the analytical framework of Nonaka and his colleagues and the knowledge management strategies of Hansen, Nohria, and Tierney, is that Nonaka explicitly deals with the shifts from individual to collective competence and vice versa. Socialization involves a "transfer" of largely tacit knowledge from the collective to the individual level; externalization involves individuals articulating their tacit knowledge, thereby making it accessible to others; combination involves a regrouping and further development of collectively available explicit knowledge; and internalization involves a process whereby individuals internalize what used to be explicit knowledge. The final process can involve the internalization of written rules of conduct or company values, for instance, but also takes place when people develop skills, such as when experienced drivers know what the traffic signs mean and what actions are required, even without thinking consciously about what they are doing.

In my view, one of the biggest problems with the knowledge management "hype" we experienced in the late 1990-ies was that it focused almost exclusively on what Hansen, Nohria, and Tierney called "codification", or the processes of "externalization" and "combination" in Nonaka et al.'s SECI-framework. When asked about it, everybody knows that in order to do a good job, you need both explicit knowledge and a large number of tacit skills and aptitudes (or talents). Hence, the development of better IT-support systems is good because it improves the support, but it can never be the complete answer to the question of how you develop your intangible resources in such a way that you may gain sustainable competitive advantage. Managers who think that they can manage *knowledge* without all the intrinsically subjective processes involved in the management of *people*, are rather naïve, to put it mildly. And in professional service firms, where routines cannot substitute for professional judgment, it is obvious that the support of people is the key process in resource development.

Finally, recent findings in my study of competence development in professional service firms in Norway, where Siw M. Fosstenløkken's Ph.D. dissertation study (forthcoming, 2005) was an important part, highlight the importance of separating the experiences of juniors from those of senior professionals, and in particular partners. Fosstenløkken found that a very important part of competence development happened in the direct interaction with clients (see also Fosstenløkken, Løwendahl & Revang, 2003 for a discussion of these issues). Access to client meetings at an early stage of the project turned out to be an important facilitator of competence development. In large projects and in large firms, such access is often limited to the seniors only, whereas the juniors get their instructions from the senior client contacts. As a result, seniors may think that juniors have many more opportunities to develop their competence than what the juniors themselves think. On the other hand, both juniors and seniors tended to underreport actual competence development, precisely because it happens as a byproduct of daily operations, and therefore people are not conscious about how much learning actually takes place. Fosstenløkken's findings indicate that professional service firms may need to improve their ability to articulate and visualize the competence development that results from the projects, especially vis-à-vis the juniors. And they also indicate that a conscious, and possibly also explicit, attention to the allocation of juniors to different (parts of) projects such that their portfolio over time constitutes a fruitful competence development path, is important. This is yet another managerial responsibility for the already overburdened professional managers, but because it is important both for resource development, professional retention, and in the long run professional recruitment, this responsibility may be dangerous to neglect.

What is strategy in professional service firms?

Given the high degree of innovation, the responsiveness to unique client needs, and the unpredictability of which target projects will be won by the firm, strategic management in professional service firms cannot be centered on the development of detailed long term plans. That, however, does not mean that the development of strategy is redundant or impossible. Strategy is necessary in order to achieve coordinated activities in a highly decentralized and non-routinized structure, where precisely the lack of detailed plans makes an agreement on goals and priorities fundamental to the achievement of a "pattern in strategic decisions" (Mintzberg, 1978). All the firms of my dissertation study had seen the consequences of a lack of pattern in key decisions in the past, in particular in terms of the lost opportunities in overseas markets when chances of long term relation building and exploitation of local learning have been forfeited. Projects had been seen as isolated events rather than as building blocks for additional projects, and individual professionals had been allowed to develop competences and relationships in isolation, rather than given the responsibility and support for the establishment of an entire group of professionals with a tight connection back to the home-office. A lack of resources and priority to these issues made every investment a short term engagement.

Since the primary strategic resources of a professional service firm are the competence resources, most of the resource accumulation or competence building is done through the contracts won and services delivered, and hence a lack of strategic coordination may be disastrous for the firm if it is to develop a unique competence base for sustained competitive advantage. As stated by Sibson as early as 1971 (p.75), a "... major cause of failures in professional businesses is that enterprises react to what appear to be opportunities but which turn out to be time-consuming and costly detractions." The temptation to undertake whatever project seems "interesting" in the short term may be even more pervasive in professional service firms than in other organizations. This is no surprise, if we look at the emphasis on flexible competence resources, the typical decentralization of decision making authority, the emphasis on constant full (or almost full) employment of all professionals, and the flexibility of the firm in terms of the ease with which strategic resources (professionals) may be switched from one market to another. At the same time, the consequences of such a short-term, opportunity driven, and ad hoc strategic decision making process may be disastrous in a highly competitive environment.

Given the high degree of independent professional judgment required in client relations, and the extreme adaptation to client needs, operational authority has to be delegated to the professionals who are in direct interaction with the clients. An attempt to centralize all key decisions would probably paralyze the operations rapidly, as there is no way the (part-time) senior management could possibly cope with the massive number of decisions which have to be made. One illustration of the problems resulting from a dependence on top management sanctions was offered by one of the firms of my dissertation study: the local manager, at the early stage of establishment of a new overseas office, only needed to refer directly to the president. He was a senior and highly respected professional with long tenure with the firm, and this arrangement was perceived as giving him a high degree of autonomy in a seemingly "flat" structure. From the perspective of the local manager, however, the view of the situation was quite different. He felt a tendency for all strategic decisions to be "centralized by default, as top management responds so slowly that the opportunities are missed." What he gained in terms of direct access to the president, he lost in terms of decision speed. When decisions of a strategic nature were required, he felt he would actually have been better off with an intermediary director to refer to, as this director would be physically located with the president and thus be able to walk into his office and demand an urgent decision, when needed. Overworked, part-time, rarely available professional managers are generally not very efficient at making quick decisions when ad hoc situations occur in an office far away from the client they are personally serving at the moment.

The strategy formulation-implementation dichotomy has lost its meaning in professional service organizations, like in the adhocracy (Mintzberg, 1983). Similarly, strategy "is not so much formulated consciously by individuals as formed implicitly by the decisions they make" (Mintzberg, 1983:263). However, in the firms of my dissertation study it was not correct to say that strategy was controlled by "whoever decides what projects are done and how" (Mintzberg, 1983:263) nor that strategy changed continuously with every new project, at least not in the late 1980s. Strategy emerged as a pattern of decisions, as described by Mintzberg (1978), but in the firms I studied this pattern was not only the result of an organic strategy formation process. A target pattern was developed ex ante, and the responsibility for the development of this target pattern, as well as the responsibility for its realization, was delegated to someone in senior management. Whereas it is true that a professional service firm, just like an "operating adhocracy," is "never quite sure what it will do next" (Mintzberg, 1983: 263), the firms I studied seemed to have a very clear idea of what they wanted to do next.

Based on later discussions with professionals, I have become less certain about this "intrinsic shared vision" or whatever we should call it. Maybe it has to do with my maturing as a student of these topics, or maybe it has more to do with the fact that senior partners are more willing to and interested in speaking to an experienced professor about more challenging topics, than they are when a Ph.D.-student comes around asking fairly naïve questions. I have seen at least three different types of challenges arising from the inherent flexibility in PSF strategic decisions:

First, lack of homogeneity and common direction. Every senior (and maybe even junior) moves in whatever direction he/she thinks is most appropriate or most fun, and the firm ends up with a fragmented strategy, less than optimal competence development, and a rather "fuzzy" reputation. One reason for this problem may be that management is unable or unwilling or insufficiently empowered to cut through the different interest groups within the firm; they simply do not dare to say that for our company's future, for example telecom clients are less important than oil companies, or that economics-based industry analyses are going to be given less priority, whereas process-related consulting is going to be invested in. When all investments are made in people, it takes strong management to prioritize one employee (and peer!) group over the others. The problem here is a lack of management with sufficient legitimate power to set the direction and interfere if partners or other professionals undertake activities that are not in line with the collective priorities.

Second, an unwillingness to turn down project offers with tempting financial implications, but which either the firm cannot deliver at a sufficiently high quality (expertise lacking) or the firm does not want to be known for. One example from a local law firm illustrates this situation: Projects were few, and several corporate lawyers were less than fully employed. One partner suggested that two-three of them could sell their services to firms after bankruptcy, an area of the law where the firm had never had any expertise before. They did their homework well, gained some contracts, and actually did a pretty good job. In the process, they also hired a couple of specialists on bankruptcy law. All of a sudden, the company had a new strategic area, well known among certain groups of clients. Should they close it down, now that "normal business" was back to normal? In this case, they didn't. But it is unclear whether or not this strategic move was the most appropriate, i.e. most profitable, most attractive to new potential recruits, most favorable to their firm reputation, etc. The strategic implications were never explicitly discussed and decided on in a partner meeting.

Third, lack of dynamics, inertia or stagnation. In this case, all professionals are busy taking care of their own traditional share of the "turf", nobody interferes with the business of others, and client projects are largely small variations on "business as usual." As a result, you see a very low degree of innovation, organizational- and personal development. The problem here may be that nobody is strong enough or courageous enough to stick his/her neck out and challenge the established ways of working. In some firms, recruiting has also come to a standstill, maybe because many of the seniors fear that the young "radicals" will upset their comfortable status quo? Partnerships may be particularly vulnerable to the challenges of inertia and lack of constructive development and change, as it may be very difficult to get partner consensus on major changes involving both their own working practices and their wallets.

Senior management is responsible for controlling the development of strategy, building consensus on a vision as well as the operating priorities, enhancing strategic focus and a clear pattern in decisions, and reinforcing the common goals of the firm and its professionals. This is no easy task. A stable strategy is likely to be as important for a professional service firm as for any other firm. Strategy, however, needs to take into account the demands on flexibility and responsiveness to client needs, as well as the

high degree of independent judgment exercised by individual professionals in operating decisions of strategic importance. Strategy cannot involve
a top down formulation and implementation of plans and procedures, but
rather involves choosing focal competence areas and client groups as well
as geographical markets. As neither expertise nor information is necessarily at its maximum at the top of the managerial hierarchy, the choices of
priorities need to be made through a consensus-based decision making
process. All key professionals must be well informed and have sufficient
faith in the decision makers' ability to make the right decisions (Webber,
1990). Strategy sets the priorities which allow the individual professionals
to make independent judgments and decisions, while remaining confident
that the decentralized decisions will exhibit a pattern favorable to the firm.
In addition, clear strategic priorities and goal consensus are required in
order for the firm to achieve coordination combined with a high level of
local responsiveness to client demands, as such responsiveness can only be
achieved through a delegation of decision making authority to the professionals interacting with the client. Hence, the development of a stable
strategy is not less important in a professional service firm than in non-
professional firms, but the strategy content and the priorities emphasized
may be different.

Unless the firm accepts to operate as a loose network with only a minimum of coordination and sharing of resources, local decision makers
must have a common set of goals and priorities in order for the firm to
achieve a strategic focus for both its resource accumulation and its
resource utilization. Strategy in professional service firms thus primarily
involves the development and communication of a consensus-based

- vision,
- clear goals, and
- set priorities.

Strategy is not so much focussed on how the goals should be achieved, as
on what should be done and in which prioritized sequence. All firms have
limited resources. In professional service firms, the utilization of scarce
resources involves both the use and investment of limited financial
resources and the utilization of competence resources, including the time
and energy of key professionals. Every time a professional service firm
undertakes a new project, it forfeits other projects and hence incurs
opportunity costs both in terms of the leverage it can get from its present
resources and in terms of the resource accumulation resulting from the

projects. As a result, all decision makers need to know and respect the priorities set for the utilization and accumulation of strategic resources, given the goals of the firm and the strategic vision. Without clear and well-known strategic priorities, the competence accumulation within any one competence area of the firm is likely to be ad-hoc and unsystematic, rather than truly cumulative in areas of strategic importance.

The VCPs of PSFs-framework

As mentioned in chapter II, I have recently developed a more comprehensive model of value creation in professional service firms, together with my colleague professor Øivind Revang and doctoral student Siw M. Fosstenløkken (Løwendahl, Revang, & Fosstenløkken, 2001). This model can be used to summarize what has been said so far about strategy and resources, and can be seen as a revised and more strategically focused version of the model presented in figure 3 earlier in this chapter. We have termed it "The VCPs for PSFs framework", where VCP is short for Value Creation Processes and PSFs is short for Professional Service Firms. The model consists of three central components: strategy/domain choice, service delivery, and resources. These components illustrate a 'snap-shot' taken at a given point in time. In addition, dynamic processes are illustrated by the arrows in figure 10. A presentation of each of the components and arrows is given below.

Strategy/Domain choice. At any given point in time, professional service firms have made their domain choice (Levine & White 1961) in terms of strategies concerning prioritization of clients and projects, – "what" is delivered, to "whom", "where", and "how"? These choices do not need to be consciously or explicitly made, but through recruiting and a preference for particular types of projects, a pattern will normally emerge. A strategic portfolio of clients and projects allows for additive improvements of the competence base, whereas without focus, projects, competence development, and recruiting are likely to be ad hoc (see figure 3 earlier in this chapter). Hence, it is important to pursue and secure the right kinds of projects and clients. This component is similar to the first process in figure 3, except that here we focus on strategic priorities in terms of which projects and clients to target, rather than the selling process per se.

Service delivery. When it comes to service delivery, path dependency is prevalent. Previous projects may enhance both the competence and the reputation of the professional service firm, thereby allowing the firm to win the most favorable projects in terms of both resource development

Figure 10. The VCPs of PSFs–framework

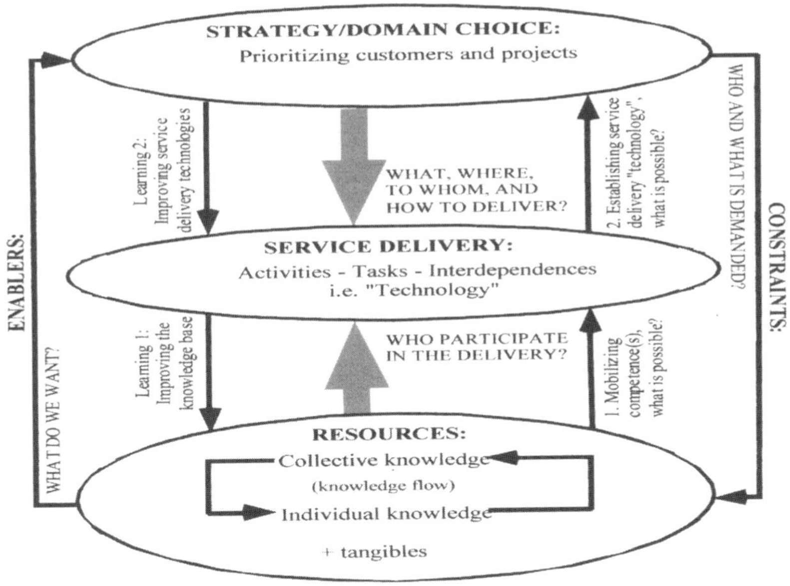

Source: Løwendahl, Revang & Fosstenløkken, 2001:925

and profitability. On the other hand, previous projects may constrain strategic development, as previous experience limits both the types of projects people have adequate competence to compete for, and the reputation, allowing the firm to sell a "credible promise". In this respect, value creation processes may be seen as a key bridge to client markets. Professionals often deliver services that require specific combinations of competence, and whereas some services involve competence development, others do not. For the professionals involved, competence development may add value directly, in terms of individual, collective, and/or organizational learning. Further, different types of services involve different task characteristics, lead to different interdependencies and coordination needs, and require different types of knowledge bases. In light of Thompson (1967), these aspects constitute different types of organizational technologies. Such technologies are classified by increasing complexity and cost of coordination, based on the interdependence between tasks. Many tasks carried out by professional service firms, because they require a high degree of customization, take on the characteristics of "synthetic organizations" (Thompson, 1967). These are effective but not efficient, because they cannot calculate in advance the extent of the problem to be solved or the full array of resources needed. Examples of such organizations include human aid projects, such as those set up by international humanitarian organizations after the Tsunami in South-East Asia in December 2004. Is it true that for professional service firms, which deliver highly customized services, only the most costly form of coordination is applicable? Does the firm need to remain inefficient and costly to operate, or can modes of coordination and collaboration be developed which reduce costs without reducing customization? In this respect, the composition of the resources plays a crucial role for competitive advantage. This service delivery component is similar to the second process in the model in figure 3.

Resource Base. The resource base consists most importantly of people, and with them a set of competences. These competences are based on individual expertise and skills, as well as collectively developed routines, procedures, and ways of doing work together. In addition to competence development, recruiting can be used as a strategy to strengthen the resource base by e.g. providing the firm with other types of competences compared to those represented by current employees. As a supplement to employment, firms can also hire people with particular competences on a temporary basis. The resource base component is similar to the third process of the model in figure 3.

The outer arrows. The domain choice and the resource base represent contextual components, which both enable and constrain the value creation processes for each specific project, as illustrated by the outer arrows of figure 10. From a short-term perspective, the components set limits for the types of projects the firm can win, and what it is able to do based on its resources. In other words, they constrain what the professional service firm can offer clients, which clients are likely to be convinced by a project proposal, and what kinds of projects and service deliveries can be successfully completed. On the other hand, reputation, client relationships, and expertise may enable them to gain advanced projects within its area of domain choice. As a result, professional service firms must compete actively in two markets simultaneously: the market for clients and the market for professional resources (Maister, 1982; 1993; Løwendahl & Revang, 1998).

The inner arrows. The two broad arrows illustrate the processes by which domain choices and resource mobilization combine to create value for and with the client(s). As a by-product of these services, value is created both in terms of options for domain enhancement (vertical arrows pointing up from resources, via service delivery, to strategy/domain choice), and in terms of learning (vertical arrows pointing down from strategy/domain choice, via service delivery, to resources). Based on the right matching of people and projects, service delivery experiences can result in opportunities to alter the domain choice in terms of going after other types of clients and projects. The strategic focus in terms of which projects the professionals want to undertake determines the priorities among projects. As a result, experience from projects affects individuals through at least two learning processes: First, the resource base may improve through experience (Itami, 1987). Second, experience can be used to improve the design and management of service delivery. These processes are referred to as Learning 1 and Learning 2, respectively. In terms of Learning 1, competence is developed as a by-product of service delivery to clients. This process can be described as "learning by doing" or "reflection in action" (Schön, 1983). Learning 2 can also, in Thompson's (1967) vocabulary, be seen as as establishing service delivery technology.

The model as a whole. The VCPs for PSFs framework highlights a number of key factors related to both strategy and resource development in professional service firms. First, it reminds us that setting priorities for target clients and projects is critical to long-term success. Secondly, it highlights the fact that strategies (defined as priorities) are never created in a vacuum. The professionals who have been recruited, and in particular the partners, constrain the choice of target clients and projects, both by what they know and by what they want to do. At the same time, the clients and other external stakeholders also set limits to the choice of strategic priorities, through what they consider to be a "credible promise", based on previous experiences and reputation. Third, it reminds us that strategies for professional service firms have to deal with two markets simultaneously: The market for services (determined by the clients) and the market for highly qualified professionals (Maister, 1982; 1993). And finally, it highlights the importance of orchestrating learning processes both in order to improve the knowledge and skills, individually as well as collectively (i.e. the resource base), and to improve the processes ("technologies") used in service delivery. When services are customized and idiosyncratic, it is difficult to create routines and procedures for how they are to be delivered. Still, the way projects are organized and staffed, the way tasks are distributed and coordinated, etc., are all parts of service delivery processes that can, at least to some extent, be perfected at the macro level.

Structuring the professional service firm

The challenges involved in structuring professional service firms are substantial. As discussed in Chapter III, contrary to Weber's (1947) bureaucracy, the professional organization has no simple hierarchical structure in which the best expert has been promoted to the highest managerial level with the highest authority and responsibility. Expertise is multidimensional, is frequently not linked to seniority and administrative experience, and operational authority may be unrelated to hierarchical position.

The basic problems of organizational design involve definition and allocation of tasks and responsibilities to individuals, coordination of tasks and activities which are interdependent, and supervision and control of activities and results. In professional service firms, the definition and allocation of tasks depends on the requirements of each client and project. The flexibility and responsiveness required make it impossible to define stable tasks and responsibilities linked to each organizational position as well as to allocate people to these positions. Such a stable set of tasks and responsibilities is also undesirable, as it reduces the flexibility of the firm in picking the best person available every time a new contract is won and the requirements of a new client have been defined. Moreover, it reduces the ability of the firm to build on the individual strengths of each professional. Picking the best person available for each task involves encouraging individuals to combine tasks in a flexible manner. It also involves making certain that responsibilities for support as well as control are allocated to the best person available for those tasks.

The professionals interviewed did not see any problems connected to their lack of formally defined job descriptions and responsibilities. As long as they knew who to report to or request support from for each of their tasks at any given point in time, they did not mind facing a highly complex matrix in terms of the formal organizational structure. This emphasis was enhanced by clear goals and priorities, in particular in terms of satisfying the client first and worrying about "red tape" afterwards, and by a top management focus on what is done and why, but only rarely on how a professional chooses to approach a task.

Rather than emphasizing the development of an appropriate organizational structure, the firms encouraged strong networks for informal coordination beyond the formal structure. The formal structure establishes broad responsibilities and channels of communication, and clusters activities and people with frequent needs for coordination. But since the tasks keep changing and the dimensions which need to be coordinated are numerous, coordination through formal channels can only incorporate a small part of the total coordination needed at any given time. Rather, it is the informal coordination that matters, and this is enhanced by professionals who know each other well and pay attention to "getting around a lot" (President Moran of CDM International).

On the other hand, even the flexible and project based professional service firm is required to develop and present images of their formal structure. Said Derish Wolff, one of the engineering design firm presidents: "Only outsiders ask for our organization charts. Our own people know how little these papers can tell you. I am sure I have one in a drawer somewhere here in my desk, but it really won't help you understand what we do or who is in charge. Even yesterday's chart is obsolete!" Morten Tarøy, the Marketing Director of Norconsult, expressed the same concerns: "We have to present our organization to our clients", said Mr. Tarøy, "as they want to know who is in charge and who is the boss of the people we assign to their projects. But in most cases this information is irrelevant. Our best engineer for a given project may formally belong to a totally different department than that of the project, especially if he is an expert in more than one area." In Norconsult, they tried to present the assigned engineers in loose-leaf binders, where the relevant engineers for a given project were presented with their CVs as well as their positions in that particular project. Still, clients wanted to know their formal hierarchical authority. It seems to be very difficult for outsiders to develop an image of who is in charge in an organization, without holding on to the traditional hierarchical map of formal tasks and responsibilities, even though we do recognize that they may not be very meaningful in complex firms. The following two "charts" illustrate this dilemma quite well. In Figure 11, the formal organization chart of top management at the US-based engineering design firm Camp Dresser & McKee Inc (CDM) is presented.

At first glance, this chart looks like any other organization chart. For our purpose, some of the functions have been highlighted and the others only include titles. The chart gets to be very interesting if we look at the names written in some of the boxes, especially if we think of the chart in the traditional way, as representing the formal lines of authority and reporting. Mr. Moran, who was my primary contact at CDM during my dissertation study, was the President of CDM International. However, if we look at this organization chart, we see that he was also the General Manager of the subunit called Geo Systems, and he was the Senior Vice President in charge of Business Development. In addition, he was one of the directors of the board of this employee owned firm. Hence, for different purposes he had three different business cards, and in extreme cases

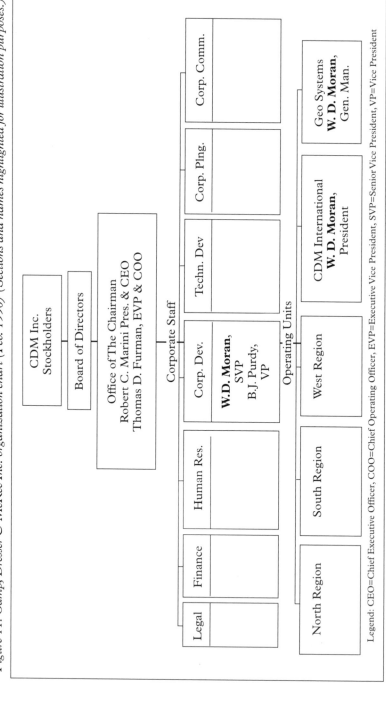

Figure 11. Camp, Dresser & McKee Inc. organization chart (Feb. 1990) (Sections and names highlighted for illustration purposes.)

Legend: CEO=Chief Executive Officer, COO=Chief Operating Officer, EVP=Executive Vice President, SVP=Senior Vice President, VP=Vice President he would end up sending memos to himself!

For people used to working in project organizations this is no surprise. They are familiar with the fact that professionals may be involved in more than one task or set of tasks, as their time can be divided into an infinite number of units, each of which can theoretically be assigned to a different task or project. They report to different people for different issues and abide by different deadlines and budget constraints depending on what project they are presently allocating their time to. If the traditional hierarchical image of a higher level of management supervising the lower levels is applied, however, such an organization resembles total chaos. Hence, we need different images that are more appropriate to the flexibility of this setting, at the same time as we respect the need of the client or other stakeholders for a clear definition of who is responsible for all the issues that are relevant to them. Tore Gulli, who was the Managing Director of IKO Strategy, a subsidiary of the Norwegian management consulting firm the IKO Group, attempted to create such an image, as illustrated in Figure 12.

Figure 12. Professional service firm organization.

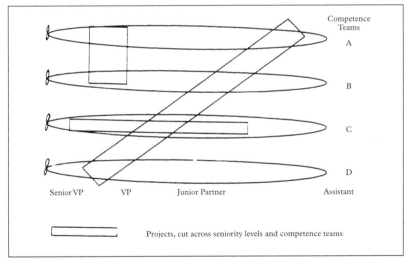

Mr. Gulli viewed his professionals as grouped or clustered based on a number of independent dimensions, of which seniority and formal authority were only one element. He preferred to draw this dimension horizontally in the picture, in order to highlight that seniority is not superiority. He then drew the different professional groups as zeppelins, moving horizontally, driven by a propeller which was the senior professional in charge of professional development of all members of his/her group. The professional groups were based on previous education and experience, and professional development hence meant that, for example, an industrial organization economist would be expected to keep track of research and development within his own area of expertise, read the relevant research journals, keep in touch with his peers and professors from university, etc. Additional dimensions to be considered when project teams were composed included industry expertise and experience, such as in the areas of banking and finance, and, when appropriate, international experience. The boxes cutting across the different zeppelins indicate temporary project teams, which typically were composed of people from different professional groups and with different levels of seniority. As the size of the boxes indicate, some projects involved many people, whereas others only involved two or three. And some people were involved in several projects simultaneously.

Although the figure shows an unorthodox and far from perfect image of the organization structure of a professional service firm, it illustrates a number of dimensions which are impossible to capture in the traditional organization chart. New and creative images as well as flexible and fluid structures are required if the professional service firm is to avoid creating unnecessary red tape through formal reporting routines which are not adapted to the reality of the projects. There are no general and easy answers to the search for the optimal organization structure, and more research is both needed and under way, designed to understand better the underlying mechanisms driving division of labor, underdelegation, allocation of responsibility and authority, and coordination across interdependent functions. Some recent research developments look particularly promising in this respect, as a stream of researchers have decided to focus on the micro-processes of organizing and strategizing in different contexts (see e.g. Journal of Management Studies (2003), special issue on micro-strategy and strategizing, edited by professors Johnson, Melin and Wittington, or the forthcoming special issue of Human Relations (forthcoming late fall 2005) on strategizing from a practice perspective, edited by professors Jarzabkowski, Balogun, and Seidl). Another interesting path which is currently explored by myself and my colleague professor Øivind Revang, builds on Thompson's early work on organizational technologies, interdependencies, and coordination mechanisms, and attempts to distinguish between tasks or activities that can be preplanned and activities which must be handled in an ad-hoc fashion. We are currently exploring different ways of coordinating ad-hoc activities, and in line with the stream of research on micro-strategizing, we also believe in looking at the micro-level of the activities first, rather than looking at "grand" organizational designs or general principles. For the time being, the creative search for what works best for a given firm at a given point in time seems to be the only pragmatic advice available, in addition to the recognition that every solution is temporary. It only lasts as long as the set of tasks and people is the same, and this is one of the dimensions where professional service firms differ substantially. In the following chapter, these differences, in terms of stability of tasks and structures, will be discussed in further detail.

These problems are naturally multiplied in the case of multi-office, not to mention, multinational professional service firms. When the number of offices, the size of each office, or the number of and geographical distance between regions and countries increase, the complexity of the organizational challenges also increases dramatically. The challenges involved in the development of common strategic priorities and a flexible organization structure for international operations will be briefly discussed in Chapter VII.

Conclusions

Even if it is extremely difficult for professional service firms to plan their operations in detail in both a short term and long term perspective, it is clearly possible and helpful to develop strategies that help the professionals focus their attention on the areas that are given the highest priority. The resource based perspective allows for a careful analysis of both the resources available, the resources needed, the success of resource accumulation and utilization, and the management of the vulnerability resulting from mobile professionals who know their alternative options very well. In this chapter, all professional service firms have been considered as a single category, as they are all firms with an extreme dependence on individually controlled competence resources and reputation. In the following chapter, these insights will be further developed, as we recognize that professional service firms are heterogeneous, both between and within industries. They differ in terms of types of tasks and clients, in terms of size and maturity, and in terms of the types of resources that make up the foundation for most of their value creation. Finally, they also differ in terms of their ability to develop and maintain a clear strategic focus, as regards target client groups, primary service offerings, and optimal resource base. The following chapter explores three potential "equilibrium" positions for professional service firms, as well as the tensions pulling the firms away from their most appropriate configurations. Again, the conclusion is that managerial attention as well as competence is required for the firms to remain efficient and effective in the long run.

Suggested Readings

Amit, R. & Schoemaker, P.J.H. 1993. "Strategic assets and organizational rent." Strategic Management Journal, 14, pp. 33-46

Barney, J. B. 1991. "Firm Resouces and sustained competitive advantage." Journal of Management, 17, pp. 99-120.

Empson, L. 2001. (Ed.) Special issue: Knowledge management in professional service firms. Human Relations. 54(7).

Fosstenløkken, S.M. forthcoming 2005. Competence development for competitive advantage – a study of four professional service firms (tentative title). BI Norwegian School of Management Ph.D. Dissertation Series. Oslo, Norway.

Fosstenløkken, S.M., Løwendahl, B.R. & Revang, Ø. 2003. "Knowledge development through client interaction: A comparative study." Organization Studies, Special Issue: Knowledge and Professional Organizations. 24(6): pp. 859-879.

Haanes, K.B. 1997. Managing resource mobilization: Case studies of Dynal, Fiat Auto Poland, and Alcatel Telecom Norway. Ph.D. Thesis, Copenhagen Business School.

Hansen, M., Nohria, N. & Tierney, T. 1999. "What's your strategy for managing knowledge?" Harvard Business Review, March-April, pp. 106-116.

Hedlund, G. & Nonaka, I. 1993. "Models of knowledge management in the West and Japan." In: Lorange, P., Chakhravarthy, B. Roos, J. & Van de Ven, A. (Eds) Implementing strategic processes: Change, learning and cooperation. Oxford: Blackwell. pp. 117-144.

Hinings, C.R.(Bob) & Leblebici, H. (Eds). 2003. Special Issue: Knowledge and Professional Organizations. Organization Studies. 24(6).

Itami, H. 1987. Mobilizing Invisible Assets. Cambridge, MA: Harvard University Press.

Jarzabkowski, P., Balogun, J. & Seidl, D. (Eds) forthcoming late 2005. Special issue on Strategizing: The challenges of a practice perspective. Human Relations.

Johnson, G., Melin, L. & Whittington, R. (Eds) 2003. Special issue on micro-strategy and strategizing. Journal of Management Studies. 40.

Johnson, G., Melin, L. & Whittington, R. 2003. "Micro-strategy and strategizing: Towards an activity-based-view. Journal of Management Studies. 2001. Special issue on micro-strategy and strategizing. 40: pp. 1-22.

Kogut, B. & Zander, U. 1992. "Knowledge of the firm, combinative capabilities, and the replication of technology". Organization Science, 3, pp. 383-397.

Løwendahl, B.R., Revang, Ø. & Fosstenløkken, S.M. 2001. "Knowledge and value creation in professional service firms: A framework for analysis." Human Relations. Special issue: Knowledge management in professional service firms. 54(7): pp. 911-931.

Løwendahl, B. R. & Nordhaug, O. 1984. OL 1994 – Inspirasjonskilde for framtidens næringsliv? Oslo: TANO.

March, J.G. 1991. "Exploration and exploitation in organizational learning." Organization Science, 2: pp. 71-87.

Mintzberg, H. 1983. Structure in fives; Designing effective organizations. Englewood Cliffs, NJ: Prentice Hall.

Mintzberg, H. & A. McHugh. 1985. "Strategy formation in an adhocracy." Administrative Science Quarterly 30: pp. 160-197.

Morris, T. & Empson, L. 1998. "Organization and Expertise: An exploration of knowledge bases and the management of accounting and consulting firms". Accounting, Organizations and Society, 23 (5-6), pp. 609-24.

Nonaka, I. & Takeuchi, H. 1995. The knowledge creating company. New York: Oxford University Press.

Nonaka, I., Toyama, R. & Konno, N. 2000. "SECI, Ba and Leadership: A unified model of dynamic knowledge creation." Long Range Planning, 33(1), pp. 5-34.

Nordhaug, O. 1994. Human Capital in Organizations: Competence, training and learning. Oslo: Scandinavian University Press.

Penrose, E. T. 1959. The Theory of the Growth of the Firm. New York: Wiley.

Prahalad, C. K. & Hamel, G. 1990. "The core competence of the corporation." Harvard Business Rewiew 63:3 (MAY-JUN) pp. 79-91.

Prahalad, C. K. & Hamel, G. 1994. Competing for the future. Cambridge, MA: Harvard Business School Press.

Spender, J.-C. 1996. "Making knowledge the basis of a dynamic theory of the firm". Strategic Management Journal, Winter special issue on Knowledge and the Firm, 17, pp. 45-62.

Tsoukas, H. 1996. "The firm as a distributed knowledge system: A constructionist approach". Strategic Management Journal, Winter special issue on Knowledge and the Firm, 17, pp. 11-25.

Webber, A. W. 1990. "Consensus, Continuity, and Common Sense: An Interview with Compaq's Rod Canion." Harvard Business Review 68:4, (July-August) pp. 114-123.

Wernerfelt, B. 1984. "A resource based view of the firm". Strategic Management Journal, 5, pp. 171-180.

Winter, S.G. 1987. "Knowledge and Competence as Strategic Assets." In Teece, D.J. (Ed.) The competitive challenge. New York: Ballinger .pp. 159-184.

V. Three generic types of professional firms

Why is the dream of a wealthy owner inappropriate in so many cases?

Introduction

So far the discussions have focussed on professional service firms in general, as if all professional service firms can be "lumped together" in a single category and treated as similar. This, however, is not the case. Professional service firms differ substantially on a number of key dimensions, and these differences exist even if we compare firms from a single industry and isolate the sample to firms of approximately the same size and level of maturity. If we compare the firms across industries, the differences become even more striking, and the implications of these differences are interesting to explore further. Unfortunately, to date most writers on professional service firm management have generalized their insights from firms in one industry and assumed their findings to be valid across firms with very different priorities.[1]

Based on my discussions with professionals from many types of firms and industries, I suggest that professional service firms may actually have a choice between three different generic strategies. Each strategy leads to a different set of challenges and opportunities, but the shift from one generic strategy to another is likely to be very difficult to accomplish. Regardless of industry, these three strategies seem to coexist, and it seems to be possible to be highly successful both in the short and the long run with any one of the three strategies. However, it does not seem to be possible to pick "the best of all worlds" by choosing the elements that are most attractive from each of the modes, as they are fundamentally different in terms of their underlying competitive dynamics. The need for clear priorities makes it impossible to win on all fronts simultaneously. At the core of these differences lie fundamental questions of priorities, both in terms of which types of resources are developed for competitive advantage and in terms of what kind of market emphasis is promoted. In most cases, these

---

[1] Since 1997, as stated in the preface, many more researchers have become interested in the understanding of professional service firms, and a lot more research has been published. The tendency is still that people study a single industry or even a single case, but more comparative studies have also been published. Please refer to the appendix on current research for more information about this development.

priorities seem to result from a combination of emergent characteristics (including luck) and explicit choices made at critical transition points. In order for the firm to avoid the pitfalls inherent in a bottom-up attraction to all opportunities available, however, it needs to have explicit priorities and pay conscious attention to these different strategic patterns.

This chapter starts with a discussion of five fundamental dimensions which create different challenges for different types of professional service firms. These dimensions are partly industry specific and partly strategic. The next section discusses two drivers of firm heterogeneity normally referred to as explanations of major differences, namely the different stages of firm maturity and growth. Following this discussion, I explore another set of fundamental dimensions driving differences across firms even within a single industry, namely the combination of the role of the professionals in value creation and the strategic focus in terms of what kind of superior value the firm seeks to deliver to its clients. Since we are talking about services, the distinction between what is delivered and how it is delivered is of little importance here; it is more critical to know whether the firm builds its competitive position from unique client relations, unique solutions, or a unique ability to solve new problems creatively. When these two dimensions are combined, three generic strategic types of professional service firms emerge, and these are further discussed in the following section. Finally, in the last two sections, the difficulties involved in maintaining a balance and avoiding the pressures pulling the firm away from its target focus are discussed in detail. The main point of this chapter is to highlight the flexibility inherent in the professional service firm, but also to focus on the dangers inherent in copying other firm strategies without consciously weighing the possibilities inherent in the new strategy against the losses that are likely to result if the new strategy involves a shift in strategic mode.

Professional services are not all the same

It is obviously not a good idea to "lump together" all professional service firms into a single category. Unfortunately, however, this has been the case in a large number of studies, and this generalization based on a single type of firm is likely to lead to inappropriate recommendations if managers try to indiscriminately apply these conclusions to their own firm. However, I do not believe there has been much damage done, as the managers of professional service firms are used to reading models and theories with a critical eye. They often discard new ideas as soon as they see that they are built on an industry or a market reality which is different from that of their own firm. In fact, the danger among practitioners seems to be the opposite of that of academics; practicing managers typically complain that their firms are so unique that generalizations are impossible to make, whereas academics often seem to generalize from a single type of firm, at least implicitly.

Many earlier studies of professional service firms based their insights on the largest international accounting or auditing firms, the so-called "Big Eight" at that time. These firms provided excellent starting points, as managing partners were positive to academic studies and they genuinely wanted to improve the strategic management of their firms. One of the very first professional service firm cases to be presented in a general strategic management textbook was "Peet Russ Anderson & Detroit", a constructed firm which carried with it a large number of the key characteristics of "the Big Eight" (Quinn & Mintzberg, 1991). Similarly, the Academy of Management Journal article discussing a study of "P2-form" (Greenwood, Hinings & Brown, 1990), explores the unique characteristics of professional service firms based on a small sample from a single industry, namely a few of the large international auditing firms.

Another stream of research attempted to look into the underlying characteristics of management consulting firms, but given the difficulties of getting access to such firms and being allowed to write about how they manage their affairs, these studies rather came out in the form of "The consultant to consultants' book on how to manage the consulting firm", such as Sveiby & Risling (1987). Their book was based on their insights as participant observers who were more participants than researchers in that particular setting, since they were consultants to the firms they describe. These studies were extremely important in terms of setting the agenda of critical issues, and yet they often led us to generalize insights from one industry to another and from one type of firm to another.

Maister's (1993) seminal book on professional firms at least carries with it insights from more than one industry, with particular emphasis on law firms and management consulting firms. But even Maister tends to generalize his insights to all partnerships primarily delivering ad hoc services to different types of clients, and this generalization is more implicit than explicit.

In the following, five critical dimensions that make firms fundamentally different will be explored. These are partly industry specific and partly strategic, as firms set their own priorities in order to develop or maintain their competitive advantage.

1) Repetitive versus ad hoc service delivery.

One of the most fundamental differences between firms, in my opinion, has to do with the extent to which the firm can expect the clients to continue to buy more or less the same service repeatedly. Auditing firms offer an excellent illustration, as all firms are required by law to have a reputable auditor. Hence, demand is relatively stable, even though it is true that as a result of client firm mergers and aquisitions the total volume of contracts has been reduced. For the client, the question is one of whether or not to continue with the same auditing firm, and the firms are compared to each other and also expected to be able to put up bids that can be compared for a similar set of services. The situation for the insurance brokerage firm is very much the same, as the client can only rarely decide not to be insured. The overall demand exists, and the competition is more focussed on out-competing competitors than on creating additional demand, even though both types of client interaction exist in both industries.

At the other extreme, the management consulting firm is typically in the situation of developing and offering services that may enhance client firm value creation, regardless of whether or not the clients knew that they needed this service. In these markets, the situation is much more fragmented, and few competitors are seen to offer the same type of service and hence to be comparable to the extent that they can be asked to bid for a contract. Projects are to a large extent ad hoc and may easily be postponed by the client for years, or even cancelled.

For law firms, the situation seems to be a mix of the two, as firms both need legal counsel on a continuous basis and ad hoc support if critical situations arise. In engineering design, most of the projects are awarded after complex bidding procedures, in which both the designs and the prices are compared. Still, the projects are largely ad hoc and may be postponed for years or even decades. In Norway, many such projects are well known, including the infamous construction of the new Oslo airport, which is now finally in place at Gardermoen after decades of political discussions and reversed decisions. A more recent example is the National Opera-house in Oslo, which is currently (2005) being built after decades of debates about location as well as architecture. A similar process has taken place for the national museum of art. For the engineering design and the construction companies, keeping alert for decades seems to be the rule rather than the exception when it comes to large government projects.

This dimension of ad hoc versus continuous services is primarily a characteristic of the industries, but is also a strategic variable, in particular in terms of the types of clients and projects sought by the firms. To take an example from engineering design, when the US based firm CDM decided to enhance their focus on environmental protection by shifting more of their project portfolio from waste water treatment to hazardous waste, they also made a strategic shift from a niche with predominantly municipal or governmental clients to large corporate clients. Hence, the shift also involved a shift from traditional competitive bids to more of an industrial partnership with firms in need of their expertise.

One of the major differences between ad hoc project oriented firms and firms delivering relatively stable services lies in the possibilities of ex ante planning. The more planning you can do, the more appropriate are formal organization structures and a traditional routinization of tasks and procedures. In addition, the relevant vocabulary used in the firms is affected. Ad hoc project oriented firms discuss projects, whereas firms delivering services on more repetitive contracts talk about client representatives, key account executives, etc. The competitive dynamics are very different for firms where the key issue is that of winning and keeping client accounts, compared to firms offering more ad hoc based services where the key is winning (or even creating) a new and challenging project to which no previous supplier has any established claim.

2) Individual versus team-based delivery.

Another critical dimension has to do with the average size of the projects. This is both a fundamental and a strategic dimension in most industries. There is an obvious connection between the size of the project and the required minimum size of the firm, and hence not all types of firm can compete for all types of contract. Firms may develop different niches, as is common in management consulting. Some firms explicitly target small and medium sized firms and their relatively small projects, whereas other firms, such as McKinsey & Co., target the large corporations. The extreme example of an individually driven management consulting service may be "management-for-hire". Here, one consultant is hired for a relatively long period of time (3-6 months, sometimes even a year), whereas the rest of the company hardly matters at all to the client. Large projects requiring the cooperation of a large number of professionals over long periods of time tend to upset the basic structure of the firms to a much more fundamental extent than relatively small projects that are undertaken by a single or a few professionals (even part time) and completed after a few weeks. An example of an extreme project was the involvement of the US based engineering design firm Parsons Brinckerhoff in the joint venture which gained the design contracts for first "BART", the subway project in San Francisco, and later "MARTA", the subway project in Atlanta. Both of these projects were so large that they were undertaken as joint ventures. As a partner in these projects, Parsons Brinckerhoff contributed hundreds of their engineers for decades, and although the firm had a total of approximately 2700 engineers employed in 1990, with 2200 in the US, it is obvious that this project turned the firm upside down for a long period of time. It also substantially affected their income and had a tremendous effect on their reputation. Whether they liked it or not, their predominant image in the eyes of the public after these projects was no longer focussed on general transportation, but rather on mass rapid transit with particular emphasis on subways.

Communication consulting is a good example of an industry where many assignments are very small, such as e.g. press releases, typically involving one consultant a small part of a day. Yet they also have more long-term contracts, e.g. when they train middle managers in crisis handling, or support top management in the development of a communications strategy. Similarly, large corporate law firms offer excellent examples of firms handling both small and large assignments within the same organization. Sometimes the client just wants quick advice from a senior; one or two hours of one lawyer's time. Other times the firm is involved in large projects, such as e.g. when carrying out a due diligence investigation prior to a major acquisition by a client. Here, it is not unusual that more than 20 lawyers, associates and partners alike, are involved for several weeks (and more or less day and night).

3) Personal versus proposal-based service sales.

Another key dimension making firms and projects different, results from the characteristics of the typical sales process. Whereas engineering projects are generally, though not always, awarded on the basis of public bidding processes, most management consulting contracts are based on a personal interaction between senior professionals of the consulting firm and senior decision makers at the client firm. Again, these buying characteristics may differ substantially across firms even within an industry, as was clearly illustrated in the case of the insurance brokerage firm Sedgwick James. The UK-based firm Sedgwick had a tradition of selling on the basis of their very strong reputation as a firm, and clients wanted to deal with Sedgwick but did not necessarily ask for the same insurance broker every time they needed a new service. They trusted the firm. Their US-based partner in the merger, however, had exactly the opposite tradition, where individual brokers carried with them a long established and personal portfolio of clients trusting them as individuals much more than they trusted the firm. There were cases where the brokers placed insurances with competitors if they found better alternatives outside their own firm, and this was only seen as a sign of loyalty and trustworthiness by the clients. If a broker left the firm to work for a competitor, the danger of losing the majority of the portfolio of clients was also substantial.

Proposal selling and bidding processes are typically much less dependent on the sales abilities of individual professionals, and the required competences are different. Personal selling to clients requires experience and skills in social interaction, whereas the more objective and distant bidding processes require skills and expertise in the development of convincing documentation without giving away too much of the actual solutions. On the other hand, price competition is typically much more fierce in the more "objective" proposal selling or bidding processes.

4) Remuneration by man-hours versus by lump sum

Both industries and projects vary in terms of the contractual terms as well as how payments are made. The most common is probably either a contract involving a complete sum for the entire project, subject to increase if parts of contract terms are altered in the process, or payment by the hour. In law and engineering consulting there is, at least in Norway, a strong tradition favoring the calculations of total fees based on the number of billable hours put in by juniors, seniors, partners, etc. The billable hours model is positive in that it forces the professional service firm to explain to the client how many hours have been spent on the project, by whom, and what have they done. On the other hand, the billable hours model has a built in paradox, in that e.g. investments in efficiency enhancing technology involve high cost but the cost is not compensated in the price of the hours billed. Fewer hours, higher delivery cost, and higher efficiency can result, and consequently less profits for the professional service firm. In other words, incentives to maximize productivity are not always perfect.

Some industries and/or firms have tried more creative ways of billing the clients. One example was Parsons Brinckerhoff's at that time highly innovative key system for hotels. The simple principle was that when the key was dropped in its appropriate keyhole at the reception, light, heat etc. in the room was turned down, as the guest had obviously gone out. When the key was collected again, all settings went back to the same as before the guest had left. And temperature was so rapidly adjusted, that the guest hardly noticed the difference. For these projects, the firm developed a form of contract where they stipulated the annual energy savings for the building, then proposed to install the system for a fee calculated based on the energy savings over the first 5 years, typically with a higher percentage the first 2-3 years than in the last years. As a result, many clients were able to buy the system, even without providing any cash up front. All costs were covered by energy costs saved – i.e. subsequent budgets were smaller, not larger to cover the investment.

In a few particular contexts, even contracts involving the principle of "no-cure-no-pay" have been employed. In most professional service firm-contexts, however, this is a highly risky type of contract, as the quality of the final process and outcome is so heavily dependent on the quality of the input of the client.

5) Application of existing versus development of new solutions.
Finally, the dimension of repeat services as opposed to new solutions to new problems is a critical dimension to consider. Again, firms differ across industries, at the same time as firms within the same industries also choose different strategies. For instance, whereas some firms in engineering design are criticized by their more innovative peers for "pulling the old drawings off the shelves," they earn well by applying the same principles to multiple projects. Other firms are almost embarrassed to admit that they do have communication systems allowing them to reuse parts of earlier drawings and designs for new projects "if the conditions are really the same." For them, innovation and creativity is critical, and reuse of old solutions feels akin to cheating.

Again, the implications for planning and firm organization are fundamental. Needless to say, the more repetitive the operations, the easier it is to plan and predict the project resources needed. The more innovation required, the more uncertainty involved in the service delivery process. I will return to the strategic implications of these dimensions later in this chapter.

The maturity and size of the firm

The maturity of the professional organization has substantial impact on the managerial challenges involved, and the same is true for the size of the firm. Many of the professionals interviewed suggested that there may be a sequence of stages through which professional service firms evolve as they grow, provided they survive each stage. This maturity may also account for some of the heterogeneity of firms within an industry. Three fundamental phases in the evolution of a professional service firm were suggested, and hence two major transitions, after the foundation of the firm:

1. The firm as a collection of individuals who make decisions independently, possibly after informal discussions.
2. The firm as a small, informally coordinated organization with part-time managers making decisions after consulting all key professionals. Organizational goals are developed, but need not be explicitly stated.
3. The multi-office firm. Formal structures and full time management become fundamental to performance.

The level of complexity of the organizational challenges increases substantially from one stage to the next. Many professional service firms remain in the first mode of operations even after the retirement of the founders, as each senior partner develops and maintains his/her own group of professionals and established client relations.

Firms where the senior professionals are highly successful at the first stage and decide to develop the firm, as opposed to only developing their own client and competence bases, face a difficult shift. They need to change from a group of loosely linked professionals to a firm with coordinated activities at all levels. In many cases, this shift also involves a shift in ownership structure, from a partnership to an incorporated company. As a result, it is no longer enough that the partners meet regularly and report on their own progress; all key professionals need to know and accept the priorities of the firm, and formal as well as informal structures must be developed in order for the firm to achieve the required coordination.

Finally, many successful firms grow beyond the stage where personal interaction among the senior professionals is sufficient for the coordination of activities and the development of consensus on key strategic priorities. In order to succeed through the next transition, a growth strategy needs to be developed. Management as well as key expert time is clearly limited, and the firm has to set priorities in terms of the services, competences, and key client groups to be focussed on for future growth. Again, the transition is likely to be difficult, as the – now large – number of professionals need to agree on priorities and accept reduced flexibility and personal discretion for the benefit of the firm as a whole. For example, Bobrick (1985) describes this strategic shift at the US based engineering design firm Parsons Brinckerhoff, after the firm had survived in the first mode of operations well into the 1970s. The firm seemed to jump directly from the first to the third stage, as the transition to highly coordinated activities happened only after the firm had grown (relatively) large and had numerous offices. The second phase could be avoided, as each of the professional specialties was run almost like an independent firm with its own senior managers in charge. Through this minimization of coordination across specialties, they avoided the second stage but naturally also incurred additional costs due to the inefficiency of running so many sub-specialties without easy transferability of slack resources across areas of expertise.

Two fundamental dimensions of firm heterogeneity

Industry differences and differences due to firm size and maturity are, however, not sufficient to explain why so many different types of firms co-exist in professional service industries. The large, multinational accounting firms coexist with very small, local auditing firms, and both may be highly profitable simultaneously. In IT-consulting in Norway, the story of Pharos illustrates how a new firm with only thirteen partners and no juniors could be highly profitable and deliver high quality services despite the competition from global firms such as Accenture, IBM and Cap Gemini Ernst & Young. In management consulting, individual consultants and mini-firms co-exist with large firms such as McKinsey, BCG, AT Kearney and PA Consulting. And among law firms, despite what seems to be a very strong trend towards mergers and acquisitions more or less similar to that of the auditing firms a couple of decades ago, we also see well known senior lawyers in Norway establish a new small law firm. A similar trend can be seen in advertising as well as communication consulting; senior level professionals leave the large firm in order to establish small, nimble, niche-specialized companies which are sometimes highly successful and then later experience the same development as the large firm – with spin offs or new mergers. The entry and exit barriers are small in professional service industries, perhaps with the exception of developing client trust and reputation. When one or a few of the professionals have a strong enough reputation as individuals to start up a new company, assignments and client loyalty may be in place even at the start up.

How can it be possible to be profitable as a small firm, if there are genuine economies of scale and/or scope in these industries? Why do professionals continuously establish new small partnerships at the same time as their peers merge large firms into even larger international companies? Why are some firms partnerships and others corporations? Why do some firms develop traditional hierarchical structures of supervision, control, and promotion (or even "up-or-out", as is the well-known principle of McKinsey, borrowed from highly reputable academic institutions in the US), whereas other firms attempt to maintain the flat structure of "a federation of equals" (Palmer, 1987)?

I suggest that there are two fundamental dimensions driving these strategic choices, and that the options available are not as many and independent as they may appear. Again, these dimensions are based on what I consider to be the two most fundamental strategic issues to be resolved in professional service firms, namely A) the role of the professionals employed, or in other words: the characteristics of the resource base utilized for value creation, and B) the types of projects targetted for value creation, or in other words: the strategic focus.

A) Resource base and/or the role of the professionals.

From a resource based perspective, there is a fundamental difference in terms of what kind of strategic resources are critical to firm value creation. Some firms rely primarily on intangible resources that are controlled by individual professionals, whereas other firms rely primarily on organizationally controlled resources such as complex data systems, excellent practices and procedures, etc. In the extreme case, the individually controlled firm can be organized as a network or "federation of equals" (Palmer, 1987), even to the extent that each partner is his/her own profit center and only pays a predefined fee for the utilization of the common office space. The other extreme involves firms where well established methods and other types of organizationally controlled resources enable the professionals to work together for a much higher joint value creation than what could have been created by summing individual efforts. Famous illustrations of the latter include McKinsey & Co in management consulting and the large multinational firms in auditing. These are firms which invest substantial amounts of effort on the development of firm specific procedures, methods, and data bases to support their work, as well as on training newly employed people in these methods and enforcing their commitment to the unique organization culture or "way of doing things".

When the firm's value creation is strongly dependent on individual professionals who are not substitutable, the firm needs to pay particular attention to individual needs in order to motivate and keep the best people. Table 3 illustrates how individual priorities may be incorporated into

Table 3. Individual vs organizational priorities

Individual priorities	Organizational responses
Priority to professional goals	Internal ownership; Professional experts as leaders
Professional challenges	Strategic priority to challenging target clients and projects
Improved competence	Investment in competence enhancing contracts; The learning organization – learning from clients, peers (academe); Competence exchange and training within the firm; Career systems enhancing learning; Incentives enhancing added competence
Satisfied clients	Emphasis on service quality; Priority to quality over profits; Support systems for quality control
"Decent pay"	Strategy and growth for high performance; Ownership, incentives, profit sharing
Own goals heard and respected	Consensus-based decision-making; use of task forces; mechanisms for "voice" rather than exits; managers who listen more than they talk
Constructive conflict level	Mechanisms for conflict resolution; Tolerance for diverging opinions; "Voice" as a norm
Support	Team structure; Physical support (computers etc.); Support staff; Clear responsibilities of managers
"Fun"	Team structure, supporting colleagues; Tolerable "red tape" level, sufficient individual freedom; Clan based/trust based control
Professional esteem/respect	Career management, ownership, learning, participation in external networks
Pride, strong ethics	Emphasis on ethical behavior

organizational goals and procedures in order to reduce the potential conflict of interest and ensure that the most mobile people do not choose to leave the firm.

Maister (1993) classifies professional service firms into three categories in terms of whether the basis for their sales is expertise (brains), experience (grey hair) or efficiency (procedures). In my view, the difference between expertise and experience is not strategically critical, as both of these are professional inputs controlled by individuals unless they are combined into team efforts through methods and procedures. Hence, I would classify both expertise and experience as individually controlled resources, whereas procedure or efficiency seems to be the same as the organizationally controlled resource base, where profits can be generated through replication and efficiency enhancement. This illustrates the second fundamental dimension, namely how the firm seeks to develop its primary source of competitive advantage. The resource base of the professional service firm may be predominantly *individually controlled, organizationally controlled,* or *some combination.* The type of resource base both determines the potential for competitive advantage of the firm, and affects the firm's domain, whether deliberately chosen or emergent.

B) Strategic focus or type of project.

The other fundamental dimension, then, concerns the source of competitive advantage for the firm, or what may be called the firm's strategic focus. If we refer to Chapter II, different challenges for professional service firms were spelled out based on characteristics of the input (or now we would say the resource base), the interaction, and the output. Even if all of these characteristics must be attended to, there seems to be a clear tendency among the firms to develop a competitive strength primarily in one of these areas. What makes the firm able to deliver superior value to a client may depend on its unique relationships to specific clients, on its unique solutions which competitors are unable to duplicate, or on its ability to utilize the professional inputs for the development of creative and unique solutions to each particular problem presented.

Firms primarily emphasizing the interaction with the client typically try to develop long-term relationships with given clients or client groups through personal selling efforts by senior professionals and tend to put substantial effort into the development of strong interpersonal ties between client firm representatives and professionals. In such extreme cases, the firm consists of a set of loosely coupled network relationships between individual professionals and individual client representatives, such that clients are loyal to individual professionals, rather than to firms. In the extreme case, we may even question whether or not this really is a firm, as opposed to individual professionals sharing an office.

Firms emphasizing the output, on the other hand, develop unique solutions that are marketed almost like products, without much attention paid to who is delivering what to whom. Markets are primarily expanded through the search for new geographical areas or new client niches where the same or similar services are needed. Also in this category, the extreme case exists, where the firm primarily sells a specific type of solution and approach, such as the famous management consulting example of the BCG-matrix. More recent examples from management consulting include the balanced scorecard, systems for managing knowledge, and ways to measure, document, and improve intellectual capital. In IT-consulting, SAP implementation is another example.

Another example often mentioned to me in the interviews, was the consulting firm Alexander Proudfoot, which was described as specialized in delivering a team-based service leading to major restructuring and cost cuts. If the appropriate solution to the client firm's main problem is not reduced costs and improved efficiency, such a firm should not be hired. If we go back to the introductory chapter and the definition of professional services as altruistic services to the client, the extreme case here probably falls outside of our definition of a professional service firm and should rather be called a knowledge based service selling firm.

Finally, the primary emphasis on inputs may be the most obvious dimension for professional services, as precisely the resource base in terms of professionals and their approaches is a salient characteristic of these firms. To the extent that the firms rely primarily on the professional interests of their members or partners, the sales may be said to be problem driven or promise based, as they primarily sell their ability to solve unique problems through the creative inputs of their professionals.

Professional service firms may develop a competitive advantage based on their superior client responsiveness or ability to handle relationships, their superior ability to solve complex problems, or their superior ability to deliver a given set of solutions more efficiently than competitors. Naturally there is an interdependence between these focal strategic dimensions and a relative emphasis on the different types of resources, and this connection is particularly salient in terms of input based value creation. When the two dimensions are combined, theoretically we may see nine possible combinations. In Figure 13, the types of resource base of the firm are presented vertically, whereas the three types of strategic focus are presented horizontally.

Figure 13. Internal and external foci.

Res. base \ Strategic Focus	Client Relations	Creative Problem Solving	Adaptation Of Ready Solutions
Org. Controlled Resources			B
Team-Based Individual + Collective		C	
Individually Controlled Resources	A		

In my dissertation study, I did not see all nine possible combinations. Rather, the three most successful combinations seem to be represented on the diagonal starting from the bottom left hand corner. As illustrated in the figure, firms with a competitive advantage in terms of client responsiveness seem to focus on a limited set of established client relations, and these relations are frequently developed by individual professionals within these firms. On the other extreme, firms with a competitive advantage based on their ability to deliver a set of superior solutions typically have a resource base dominated by organizationally controlled resources and target a broad set of clients in the marketing of these services. The intermediate position involves firms specialized in superior problem solving for a certain type of complex problem, where expert professionals are supported by strong organizations in their creative attempts to solve the unique problems of each individual client. As a result, the number and types of clients are typically limited, but not as limited as in the case of client responsiveness.

These are the three generic strategies identified, which will be discussed in further detail in the following. First, however, I would like to highlight why these three combinations seem to be more viable than the other six.

Value creation and firm evolution

In Figure 3 (Chapter II), the value creation processes of professional service firms were discussed and illustrated as a sequence of three different processes: First, selling a credible promise. Secondly, delivering the promised value (without exceeding budgets). And thirdly, learning from the process in order to improve future value creation. In the early stages, professional service firms are primarily driven by the competence, reputation, and connections of founding professionals, and sales are highly personal. Hence, the firms are typically located in the bottom left-hand corner (type A) of Figure 13. However, as they interact with the clients, they develop solutions as well as approaches to problem solving, and even at this early stage a strategic choice becomes evident, even if it seems to be implicit, rather than explicitly made in most firms. The firm may invest in further improvement and sale of the solutions developed, or it may search for new projects requiring new solutions. As the firm recruits new people, it also sets the direction for its strategic development. It may recruit professionals who are similar in order to enhance their total expertise and be able to take on ever more challenging projects, it may recruit additional senior professionals with their established relationships and reputation in place, or it may recruit juniors to assist the process of service delivery and spend time and effort on the development of procedures to secure high quality output from these young assistants. The focus on expertise and more challenging projects takes the firm into the second box on the diagonal (type C) and leads to new requirements for coordination and team building. The focus on junior assistants takes the firm into the third box on the diagonal (type B), but requires the firm to develop sellable solutions and collective competences (e.g. procedures) that enable these juniors to deliver a high percentage of the value creating activities.

However, it is not necessary to make these transitions, and many firms remain successful in the bottom left-hand corner. If they recruit other independent and self-sufficient professionals with established client networks, the firm can grow into a conglomerate of individual practices, with almost no investment in joint procedures and learning activities. No solutions need to be consistent across professionals, and no learning is transferred to collective competences in order to make juniors able to deliver senior quality without constant supervision. Both efficiency and effectiveness are taken care of by each individual professional, and if one professional delivers inadequate quality, his/her own revenues and reputation automatically suffer.

If the firm does make the transition to established procedures and solutions, again the efficiency and effectiveness of the firm are relatively easy to ensure. These firms strongly resemble traditional manufacturing firms and through the usual hierarchical organization both efficiency and effectiveness can be supported by traditional mechanisms of division of labor, supervision, and control. Relationships to clients are taken care of by senior client representatives, and operations are separated from sales and solution development.

The most difficult position to maintain seems to be the one in the middle, where coordination is required for team cooperation, learning must be institutionalized, and client interaction may occur at all levels. Yet the formal hierarchy cannot be relied upon to solve coordination challenges. When services are primarily innovative and ad hoc, by definition they cannot be routinized and preplanned. As there are strong pressures pulling the firm in both directions, a great deal of managerial attention and effort is required in order for the firm to maintain its position. This is particularly true for firms in the middle box of the diagonal but also for firms in the other two diagonal positions. These pressures and challenges will be discussed at further length later in this chapter.

Three generic strategies for professional service firms

As discussed in the previous chapters, the strategy chosen manifests itself primarily in terms of target projects and professionals, both of which affect competitiveness and resource accumulation. However, consciously or indirectly through prioritized alternatives, firms may choose different strategies, depending on which set of core resources they prioritize. Naturally, this choice is dependent on the strengths of the firm at present, its competitive position, the client service needs the firm attempts to satisfy, and the target competitive position for the future.

In terms of leveraging existing resources, a firm may base its competitive advantage in organizational competences such as sophisticated data bases, patented computer models, and common procedures or in highly reputable individuals and their networks of relationships. Similarly, firms may choose different sets of strategies for the accumulation of assets for future competitive advantage, depending on their target future assets. Naturally a strategy aimed at developing client- and industry-specific organizational competence, such as sophisticated data-bases, will have to target the accumulation and organization of information about the chosen firms and industries. Strategies based on individual competences, on the other hand, need to focus on keeping, recruiting, and motivating the people who embody such individual competences.

These strategies require different combinations of organizational structures and control mechanisms, in particular since the uncertainties and vulnerabilities which result from the strategies are very different. Strategies based in technology or sophisticated models are based on resources that belong to the firm, but lead to vulnerability to imitation as well as obsolescence. Strategies based in competences embodied in individuals, on the other hand, make the firm vulnerable to the exit of these individuals.

Figure 14 below illustrates how the positions on the diagonal are more naturally profitable than the other six alternatives.

Figure 14. Optimal positioning on diagonal.

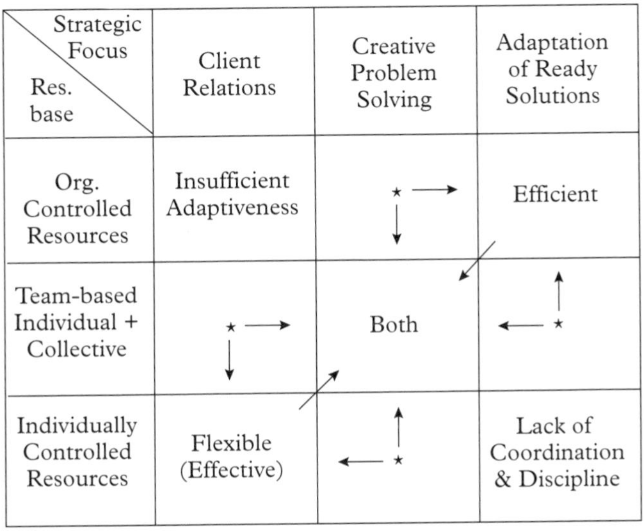

Strategic Focus / Res. base	Client Relations	Creative Problem Solving	Adaptation of Ready Solutions
Org. Controlled Resources	Insufficient Adaptiveness	⋆ → ↓	Efficient
Team-based Individual + Collective	⋆ → ↓	Both	↑ ← ⋆
Individually Controlled Resources	Flexible (Effective)	← ⋆ ↑	Lack of Coordination & Discipline

⋆ Indicates intermediate positions with potential for
improved performance by moving into diagonal cells.

Firms in position A combine individual competences and relationships with responsiveness to all client demands. They are highly flexible. Firms in position B develop organizational competences to enhance efficiency and have routines and procedures that allow them to replicate solutions consistently. In the upper left-hand corner, the collective resources cannot be sufficiently leveraged, as the client responsiveness requires flexible tailor-making. In order to increase flexibility, the firm is likely to be better off by reducing its emphasis on procedures and returning to individual relationships, hence moving the firm to position A. In the bottom right-hand corner, it is impossible to replicate solutions efficiently and consistently while the individual professionals make autonomous decisions with very little coordination. Common procedures will make the firm more efficient, hence moving it to position B, or the firm adds on new flexible services and instead moves to position A. Similarly, all the middle positions off the diagonal offer potential for improvements by cultivating the strengths and prioritizing one of the "clean" positions A, B, or C.

In order to avoid the difficulties involved in the management of a firm serving multiple niches, some firms decide to establish separate strategic business units (SBUs) in order to allow each value creation process the necessary focus to maintain one of the generic strategies. An example of a firm which set up independent SBUs in order to approach different markets with different strategies, was the IKO group. This strategy worked very well for a number of years, until the markets turned severely competitive and a couple of the SBUs found they were cannibalizing each other, fighting over the same limited number of clients. The splits of large accounting and consulting firms such as the then highly reputable Arthur Andersen (where the auditing part is now closed down, many good auditors have gone to competitors, and Accenture – the consulting part – is alive and well), Ernst & Young (where the consultants were "sold" to Cap Gemini), and Price Waterhouse Coopers (where the consulting part was taken over by IBM) may also reflect the difficulties of maintaining two very different strategic modes in one firm. Whereas consulting practices are largely ad hoc and require substantial flexibility, auditing practices are continuous and require long term client relationships and stable operational routines.[2] In the following, the three different strategies are discussed in further detail.

A) Client Relation Based Strategies

Client relation based strategies emphasize the firm's unique ability to understand and help particular client groups. As such they are likely to be highly focussed in terms of target client groups and less focussed in terms of professional competences and the scope of services offered. If the firm perceives a potential for better serving existing target clients by adding

---

[2] There are other obvious reasons for the split in this particular case, though. The firms were particularly concerned with the effects on reputation of discussions of conflicts of interest in the press, if one firm is first advising and later auditing the same clients. Separate firms make the claims for independent and objective service delivery more credible.

additional competences to the team, the firm is likely to hire professionals who have those competences, rather than let the client buy those services elsewhere. The primary strategic assets of these firms are the professionals' reputation among target client groups and their strong relationships with key client groups. Growth is based on the development of new relationships of trust and confidence to new clients, and thus the professionals with the highest status and authority are those who are able to build such confidence and win new clients. Seniority and experience with the key client groups are crucial factors, and young professionals, to the extent that they are hired at all, can only be trained through years of apprenticeship working with the seniors in close interaction with the clients. The organizational structure must be extremely flexible, and the informal interaction required at any point in time drives the coordination within the firm. The formal structure, however, is only a minimal skeleton. Formal procedures and requirements for coordination are likely to be ignored, unless they are seen by the professionals as beneficial in their efforts to deliver the best quality service to the client.

Senior professionals and top management spend most of their time with clients: building new relationships, making certain the client is happy with services delivered, and exploring possibilities for additional contracts with the same clients. Internal issues are only taken care of to the extent that it is absolutely necessary; the development of the firm, its organization and its strategy, are not highly emphasized and do not lead to an increased respect among the professionals. Administration and management are primarily classified as costly overheads and barely tolerated. If coordination is required, it is likely to be achieved predominantly through "price" (Bradach & Eccles, 1989), i.e. through the establishment of financial incentives which help align the individual activities with the overall goals of the firm.

The firms following a client relation based strategy seem to be the firms that most resemble the "operating adhocracy" described by Mintzberg (1983) in that very few activities can be planned in advance, and the strategic decision making authority rests in the hands of the senior professionals who interact with the clients. However, synergies may still be achieved through clear priorities on client groups that allow the firm to build its competences cumulatively, even though the competences are individually controlled and client related. This is primarily achieved through the new professionals recruited. In addition, the firm may develop strategies that tie the professionals to the firm, thus reducing the probability of their exits. The shared knowledge about key clients may be increased through internal training programs and seminars, client information data bases, team cooperation in service delivery, etc., thus reducing somewhat the dependence on specific key individuals.

Performance in these firms is primarily measured in terms of client satisfaction and the retention of clients and number of "follow-on contracts" with a given client. The firm is unlikely to have external owners, as the firm itself has little value beyond what is created by the professionals. Senior professionals are likely to be partners or stock owners, and all strategic decisions are based on consensus. Top management, if such roles are assigned, has very little power and control over the activities of other senior professionals. Since client satisfaction is the number one goal for operations, this is not seen as a problem. As long as the client is satisfied, the independent judgment of the senior professional is also trusted to be the best for the firm.

Two firms that were included in my dissertation study were extreme in their emphasis on client relations, namely the partner company of the IKO Group in the UK, Harold Whitehead & Partners, and the American partner in the insurance brokerage firm Sedgwick James; Fred S. James. The dependence of Fred S. James on its individual brokers has been previously described. In the case of Whitehead, the situation was more extreme, as single consultants had worked for the same clients for decades. Whenever the client needed a consulting service, the client representative would contact the same senior consultant and he would decide whether or not this was a service his firm was capable of delivering. In some cases they would hire experts to support them in the project; in extreme cases they would put the client in contact with another expert firm. For the client, however, the consultant served somewhat like an in-house counsel, that is like a lawyer hired on a permanent basis to provide advice on any legal problem that might occur in the client firm. The senior consultants knew the firm so well that they also knew how to define its problems and where to seek appropriate expertise. As a result, the nature of the services delivered was highly flexible, whereas the number of clients was rather limited. Naturally no clients were continually in need of consulting advice, and hence they floated in and out of the portfolio of present projects. The relationship, however, was maintained, and this interdependence was seen as positive for both the client and the consulting firm.

B) Solution or Output Based Strategies

Firms basing their strategies in superior collective capabilities or solutions have developed a core portfolio of such services, methods, or solutions. Growth is achieved through the addition of new markets and client groups where similar services are needed. The core strategic resources of these firms are embodied in organizational competences, as exemplified by the computer software developed by professional groups within CDM and Parsons Brinckerhoff, or the well known example of the BCG-matrix. At both CDM and Parsons Brinckerhoff, however, the core strategy was based on superior problem solving expertise (type C). These particular solutions were seen as support for the professionals rather than as "products" to be sold in a solution based strategy. When firms following solution based strategies want to add new solutions to their portfolios, this can be accomplished either through internal R&D departments or through acquisitions of firms with appropriate solutions.

Given the high degree of emphasis on organizational competences, the firm as such may also have a high value beyond the value added by each individual working for the firm. As a result, external ownership is possible. However, as long as capital intensity is low, external ownership is not likely to be the dominant mode. On the other hand, the firms following this type of strategy are also likely to be the firms most willing to increase capital intensity in order to support their R&D divisions and the marketing of solutions, and such capital investments may yield high returns, even after the highly salaried experts developing new solutions have been paid.

Since the people developing the services or solutions do not need to be externally oriented and interested in sales, top management has substantial authority in these firms. Activities need to be coordinated to a great extent, and the formal organization is likely to be more important to actual behavior than in firms following either of the other two strategies. In the extreme, these firms may evolve from solution driven professional service firms to knowledge based service sales organizations. Their main vulnerability is to solution obsolescence. Hence their main challenge is the motivation of the people involved in R&D activities to create new solutions that are relevant and value adding to a large group of clients.

In addition to the examples mentioned above, where subsections of the U.S. based engineering firms were basing their strategies on unique solutions, the IKO Strategy subsidiary was explicitly investing in the development of unique methods or solutions, particularly for clients within a limited number of industries. The UK based partner in the merged insurance brokerage firm Sedgwick James; Sedgwick, also had very strong collective routines, solutions ("products"), and a collectively oriented client loyalty and firm reputation. Other well known examples include McKinsey and Accenture. In general, it is fair to say that when clients accept contracts that do not name the professionals who are going to be involved in service delivery, this is a clear sign of a successful development of collective routines and firm reputation.

C) Problem Solving or Creativity Based Strategies

The problem solving based strategies result in the most complex firms typically delivering services involving a high degree of innovation. One reason for this is the fact that the professional competence in terms of problem solving capabilities, creativity, and expertise cannot be converted to organizational competence, even though it may be used to develop collective competence, such as team and organizational methods or new software support. The expert developing the solution is unlikely to be made redundant by the development of organizational competences. In fact, the more the key professionals use their competence for the benefit of the organization at large, the more important they become for the continued welfare of the organization. As a result, the creativity based problem-solving firm cannot avoid dependence on key individuals. It can develop organizational competence assets such that the firm's survival does not depend on a few key professionals, but it cannot develop a competitive advantage without central individuals unless it alters strategy. These organizations have to develop strategies and structures that make the most of the strengths of the individuals and simultaneously develop the organization. They cannot emphasize one and ignore the other.

The top managers of the problem solving based organizations are likely to be the most highly recognized professional experts, or rather the best professional who is willing and able to accept managerial responsibilities. The firm is likely to prioritize professional goals and hence is unlikely to have external owners. New offices are typically set up based on a consensus on goals and developed from internal resources; acquisitions are quite rare, except in terms of small and highly specialized niche firms with a similar strategy. Respect and authority follows the best professional expertise. Senior managers, however, have to balance the demands on them as professional experts responsible for convincing clients of the (true) quality of their problem solving capacity with the demand for coordinating internal operations. The firm needs to be coordinated to a relatively high extent, particularly in terms of support structures and a sharing of the best professional resources across divisions and locations. But as strong professionals only accept control by a manager or an organization to the extent that they feel the control is to the benefit of their own and the firm's professional development, management needs to spend a great deal of energy on internal issues, including the development of consensus on goals and priorities.

The organizational structure involves both a structure of authority and respect, based in particular on professional expertise, and a structure requiring a high degree of flexibility and adaptation to the decisions of the key professionals. Decisions are typically not controlled from the top, except to the extent of developing the common pattern in decisions. Even this is a pattern which results more from top management listening to professional aspirations and concerns of key professionals, than from the aspirations of top management in isolation. Coordination is achieved through mutual adjustment.

In the sample included in my study, both U.S. based engineering design firms were clear examples of such complex firms with a competitive advantage based in unique problem solving expertise within a limited number of areas. At Parsons Brinckerhoff, the most highly esteemed engineers were promoted based on the criterion of being "among the best experts in the world within their area of expertise". At CDM, the expertise was so highly recognized within the water treatment area, that the firm's experts were asked by U.S. Government Agencies for professional advice before a new Water Treatment Act was proposed. Both firms had close connections with some of the best universities in their areas of expertise and supported the training of young engineers. They also invested substantially in the professional development of their own best people, including support for research and publications in academic journals.

A Comparison of the Three Strategic Modes

The three types of competitive advantage and resultant strategies are not mutually exclusive. However, it seems to be difficult for any firm to deliver superior performance based on multiple strategies simultaneously. The managerial and organizational challenges involved differ too much. Table 4 below indicates how the three types of strategies differ on a number of key dimensions.

The stronger the dependence on individually controlled assets, the more important it is for the firm to develop a structure that supports the individual professionals and increases their loyalty to the firm. When the firm is dependent on the sale of solutions, the development of new solutions for which there is a market is fundamental to high performance. In addition to the major differences in firm characteristics, there seems to be a mutual self-selection process involved when these firms recruit new professionals. Highly creative and autonomous experts tend to prefer less for-

Table 4. Three generic strategies and configurations

	Adapting Solutions	Client Relation	Creative Problem Solving
Status and authority	Hierarchical Management	Client rel.	Expert
Management focus	Internal R&D	External Sales	Internal+ External Competence development
Control	Authority	Price	Trust
Coordination	High HQ to local	Low	Medium Two-way
Performance evaluation	Sales revenues New solutions	Client satisf. % repeat buy	Innovation Capture rate for challenging projects
Org. design	Top down	Bottom up	Self designing
Org. flexibility	Low	High	Medium
Service complexity	Low	Medium	High
Ownership	External possible	Internal	Internal
Key assets	Org. control	Ind. control	Org. + Ind. control
Vulnerability	Obsolescence of solutions	Exits	Obsolescence of competence or rigidity (loss of innovativeness)
Strategic focus	Target markets	Target clients	Target projects/ problems (challenges)

malized and structured firms, whereas young professionals who seek job security and proven training programs prefer the larger, more hierarchical organizations. Some of the latter also seek employment in government agencies, where job security has traditionally been extreme. For the problem solving based firm, both the loyalty of the innovative experts and the quality of solutions is fundamental. Hence the coordination and sharing of expert resources are critical in a balance between organizational and individual demands.

Similarly, the focus of top management's time is different. For the client relation based firm, the senior managers spend most of their time on external issues, in particular on client relationship development and maintenance. The managers of a service or solution driven firm put more emphasis on internal issues of solution development and coordination of activities. Finally, the managers of a problem solving based firm need to emphasize strength in both externally oriented client management and internally oriented motivation and coordination of professional experts.

Whereas the client relationship based firm is likely to be the most difficult to coordinate, the managerial challenges are not as complex as in the creative problem solving firm. The client relationship driven firm finds a quasi-solution in reducing the amount of coordination required and allowing the professionals to make decisions relatively independently. It also recruits highly autonomous individuals. The solution selling firm, on the other hand, is better equipped to achieve a high degree of coordination but is not dependent on motivating and keeping the most independent professionals to the same extent as the other two types of firms. In addition, the firm may isolate the most creative and autonomous professionals in a small and relatively independent R&D department. The creative problem solving firm, however, has to achieve a high degree of coordination without inducing conflicts with the most independent professionals. In Table 5 below, the relationship between different professional priorities and the different strategic solutions are compared.

The primary coordination mechanism used to achieve the necessary level of coordination is also likely to differ across firms with different strategic modes. Bradach & Eccles (1989) suggest that coordination may be achieved based on price (financial incentives), authority, or trust, or any combination of these three mechanisms. Whereas the client relation based firm is likely to coordinate its relatively independent professionals primarily through financial incentives including potential or actual ownership (price), the solution based firm is likely to coordinate primarily based on authority and the formal structure of the organization. The complex firms

Table 5. Individual priorities and different professional firm strategies.

	Adapting Solutions	*Client Relation*	*Creative Problem Solving*
Priority	Job security	Autonomy	Learning, Innovation
Risk aversion	High	Low	Medium
Goal setting	Firm	Individual	Team
Primary goal	Sell or develop solutions	Pleasing the client	Enhancing competence
Authority	"The boss"	The client dec. maker	Professional expert
Reference group	Firm	Client	Academe/peers
Status/Rewards linked to	Loyalty, New solutions, Sales	Client satisfaction, Retention	Creativity, Challenging projects won and completed
Demand from organization	Org. Support	Challenging clients, Autonomy	Challenging projects, Expert colleagues
Degree of autonomy preferred	Low	High	Medium
Primary conflict resolution mode	Loyalty	Exit	Voice

basing their strategy on superior problem solving capabilities must develop a high degree of mutual trust and consensus. This allows for co-ordination simultaneously with the individual experts obtaining sufficient independence. In addition to the mutual trust, strong norms and other elements of organizational culture are required to support a high degree of individual freedom within the constraints of collective goals.

The inherent tensions of the three modes

Whereas most professional service firms start out as small firms with an extreme dependence on the competence, reputation, and established networks of individual professionals, many firms grow and develop into team-based creative problem solvers or even highly efficient delivery systems for professionally based solutions. Firms may exist at any point along the diagonal of Figure 13. Figure 15, below, expands upon Figures 13 and 14, indicating the fundamental tensions pulling firms away from the diagonal positions.

On the one hand, there appears to be a strong tension in most firms from professionals attempting to pull the operations of the firm in the direction of their individual priorities and demanding more freedom and

Figure 15. Pressures for change.

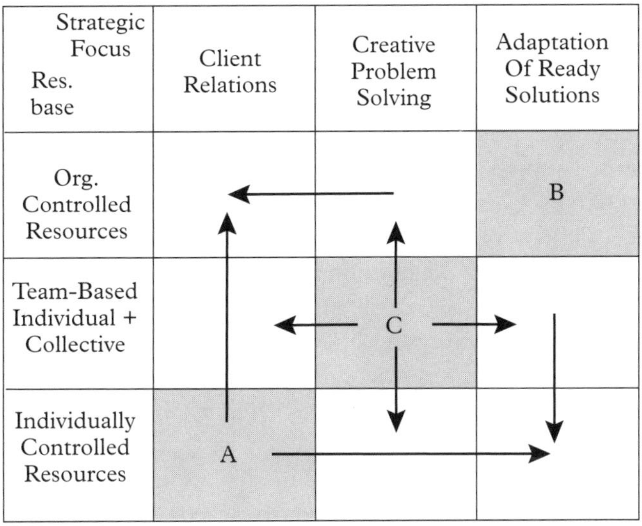

Strategic Focus Res. base	Client Relations	Creative Problem Solving	Adaptation Of Ready Solutions
Org. Controlled Resources			B
Team-Based Individual + Collective		C	
Individually Controlled Resources	A		

less submission to collective goals. Thus, firms of type B face substantial pressures pulling the resources toward the individual (bottom) corner, as well as pulling professional tasks toward the more challenging tailormade solutions in the left-hand corner. For some professionals working for firms in the second or third box on the diagonal, the temptation of relocating to a firm in the bottom left hand corner may be so great that they change employers or set up their own firms. The establishment of the Norwegian IT consulting firm Pharos offers a clear example of such a situation, where the founding partners of the new firm say they left their previous employer (an obvious type B firm) because they suffered from "acute allergy to bosses". However, even if professionals do not go to the extreme of leaving the firm, there exists an ongoing tension between the organization's need for procedures and subordination and the individual's need for freedom to choose and thus develop expertise.

Similarly, firms of type A face pressures, typically more of the administrative and profit oriented kind, demanding more standardization and replication in order to increase revenues. This can be seen, for example, when an engineering design firm tries to modularize designs and drawings in order to reutilize as many modules as possible. Standardization may increase efficiency and reduce costs and result in increased profits, at least for projects already contracted. Attempts to codify individual expertise and routinize successful approaches represent pressures pulling the type A firm up the vertical axis. Similarly, attempts to reutilize existing solutions with new clients pull the firm in the right-hand direction of the horizontal axis. Even in small partnerships, there always seems to be one professional with a stronger interest in the development of methods and routines than his/her peers. When professionals in the bottom left-hand corner are asked to develop procedures, train juniors, or (even worse) repeat the same solution several times with different clients, they typically protest. However, they may be tempted to do so, as the profit potential is often substantial.

Firms of type C are virtually "stuck in the middle" (Porter, 1980), as they face all four pressures simultaneously. If they have managed to achieve an equilibrium, the position is highly unstable. Managers develop more routines in order to control "the mavericks" and leverage solutions. Professionals find creative ways of avoiding repetition, and make ad hoc decisions even in situations where procedures do exist. To be successful, they have to balance all these pressures carefully, in order to stay in their intermediate position.

However, all firms need to manage these tensions, as there is a danger of being pulled out of the strategic mode the firm is in, towards a mix of all modes. The solution based firm may lose its most creative people and hence also lose its ability to improve and develop new solutions. For the professionals who developed the BCG-matrix or the value-chain, it becomes boring work to conduct the 150th training seminar on the same model, and they may readily start a new small partnership with much less routine work. Similarly, the small partnership which develops such (potentially) universal methods may want to increase profits, and even firms that are explicitly designed to be pure partnerships may be tempted to hire junior assistants to improve profitability. The moment they do so, however, they have shifted from individual to a more team-based type of delivery requiring more routine work. They must consciously move along the diagonal; they cannot stay in the left-hand side of the figure and maintain their flexible emphasis on each professional bringing in his/her own clients if they hire juniors who need tasks as well as payment, and who do not have their own networks of client connections.

Dynamics and challenges of changing modes

Although it may be possible to move from one configuration to another over time, this is likely to be very difficult. For example, an organization with strong client relations and no unique solutions cannot, from one day to the next, alter its strategic mode to one requiring replication of previous solutions. If it is so lucky as to "stumble over" a universal solution, it may be able to alter its strategy, provided the professionals agree to the shift. Without such luck, it will need to develop a strategy for the transition into a more solution-driven mode, including heavy investments in marketing and sales as well as R&D designed to develop and improve solutions. All such transitions have to be based in consensus on the appropriateness of the new direction, and require substantial organizational changes in order to accomplish the necessary level of coordination and integration. Hence, such shifts are likely to be extremely difficult and quite rare among professional business service firms. The larger the firm, the more difficult the transition is likely to be.

One reason for these difficulties is found in the professionals hired and their priorities. Another reason is the stability of the reputation of the firm, as its previous project and client types also determine, to a great extent, what kinds of promises the firm can credibly make. However, the type of professionals recruited, their needs, and their mobility in cases of dissatisfaction are the most fundamental reason for the "stickiness" of the strategic modes, despite the tensions pulling in different directions. The most autonomous individuals are not likely to be willing to work for a firm requiring a high degree of subordination to organizational demands. And the firm that requires a high degree of coordination and only a limited degree of innovation and independent judgment is unlikely to hire a professional "rebel." As a result, the firms end up with different types of professionals and the strategic options open to the firm without changing a number of the key professionals are limited.

Strategy as consistency and "informed choice"

Strategy in a professional service firm implies making clear priorities in terms of the kinds of professionals recruited and the types of services to be delivered. It is impossible to be successful if the firm keeps trying to be everything for everyone, and the most likely result is negative spirals, rather than positive. The professionals who are frustrated leave the firm very easily and often go into competing business, thus further worsening the negative spiral. As soon as professionals leave, the reputation effect reduces the probability of winning the best clients and projects, although for firms with strong procedures and routines, as demonstrated in the McKinsey Rome story described in Chapter IV, it may still be possible for the firm to reassure clients that quality will not suffer.

Above all, the professional service firm needs to be conscious of its strategic mode, both current and future. It is possible to move from one mode to another through long-term investments and by hiring professionals with a different set of priorities. It is not wise, however, to divert attention from the primary focus and give all individual initiatives equal impact on the future direction of firm growth. The most challenging and difficult mode is clearly the middle position, the type C firm, where pressures are extreme in all four directions. Hence, this should only be the strategic mode chosen if it is also the best position in terms of delivering superior creative solutions based on team cooperation in projects. It should not be the default mode for firms actually targeting one of the other postures but not succeeding in maintaining their focus on one of the other modes. If the firm shifts substantially without prior strategic consensus, the firm is likely to lose many of its best professionals before management realizes that the shift is actually taking place. Conscious and "informed choice" are therefore crucial for the maintenance of a viable professional firm.

Some afterthoughts for the 3rd edition

Later studies conducted by both myself and several of my students have led me to question whether or not my 3x3-model is valid for all industries and at all times. I am convinced that the two dimensions of resource base and strategic focus make sense. As regards the resource base, we see firms consisting of only seniors with individual reputations and client relations, we see firms that look more like Weber's traditional pyramid, with a strong focus on socialization and training, and the up-or-out principle applied to make "climbing" to the partner level on top highly attractive, and we also see a number of "hybrids" trying to combine the two logics. We also see, as in my first study, that firms that try to combine individual "stars" with a hierarchical structure with a large number of juniors, are the most challenging to manage and keep on track. As regards the strategic focus dimension, we see firms that primarily target repeat buys from existing clients, we see firms that try to develop models that can be modified and resold in what Hansen, Nohria, and Tierney (1999) called "reuse economics", and we see firms trying to be the most innovative, solving different problems for different clients every time. What I am less certain about, is the strict combination of the strategic foci and the type of resource base. I think some firms may continue to be successful, even if they combine reuse of some solutions with the invention of new ones, or they rely largely on repeat buys from well-known clients, but still provide highly innovative services. I have seen management consulting companies that have adopted such a mixed strategy, and that seems to work well. One extreme case may be that of IBM, which – at least in Norway – attempts to cover everything from the sales of hardware and software via the management of IT-units outsourced by other organizations, to advanced professional services in terms of problem solving and support in implementation processes. One reason why these combination strategies work may be that these are all relatively large companies that can rely on broad networks of resources and specialists, sometimes even globally. In some sense, they may resemble the large, multidivisional manufacturing companies, where different units may operate by different logics. Traditional examples are marketing relative to production relative to R&D. In the case of IBM, it is not only a question of a global network of highly qualified people, but also the question of a global network of sub-contractors and collaborating partner firms. Another reason why more combinations may be viable today may be the impact of information- and communication technology, which actually makes it possible for one single expert to be present globally in his/her problem solving work, without ever going to an airport. This was not the case in the late 1980-ies and early 1990-ies, when I conducted my first study.

However, what I am certain about, is the importance of being conscious – and probably also explicit – about the strategic priorities of the firm, both in terms of types of professionals hired and in terms of types of clients and projects targeted. The challenges of strategic management do not go away with more flexible and multidimensional strategies; on the contrary, they increase!

Suggested Readings

Hansen, M., Nohria, N. & Tierney, T. 1999. "What's your strategy for managing knowledge?" Harvard Business Review, March-April, pp. 106-116.

March, J.G. 1991. "Exploration and exploitation in organizational learning." Organization Science, 2: pp. 71-87.

VI. Firm development and growth

Why isn't bigger and global always better?

Introduction

Several key dimensions of the firm are altered when individuals with strong personal competence and a high degree of mobility control the most critical resources for firm value creation. Even professional service firms differ, however, and some have been able to develop collective resources and organization structures that are highly similar to traditional capital based organizations. For some firms, such a development is an excellent idea; for others it would be disastrous. Hence, it is crucial for professional service firm managers to define the type of firm they have developed, as well as what kind of firm they want to develop for the future.

Similarly, it is not the case that bigger is always better, nor the case that internationalization or globalization is always a sign of success. The professional service firm may, in fact, have far more options than any other type of firm, and in many cases the firm may develop a niche where it is possible to deliver superior value and be highly competitive without growing large or international or having investors as stockholders. Again, there are no general and obvious answers. Firms are highly heterogeneous, and if the strategic focus is on value creation through processes which require globalization and large size, these dimensions will be just as relevant as they are to many manufacturing firms today. This chapter briefly discusses these issues, based on the discussions of the previous chapters.

Questioning traditional assumptions

A number of the strategic "buzz words" from manufacturing seem to have spilled over onto all types of firms, including professional service firms. Despite the fact that many managers expressed concern with the lack of applicability of traditional strategic management theories and models, many professionals still appear to believe that their firms exist for the same reasons and should be judged by the same criteria as manufacturing firms. This is not necessarily true. The most successful and competitive firm is not necessarily the most profitable firm. In order to judge the success or failure involved, we need to compare performance to the goals set for the firm. If the professionals who own the firm prefer professional challenge to more money, reduced profitability cannot be interpreted as a lack of success.

Shortly before I published this book, I discovered that Babson College in Boston had developed a teaching case based on interviews and other information from Camp, Dresser and McKee (CDM) Inc (Babson College, 1993). The problem stated on the first page of the case may be summarized as follows: Top management, in 1993 led by CEO and President Tom Furman (EVP and COO at the time of my interviews), is concerned about the unstable and possibly falling rate of ROI (Return on (capital!) investment). Sales are going well, turnover is showing a healthy increase, the "hit rate" of projects won relative to proposals delivered is high, but, alas, ROI is not showing the healthy trend. Now it may be true that this should be a matter of concern to management, as it may be an indicator of deeper underlying problems. Still, the presentation had me seriously worried. Why should management be concerned with an unstable ROI in a firm where the employees own all the stock and the employees themselves state that they are more concerned with "having fun", learning even more, and delivering excellent solutions to clients, than with making profits beyond the minimum necessity? Why does the ROI keep shifting? Is it because of some fundamental problem, or is it rather the result of a healthy balancing of profitability and investments in better reputation and improved expertise? From the teaching case it is impossible to find the answers to these questions. What troubles me is that nobody seems to be interested in asking such questions; in the case it is taken for granted that an unstable ROI is a major problem for all firms, including professional service firms. That is not necessarily true![1]

Very often, not only are the performance measures imported from the traditional corporation, but the same thing is also true of the critical success factors. Underlying assumptions which are often taken for granted include, but are not limited to the following:

- there is a positive relationship between scale and low costs,
- there is a positive relationship between low costs and sales,
- there is a positive relationship between sales and profitability, and

---

[1] It is possible that the vocabulary used in the case is more the result of the mindset of the case writer or a desire to communicate general strategic concerns to young students, than representative of the actual set of priorities of CDM's top management. It is also possible that ROI is critical, if the firm is undertaking major financial investments, as may be required e.g. in an internationalization process based on acquisitions.

– there is a positive relationship between market share and profitability.

Every single one of these assumptions needs to be questioned. In some cases they do hold, but in many firms they are false! When professional service firm managers attempt to develop strategies designed to fit with the above critical success factors, they often find that they fail in more than one respect.

There appears to be no clear evidence that traditional *economies of scale* exist in professional service firms where the primary strategic resource is the competence of the individual professionals. The possibilities of developing economies of scale depend on the type of resource base of the firm, as well as its strategic focus. If the firm can develop unique software, databases, models or techniques that enhance the value creating abilities of the individual professionals (type B in the previous figures), there is a potential for economies of scale. However, for most firms the relationship between size and profitability is highly questionable. Economies of scale may exist, but they may also be eroded by increased and costly needs for complex coordination mechanisms.

Size, then, is no guarantee for increased profits. On the contrary, size also involves greatly increased coordination requirements which either foster the need for full time managers or the need for sophisticated constraint systems limiting the autonomy of the professionals. There may be substantial diseconomies of scale in professional service firms as the cost of coordination goes up, whereas there is no automatic reduction in production cost as the result of scale increases. Low fixed costs and a lack of standardization mean that there may be no gains from increased scale at all!

Similarly, there is no automatic relationship between *reduced costs* and increased sales. Sales depend on credibility, reputation, and expected service quality, and many cost reduction efforts of professional service firms have been perceived by the clients as a reduced ability to deliver high quality. One of the most extreme examples may be that of McKinsey & Co: there is certainly no reason whatsoever to believe that their sales would increase with lowered prices. The same is true for law firms in many corporate law areas. In fact, clients often look to price as a proxy for quality. When they have no way of assessing the quality of one lawyer (or law firm) relative to another, they assume that the most expensive must also be the best. For price to be an adequate proxy for quality, one would have to assume that these services are traded in (relatively) efficient markets.

Given the information asymmetry typically present in the markets for professional services, there is no reason to assume market efficiency in this case. Still, buyers of professional services often seem to think that expensive means very good, and are typically suspicious of firms offering "bargains"!

The relationship between *sales volume* and profits is also questionable. In many situations, one additional project will lead to extreme additional costs in terms of hiring and training of temporary employees, overextension of the capacity of the best experts, mistakes made due to time pressures, and reputation losses.

The relationship between *market share* and profitability also rests on assumptions of a relationship between costs and volume, in particular in terms of the experience curve leading to reduced costs as the result of accumulated volume. As a result, the largest producer is more likely to maintain the lead on competitors. In professional services there is no reason to expect such a relationship, both due to the reduced importance of costs and due to the fact that the relationship between experience and costs is dubious. If future activities are highly similar to past activities, the relationship may be important, maybe even more so than for other firms. However, if the experience rests with the individuals rather than with the firm, it is also critical to ensure that the most experienced professionals prefer to continue using this experience for the benefit of firm value creation. There seems to be a negative relationship between efficiency in terms of repeating the same procedures multiple times and motivation of the most expert professionals. The optimal learning in terms of repetitive activities is countered by the reduced probability of motivating individuals to repeat learned tasks.

Core competence in professional services

In their seminal Harvard Business Review article "The core competence of the corporation", published in 1990, Prahalad and Hamel developed a new concept which was soon to become a new "buzz word" in strategic management. Core competences are sought, not only in corporations, but in all types of firms and industries. Prahalad and Hamel define core competences as competences that

- give a disproportionate contribution to value creation (as seen from the customer's perspective)

- have long term implications and span more than a single product line, and
- enable the firm to distinguish itself from and outcompete its competitors.

In popular use, the third of these criteria is often neglected, and managers look for activities that the firm performs particularly well, rather than compare the firm's competitiveness in these activities to that of the main competitors.

Core competences are typically defined as collective, tacit, and socially complex. As a result, they are extremely difficult to copy, and hence they may provide the firm with a sustainable competitive advantage. For professional service firms, however, this emphasis on collective competences may be misleading. Firms of type B may definitely have collective core competences, and these competences may constitute the foundation for their competitive strength. From an external analysis, it seems very likely that firms such as McKinsey and Accenture do have such core competences, and that these core competences allow them to outcompete their competitors for a large number of client contracts. For firms of type A and C, however, the requirement that core competences be collective is more dubious and certainly should be analyzed carefully. To the extent that the core competence contributing to competitive advantage resides in a single individual professional, either through his/her unique expertise and experience or through his/her unique characteristics as a catalyst for mobilizing the competence of others, sustainability will depend on the firm's ability to retain such critical individuals. In Norway, several recent examples (spring 2005) illustrate this vulnerability very well. One was among our largest and most reputable law firms, where a well known tax lawyer (partner) decided to leave the firm for the benefit of a competitor. A large number of clients followed him to his new employer. Shortly after, three more tax lawyers moved to the same competitor. According to Dagens Næringsliv, Norway's largest financial newspaper, the ex-employer firm threatened to take their ex-partner to court for a substantial amount of money, and they also threatened to charge clients that switched supplier with a fee for transferring their client documents from their files to the competitor. In the end, all parties involved decided to settle quietly, out of court, and without any information to the press as to what the final agreement was. Another example concerns the large international financial brokerage firm, ABM Amro, with its Norwegian subsidiary Alfred Berg. Here, the highly profiled Nordic brokering manager left first, followed by a large number of colleagues. Friday April 15th, Dagens Næringsliv reported that 15 brokers and analysts had left the company. A few days later (April 21st), the same paper reported that the top manager of ABM Amro Equities, Tim Boyce, had resigned, as well as two more brokers located in London.

Again we see that the discussion from traditional industries may have to be extended in order to be applicable to professional service firms. Core competences in professional services are also rare, inimitable (difficult to copy) and highly valuable for the firm (Barney, 1991), and hence have the characteristics required for them to be potential sources of sustained competitive advantage. However, unless they are collective, the value creation from these competences must be linked to the firm for such values to be sustainably connected to firm performance. That link must be made through incentives tying the professionals to the firm.[2]

Measuring success

In the traditional corporation, where capital is a scarce resource and the primary goal may be defined as satisfying the requirements of the equity holders, performance is normally adequately measured through the performance of traded stock on the stock exchange. The market carefully analyzes both present earnings and future value creation, and the price of the stock is assumed to reflect the value of the firm.

When the firm has little or no capital invested, but rather relies on the present and future contributions of competent experts in interaction with sophisticated clients, such measures are at best irrelevant and at worst terribly misleading. If we return to Figure 6, value creation is measured through an increase in the value creating potential of all the firm's available resources, including but not limited to financial resources. For the traditional corporation, it is possible to include predictions of innovative capacity as well as goodwill and excellent management in the calculations of stock prices. But still, such calculations require that there is a significant relationship between the capital invested, the management employed by representatives of the owners, and the value creating abilities of the firm. When most of the firm's value creation is the result of professional competences and relationships controlled by individuals, the value of the firm may be extremely difficult to predict.

---

[2] This point was also made by an American colleague of mine, Russ Coff, in an excellent article in Academy of Management Review, 1997, entitled: "Human Assets and Management Dilemmas; Coping with hazards on the road to resouce-based theory". 22 (2), pp. 374-402.

Those who control the firm's most critical resource also gain power in the firm. This fact is also the underlying explanation for the power held by owners of the financial capital in the traditional corporation. When the most critical resource is individual expertise, owners of financial capital have very little power, and their goals of increased financial wealth receive a much lower priority. The professional service firm may decide to prioritize a number of projects with barely sufficient profits, in order to enhance the problem solving abilities and commitment of the professionals. When choosing between a highly profitable project and a much less profitable but more challenging project with substantial competence development potential, the professional firm will often choose the latter. The only exception is when the firm's owners prioritize financial results.

Not only is it misleading to measure professional service firm success in terms of ROI if most of their returns result from human investments rather than financial, but comparisons over years become misleading as well. Comparisons across firms make no sense whatsoever. Since the financial investment has little to do with the revenues generated, comparing firms on ROI may mean that the firm seems to be more successful the less capital it invests!

In order to evaluate performance, all firms need to assess the degree to which the firm reaches its goals, in a prioritized sequence. If ROI is not important to the most critical stakeholders, typically including professionals as owners, why be concerned? If a lack of challenging projects leaves key professionals frustrated, despite an excellent "bottom line", the potential effect on future value creation is far more serious than if the profits generated are below target level.

What then is "success" for the professional service firm? Success of a firm must be assessed relative to the goals of its owners. To the extent that it is owned by the same professionals who also have the ultimate power over the utilization of the critical resources, the success factors and the goals need to be defined by this group. Critical elements typically include:

- Recruiting and retaining the best professionals
- Applying competence and other resources to the best possible projects or clients, both in terms of maximizing the firm's and the client's value creation in the short run and in terms of maximizing learning and reputation building effects in the long run
- Utilizing and improving methods and procedures for minimum value loss and maximum learning over time
- Generating sufficient profits to "have fun" and continue doing what is most interesting

- Completing projects in such a way that the firm's reputation is further enhanced and the probability of winning the most challenging projects and recruiting the best professionals is improved, thus creating positive spirals.

In other words, the positive spirals of professional service firms may be illustrated in terms of five P's as in the following figure:

Figure 16. The 5P's of performance in professional business service firms.

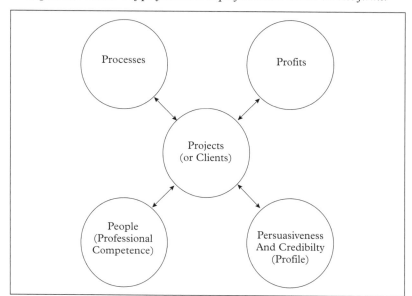

In the above figure, the five performance indicators are drawn with equal size. The relative weighting of the five factors will, of course, vary from one firm to the next, in particular across different strategic modes. The relative weighting of the performance measures is also likely to vary across individual professionals, further illustrating the importance of consensus building as regards which goals for the firm have higher priority. The center position given to Projects is no coincidence, however. Whereas firms differ substantially in terms of their priorities of Profits relative to (individual) Professional development relative to (collective) Procedures relative to firm Profile or reputation enhancement, the firms I have studied all seemed to agree on the importance of the Projects or clients. Client needs and project requirements in terms of advanced creativity or application of existing solutions were seen as driving the core of the positive or negative performance spirals of these firms. Excellent projects and challenging clients attract excellent professionals and typically also allow the firms to charge sufficiently high prices to develop improved methods and still retain an acceptable level of profits. Successful completion of challenging projects enhances profile and further increases the probability of winning the most challenging projects and hiring more highly qualified professionals. The spiral goes on and on.

On the other hand, the negative spiral also seems to be driven by clients or projects. If the firm is unable to win interesting projects, highly mobile professionals leave the firm, thus further reducing the probability of winning new challenging projects. As a result, firms accept projects that are peripheral to their strategic priorities and/or at a lower price than what they would normally accept. The fear of too many non-billable hours among the professionals typically makes the firm willing to accept projects that would otherwise have been far from their target portfolio. If the projects are peripheral to the firm's strategic priorities, the profile or reputation will also be blurred, further reducing the probability of winning the most interesting target projects in the next bidding process.

Every time a professional makes a choice in terms of what kind of service to deliver, the type of client to be approached, the type of project to be accepted, the price level and constraints involved, or the amount of innovation and creative problem solving required, (s)he also agrees to deliver services that will affect both short term resource deployment and profitability, and long term learning and reputation building. Some client projects are unlikely to succeed and, hence, with a high degree of probability lead to reduced or diverted effects upon reputation. Such projects should clearly be avoided at all costs, even if they are of minimal risk financially, i.e. in the short run. As stated by Normann (1984): "… it takes twelve rights to make up for one wrong!" In other words, it takes much more to develop a positive reputation than to destroy one. And unfortunately, just like the positive spiral, the process goes on and on.

It is extremely important, however, to be aware of the fact that professional service firms may not prioritize financial profits as their number one goal. To the extent that the owners prefer maximizing the returns on their intellectual rather than financial capital, they may consciously downplay the importance of making more profits to the benefit of more learning, more intellectual challenges, more "fun", or any other goal they prefer to set higher. The value of the firm, then, for the owners, depends upon their own relative weighting of short term versus long term priorities, as well as their own individual versus firm oriented value added. There is certainly nothing wrong with professional service firms maximizing the short term gain of the lawyers, auditors, or other professionals who are partners. The only limitation is the importance of paying attention to the professional requirement of altruistic service delivery to the client.

Acquisitions in professional services; beware of buying "an empty INC"

How would you buy shares in McKinsey? Well, you cannot, and most likely you should not. Many investors who see the profitability and growth of such firms and want a share of the pie want to invest in projects with potentially high returns. However, the problem is that the returns are not necessarily on financial capital but on "brains." Traditional investors generally do not want to add brains; they want to add capital in a limited risk situation. However, in professional service firms, the risk is normally very high for an outside investor, unless the financial capital itself actually does generate additional value. If the professionals possess the ultimate power in terms of restricting their discressionary efforts and even resigning from the firm, thus leaving an empty shell or "empty inc" for investors, financial capital holders or potential merging partners are well advised to look carefully into the types of resources they are buying into, and how they are expected to generate future cash flow. Firm reputation, organizational competences, tangible assets and cash are all available to firm owners. However, if client relations, professional competences, organizational culture and other types of value creating combinations are held by individuals, the acquisition or investment must be based on consensus with these resource holders, otherwise they are likely to withhold or reduce their discressionary efforts to an absolute minimum.

In addition, we may expect that in the case of professional service firms, the costs of the integration of firms with different cultures and traditions will be extremely high. These demotivating effects need to be taken into consideration before a merger is implemented, as both buying firm and aquired firm professionals may "fade out." Even if contracts may succeed in holding professionals for several years, there is no way a contract can prevent a professional from putting his/her most creative energy on hold. (S)he may even go into a phase of painting the house, taking up mountain climbing, or learning to play the piano, while limiting the work-oriented energy to the contractual minimum, both in terms of hours in the office and energy spent per hour.

A few scholars within the professional service firm research tradition have focused particularly on the implications of mergers and acquisitions among such firms. Among these are Greenwood, Hinings, and Brown (1994), Coff (1999), and Empson (2000a and b; 2001). For example, Empson (2001) bases her article on a comparative case study involving two mergers, each between two accounting/auditing companies, as well as one merger between two consulting companies. Her particular focus was post-merger knowledge transfer. She identified that there was both "a fear of exploitation" and "a fear of contamination." In other words, there was both a fear of letting "the others" reap the benefits of the own firm's knowledge and hard work and a fear of becoming like "the others". Para-doxically, on the one hand they did not want the others to learn from them ("take away their knowledge"), but on the other hand, they did not want to learn from their new partners and exploit their knowledge. These fears were present in all six companies.

Why internationalize? Or why not?

The original study of my dissertation was aimed at analyzing the possible strategies for globalization of professional service firms. Globalization was, and still is, a hot trend and many professional service firms seemed to feel that they needed to be global in order to be viewed as successful. For some firms this was clearly true, as they were required to respond to the trend of globalization and major mergers and acquisitions that took place among their client firms. It remains a subject of major debates, but to the extent that global client firms require centralized decisions related to their service providers, and hence also require consistent services world wide, this trend of globalization in professional services represents a real demand. However, it is doubtful that the trend of globalization is as powerful in pro-fessional services as in other types of industries. Advertising offers many interesting examples, as global firms are increasingly becoming aware of the need to match their global brands to local perceptions. In Norway we recently experienced (with great pride, for such a small nation) that our local soft drink SOLO managed to develop an advertising campaign that attracted Coca Cola's interest and caused the powerful Coke to alter their Norwegian advertising for a period of time. The SOLO slogan and ads in black-and-white fit so well with local youth: "SOLO, probably the only drink that doesn't satisfy anything but your thirst!". The success of the ad reminded both local and international soft drink producers that buyers are anchored in local markets, even though they may be international travellers and Internet surfers. The globalization of professional services is thus not likely to be as automatic as that of other services and products. The following chapter explores the topic of globalization in further detail.

Suggested Readings

Coff, R. 1999. "How Buyers Cope with Uncertainty when Acquiring Firms in Knowledge-Intensive Industries: Caveat Emptor". Organization Science, 10(2): pp. 144-161.

Empson, L. 2000. Mergers Between Professional Service Firms: Exploring an Undirected Process of Integration. *Advances in Mergers and Acquisitions*, 1: pp. 205-237.

Empson, L. 2001. Fear of Exploitation and Fear of Contamination: Impediments to Knowledge Transfer in Mergers Between Professional Service Firms. *Human Relations*, 54 (7): pp. 839-862.

Greenwood, R., Hinings, C.R. & Brown, J. 1994. Merging Professional Service Firms. *Organization Science*, 5 (2): pp. 239-258.

VII. Globalization

– Fad or genuine source of competitive advantage?

Introduction

This chapter is a slightly abridged version of my chapter entitled "The Globalization of Professional Service Firms – Fad or Genuine Source of Competitive Advantage" (Løwendahl, 2000), published in the edited volume "The Globalisation of Services – Some Implications for Theory and Practice" edited by Yair Aharoni and Lilach Nachum for the Routledge Series "Studies in International Business and the World Economy" (Aharoni & Nachum, 2000). It discusses the globalization of professional service firms contrasted with the globalization of more traditional manufacturing firms, and builds primarily on the theoretical contributions of Michael Porter, particularly Porter (1986), where he discusses globalization in terms of market characteristics as well as in terms of the characteristics of the value creating activities taking place within the firm. I argue that due to the particular characteristics of professional services, most of the traditional arguments for globalization do not automatically apply, neither in terms of market characteristics nor in terms of internal value creating activities. In particular, since many professional service firms do not compete on price and cost, and some do not even primarily maximize profits, their internationalization or globalization processes are fundamentally different from those of industrial manufacturing firms. Given their unique characteristics, it is absolutely crucial for professional service firms to analyse both costs and benefits carefully (economic as well as intangible) before a decision to go global is made. If not, internationalization or globalization may turn out not to be a formula for success; it may even reduce the probability of success in its most extreme sense, namely survival. Hence, professional service firm managers and owners should make sure a "devil's advocate" has asked all the awkward questions and that they are capable of answering them well, before a global strategy is implemented. Even though globalization may be good for some companies, it may be disastrous for others!

The following section discusses reasons for globalization in general, whereas the subsequent section applies and extends this theory to the globalization of professional service firms. The final section discusses implications and conclusions.

Why do firms globalize?

Before we discuss the globalization of professional service firms, we need to look at more general theory of globalization, and here I prefer to base my analysis on the well-established frameworks of Michael Porter. Porter (1986) discusses the evolution of global industries, as well as global strategies in response to industry (including market) characteristics. Central to Porter's theoretical framework is the discussion of the following issues:

- To what extent is the market global (as opposed to "multidomestic")?
- To what extent do the different activities (in the value chain) need to be centralized versus dispersed?
- Where should the centralized activities be located, in a global company, and in how many places?
- How should the different activities be coordinated across sites?

The first question to assess, then, regards the characteristics of the market (or industry). Porter states (1986: 17-18) that:

> "In multidomestic industries, competition in each country (or small group of countries) is essentially independent of competition in other countries. A multidomestic industry is one that is present in many countries (e.g. there is a consumer banking industry in Sri Lanka, one in France, and one in the United States), but one in which competition occurs on a country-by-country basis. In a multidomestic industry, a multinational firm may enjoy a competitive advantage from the one-time transfer of know-how from its home base to foreign countries. However, the firm modifies and adapts its intangible assets in order to employ them in each country, and the competitive outcome over time is then determined by conditions in each country. The competitive advantages of the firm, then, are largely specific to the country."

> "At the other end of the spectrum are what I term global industries. The term global – like the word 'strategy' – has become overused and perhaps misunderstood. The definition of a global industry employed here is an industry in which a firm's competitive position in one country is significantly af-

fected by its position in other countries or vice versa. Therefore, the international industry is not merely a collection of
domestic industries but a series of linked domestic industries in which the rivals compete against each other on a
truly world-wide basis. Industries exhibiting or evolving toward the global pattern today include commercial aircraft,
TV sets, semiconductors, copiers, automobiles, and
watches."

Porter argues that in order to analyse the appropriate configuration of
value creating activities in an international firm, we first need to disaggre-
gate these activities. In global markets, he says, value creation is increased
by organizing the activities in a global company, such that all activities are
located where costs are lowest and value creation is greatest, yet taking
into consideration the costs of transportation and coordination:

> "In international competition, a firm has to perform some
> functions in each of the countries in which it competes.
> Even though a global competitor must view its international
> activities as an overall system, it still has to maintain some
> country perspective. It is the balancing of these two per-
> spectives that becomes one of the essential questions in
> global strategy. (1986:19)"

Porter's logic of value creation and dis-aggregation of activities is fundamentally rooted in the value chain analysis, in which nine generic activities are
identified and supposedly valid in all types of firms (Porter, 1985; 1986: 21).
Given the nine activities, it is clear that the underlying image of the firm is
one of a manufacturing firm; a "machine metaphor" (Morgan, 1986) and a
"long-linked technology" (Thompson, 1967; Stabell & Fjeldstad, 1998).
The activities included are, as most people now know, five primary activities:
inbound logistics, operations (i.e., in most cases "manufacturing"), outbound logistics, marketing and sales, and service, plus four support activities: firm infrastructure, human resource management, technology development, and procurement. The activities are further classified in terms of their
relationship to the buyer: inbound logistics, operations, and part of outbound logistics, plus all support activities, are defined to be "upstream activities", whereas the rest of outbound logistics, marketing and sales, and service are defined as "downstream activities" (1986: 23):

"A firm that competes internationally must decide how to spread the activities in the value chain among countries. A distinction immediately arises between the activities labeled downstream ... and those labeled upstream activities and support activities. The location of downstream activities, those more related to the buyer, is usually tied to where the buyer is located." "Upstream activities and support activities, conversely, could conceptually be decoupled from where the buyer is located in most industries."

"This distinction carries some interesting implications. First, downstream activities create competitive advantages that are largely country specific: a firm's reputation, brand name, and service network in a country grow largely out of a firm's activities in that country and create entry/mobility barriers largely in that country alone. Competitive advantage in upstream and support activities often grows more out of the entire system of countries in which a firm competes than from its position in any one country.

Second, in industries where downstream activities or other buyer-tied activities are vital to competitive advantage, there tends to be a more multidomestic pattern of international competition. In many service industries, for example, not only downstream activities are tied to buyer location, and global strategies are comparatively less common. In industries where upstream and support activities such as technology development and operations are crucial to competitive advantage, global competition is more common."

How does a professional service firm create value?

For professional service firms, the value chain does not represent an ideal tool for the analysis of costs and value creation. Even at the first glance of the five primary activities, the lack of fit with the value creation processes of professional service firms becomes clear (Løwendahl, 1992; Normann & Ramírez, 1993; Stabell & Fjeldstad, 1998). Yet, although the value chain is an inappropriate model for the analysis of the value creation in professional service firms, an analysis of value creating activities and their appropriate   configuration for potential competitive advantage is meaningful. Professional service firms do not create value through the transformation of (tangible) inputs into outputs with value added, as suggested in the value chain framework. As discussed in chapter II (fig. 3), there are three core processes involved in professional service firm value creation:

1) Selling "a credible promise"
2) Delivering what has been promised
3) Learning from the selling and delivery processes, in order to improve both efficiency and effectiveness in future projects

The first core process illustrates quite clearly one of the main differences between professional service firms and manufacturing firms, namely that value creation starts with selling, or even convincing the client of the firm's value creating capabilities. For some firms, this means diagnosing and solving a problem (e.g. engineering consultants and management consultants), for others it means designing or creating something for the client (e.g. architects and art directors in advertising), assisting the client in a process involving a third party (e.g. lawyers defending a client in court), or assessing and certifying the quality of the client's own processes (e.g. auditing). Rather than the traditional sequence of design – production - marketing and sales - delivery, the efforts to win the project itself come before the design and delivery phases. As a result, the notion of "upstream" and "downstream" loses much of its original meaning, as the only activity which may be removed from the client/buyer is the final one; the internally focussed learning process.

The distinction between primary and support activities and between upstream and downstream activities is much more difficult to clearly define in a professional service firm than in a manufacturing firm. The fundamental processes involved in the creation of value for – or even with – a client involve both the choice of the right models and tools to apply, the development of new models and tools, the "mobilization" (Haanes, 1997) of the right professionals to participate in the project (mostly internally, but often also external experts), and the "procurement" of additional tools and materials to be used (hand-books, software, computers and printers, etc.). Most of the development of "technology" as well as the generation of new knowledge and improved data-bases take place as a "by-product" of operations (see e.g. Itami, 1987), and is not delegated to separate functions or roles which can be defined as "support functions".

However, there are a few functions which normally are pure support functions, such as the infrastructure (including accounting, secretarial services, desk-top publishing support, etc.). And many firms have begun to invest more in technology to improve the support functions, in particular in terms of data base development and maintenance. These are "upstream" activities in Porter's original sense; back-office activities which cannot be billed directly to the client project, but which are charged as part of total "overhead". When more professional time is allocated to such back-office functions, the nature of the firm changes somewhat and makes it more similar to the manufacturing firm than what it was originally. Implications for globalization will be discussed in the following section.

Why do professional service firms globalize?

As pointed out by Porter, global markets are less common in services than in manufacturing. Yet we do see a number of global professional service firms, even though it is rather unclear whether the competition is truly global or rather multidomestic. It seems that the character of such global competition may be both similar to and very different from that of more traditional manufacturing industries.

The underlying reasons for globalization in professional service firms probably depend on the nature of the industry, just like in manufacturing. However, there are a number of fundamental differences between professional business service firms and multinational manufacturing firms. The first challenge arises because the firms deliver to business firms, not to consumers, and this distinction alters some of the arguments in Porter's analysis above. This distinction is not, however, limited to service firms. Business to business marketing is different from consumer marketing, even in manufacturing industries. When a buyer is a person, the buyer is located somewhere. When a buyer is a firm, the buyer may be global, local, or multidomestic ("polycentric"), and hence, even though the characteristics of the services and underlying technologies may be local in nature, the buying firm may want to deal with a single professional service firm world wide. Many client firms demand consistent and common services globally, e.g. in terms of auditing and advertising, even though in both cases local expertise is critical, and "production" cannot be centralized to one country.

The demand facing professional service firms varies substantially across industries as well as within industries. Whereas consulting firms can "create" a market if they develop a creative solution which is needed, but not yet demanded by their clients, the purchase of the basic services of auditors is mandated by law. Consultants may face both global and multidomestic markets, depending on the kinds of solutions they offer, whereas law, auditing, and to a large extent advertising are constrained by local laws and consumer tastes. In Porter's terminology, the markets for these professional services are intrinsically "multidomestic" in nature, and as a result, as Perlmutter (1969) stated it long before Porter, these firms are most likely to be "polycentric".

In manufacturing, the five primary activities of the value chain make sense, as well as their sequencing. Global competition in terms of actual delivery would mean *either* that the global presence would enable the firm to become more cost-efficient than local competitors, *or* that it would be able to deliver superior quality. Yet some professional service firms are able to deliver *both* higher quality and lower price, whereas other global firms deliver services at a much higher price, without being able to document a higher quality. And still they claim that globalization gives them a competitive advantage vis-à-vis local firms. How can this be possible?

The model in chapter II (figure 3), focusses on much more than the "primary activities" of the chain (the second process in our model), i.e. producing and delivering the "product". What the two additional processes of value creation add to the analysis, is first, that global presence may make it easier for the firm to sell a credible promise (and even charge a higher price, regardless of "objective" level of quality), i.e. a "reputation effect". Here, the professional service firm may face a "chicken and the egg"-problem, as global presence may lead to a higher reputation, but on the other hand an excellent reputation may pull the firm into the global market, if the reputation transcends national borders. This is contrary to Porter's statement cited above, where reputation (connected to downstream activities) is considered to be local in nature. Secondly, global presence may enable the firm to develop broader and more sophisticated "experience records" and shared knowledge, because of the access to a broader set of academic knowledge development sources. Again, this is the reverse of the knowledge transfer described by Porter above, where a temporary competitive advantage may result from a one-time transfer of know how to the other country. In professional service firms, the competitive advantage, if achieved, results from the ability of the firm to continuously tap into the knowledge developed in all relevant centers of the world, regardless of the local market potential in these knowledge centers. You may even gain competitive advantage from being located in a place where the market is not profitable at all, if the learning from these projects adds more value to *other* markets than what is lost locally. (See e.g. Bartlett & Ghoshal, 1989, for an in-depth discussion of such organization forms).

Since the markets for professional business services are different from the markets for (consumer) goods, we need to look at the three main categories of client firms which look to global professional service firms for service provision: global clients, local clients with "global problems", and finally local clients with local problems but who still prefer global professional service firms. Each of these categories is explored in further detail below:

Global clients

Global clients may be divided into two fundamentally different sub-categories: firms which centralize the decision-making and/or the activities, and firms which demand consistent services globally:

a) Global clients with centralized decisions and/or activities

When a global client firm makes decisions about a specific category of professional service delivery at only one particular place in the world, firms which have a strong reputation in the country where the decisions are made and/or the activities are carried out, have an advantage. For example, if a large manufacturing firm with HQ in New York decides that all advertising should be run from New York, with an emphasis on globally renowned media such as CNN and National Geographic, firms with a strong reputation in New York will have an advantage even if the client is global. If the activities are centralized as well, the local advantage becomes even more obvious: If all customer databases of a global bank are managed from a central office in London, IT consultants located close to this activity center are most likely to be considered for outsourced services as well as professional assistance. In both of these cases, the globalization of the professional service firm is likely to add to the costs of delivery, without adding much to the competitive position of the firm.

b) Global clients who demand consistent services at multiple sites

When a global client firm demands consistent services all over the world, the effects on the professional service firm may be very different depending on the types of services to be delivered as well as the actual delivery process. Here a number of possible options seem to be viable:

i) consistent services delivered from a central pool of professional resources

If the services required are needed on an infrequent basis, the global firm as well as the professional service firm may agree to a contract where the professionals travel to the site where the services are needed, stay there for a limited period of time, then return to their own HQ. One example may be the maintenance of a particular type of machines, where e.g. the expert engineers may all be located in Boston, but they may travel to distant locations on a regular basis. Such professional service firms, despite their global service delivery, are likely to remain "ethnocentric" (Perlmutter, 1969). Even if the client firm is global, the professional service firm delivers its services from one single knowledge center, and does not need to worry about localization, configuration, and coordination across sites. The globalization of such a professional service firm would increase costs, and probably decrease quality, at least if the center of new knowledge development was located in Boston.

ii) consistent services developed and distributed from a single "hub" and a network of delivering units

If the services are required more frequently, the professional service firm may set up regional "hubs" where professionals trained in the specific service delivery are located. From these hubs they travel to local sites. Knowledge development and training may still take place at one "hub", such as Boston, but specialists are available closer to the client sites. As a result, the professional service firm is likely to turn "regiocentric" (Perlmutter, 1969). Yet, just like the "ethnocentric" professional service firm above, the coordination requirements are minimal. The central hub develops the new knowledge and standards, and these are implemented through regional "satellites" which know the local markets and the necessary translations, but which loyally accept the standards "dictated" from the hub.

iii) consistent services developed and distributed from a global network of multiple "hubs"

Just like manufacturing firms, professional service firms with global clients may also develop a global matrix structure with multiple hubs and different "centers of excellence", where knowledge generation and distribution is centralized. For a large management consulting firm, the knowledge center for offshore oil companies may be located in Norway, whereas the financial knowledge center may be located in New York, London, or Singapore. Each hub has a specific responsibility in terms of knowledge development and distribution throughout the entire network of local offices, and services delivered within that particular area of expertise are required to be consistent world-wide. Still, coordination across hubs is infrequent – there is one single authority per knowledge area. Such firms will benefit from being truly global, yet activities are still centralized (albeit at multiple centers, one per knowledge area), and coordination across sites is more one-way delivery and control than focussed on mutual exchange processes.

Local clients with global "problems"

Another typical category of professional service firms delivers to the local client with a global problem, such as the local municipality or government hiring the world's best architects after a bidding process. Public buildings may attract architects from all over the world, and as a result Norwegian architects could win a bid for a national library in Egypt, without any local representatives established. In engineering consulting, this is a well-known type of international activity, as e.g. hydro-electric dams and power generators are more or less the same all over the world. Similarly, if you have the required local information about geological ground conditions, a sub-sea tunnel requires the same expertise whether it is located in Oslo or the English Channel or New York. These are mega-projects with international experts flown to the site for as long as their ad hoc presence is required. Unless the problems are recurring, no local offices are likely to be established, and the professional service firm is most likely to remain "ethnocentric".

In this context, the existence of a global profession certainly helps. With a global professional knowledge base, local experts can easily judge the quality of colleague professionals from any country of the world, and international professionals can work with local professionals from any country of the world, provided they share the means of communication – be it mathematical symbols, drawings, or a common language (e.g. English). A global profession also means that world class professionals are known world wide, and hence professional service firms that employ such experts are also able to attract excellent young professionals from a global talent pool.

Local clients with local "problems"

When local clients have local problems, the industry is multidomestic, and Porter would not recommend the professional service firm to develop a global strategy. Still, some professional service firms globalize, even in industries which are fundamentally multidomestic. Why? First of all, professional service firms seem to find size and globalization attractive because these two factors serve as proxies for high quality. When clients try to evaluate before buying a service the quality of a professional expert or a professional service firm, the client typically does not have the necessary expertise to evaluate the level of the person's or the firm's expertise. But as size and global presence is typically seen as signals of successful operations, particularly in manufacturing industries, size and global presence are also taken as indicators of high professional quality, and hence serve to enhance the reputation of the professional service firm. The following proposition may be presented:

> The more difficult the "objective" judgment of professional
> service quality, the more likely it is that globalization and size
> will serve as a proxy for quality.

This is the opposite of Porter's argument about reputation being local in service industries, quoted above. And again, if a global profession exists, the assessment of quality locally is much easier than if no profession exists. Hence, where no profession exists, globalization is even more likely to serve as a proxy for quality.

Economies of scale are by definition very difficult to realize in professional service firms, since the services are customized and heterogeneous. Still, they are not entirely absent, but they are most likely to be found in activities very different from the primary activities of Porter's value chain. Economies of scale seem to exist primarily in one area in professional services, namely in the only "upstream" activity involved, i.e. what is often called "knowledge management": a global information system, globally assigned responsibilities for knowledge gathering, creation and dissemination in specific areas, and centralized "corporate universities" or development programs for all employees. These activities sound like "support activities" in Porter's framework; as a sub-set of "human resource management". But for professional service firms, these activities deal with the maintenance and development of their core resources: their professional competence, at the individual as well as at the collective levels. Knowledge management is not a support activity in professional service firms; it is core to value creation, and an activity with potential for competitive advantage. Another interesting characteristic of these activities is that they actually raise the quality of solutions while at the same time reducing the costs of gathering the necessary information for a client proposal, assessment or even report. The firm is able to deliver better quality, faster, and even at a lower cost.

In other words, in industries where traditional reasons for globalization do not apply, professional service firms may still choose global strategies, due to the potential impact of globalization on part 1) and 3) of the model described in chapter II (figure 3), namely the credibility of the promise, and the ability to learn from a large number of diverse projects in order to further enhance the professional capabilities for future value creation. However, it is particularly in this category of client markets that the professional service firm needs to be very careful in its analysis of costs and benefits from globalization. The reputation and knowledge enhancement effects are not automatic, and the challenges and costs involved in coordination are substantial.

There are also examples of professional service firms that are multinational without such operations enhancing value creation. The location of new local or regional offices is not always the result of rational analyses and strategic plans. Quite frequently local offices are established as the result of personal preferences of partners, such as when UK partner John Jones marries his Spanish fiancée, and sets up an office in Madrid. Depending on the nature of the market, this office may serve Europe, Africa, and the Middle East, or only the Mediterranean part of Europe. If Jones is successful and wants to expand, he may build a large office with many professionals, and add local clients to the portfolio. Such offices may turn into permanent parts of the infrastructure of the professional service firm. If Jones works mostly on his own, and develops new knowledge and solutions locally, the office is kept as long as it does not require support from HQ, it maintains an adequate quality, and it makes enough money to make Jones happy. Except for firm name and some information exchange, the local subsidiary is almost like an independent professional service firm. If John Jones leaves the firm and there is no other local partner ready to take over, the office is probably closed down.

Conclusions and implications

Whereas global manufacturing firms typically centralize a number of (upstream) activities in one or a few sites in order to exploit economies of scale, the economies of scale are less obvious in professional service firms, and the number of "upstream" or equivalent activities is small. In fact, many professional service firms face a number of "diseconomies of scale" if they try to centralize decisions, as the coordination across multiple sites, languages, cultures, and legal systems becomes extremely costly. However, the professional service firm organization depends fundamentally on the organization of the client firm activities it is supposed to support. If the professional service is tailored to support an upstream activity in a global client firm, the implications for the professional service firm depend on the organization of the client firm, including the number of places where the activity is located, and the extent to which it is coordinated across locations. If activities are centralized, the professional service firm may also centralize its service delivery. If the activities are dispersed but highly coordinated for consistency and efficiency, the professional service firm may also need to develop a structure of dispersed and coordinated efforts.

Porter's model (1986) focusses on key activities and where they should be located, and emphasizes the costs of *coordination* and *transportation* as important factors limiting the globalization of firms where global demand and economies of scale are not sufficient to offset these costs. In professional service firms, the situation is different. Since there are no tangible raw-materials involved, no tangible products to be delivered to the client, and even no equipment required for the delivery of a high quality professional service, the question of *location* takes on a different meaning. Most of the activities involved in value creation are "downstream", and take place in interaction with the client, typically at the client site. The professionals bring their lap-tops and their cellular phones, and hook up with colleagues regardless of whether they are at an office in the same country, at HQ far away, or even on an assignment for another client somewhere else. Hence, the costs involved in logistics and transportation are very different – in most cases all you need to do is transport the professionals to the client site. As a result, the key question is not the costs of setting up and maintaining permanent physical facilities where the activities can take place, but rather a question of duration and frequency of client demand. For ad hoc services such as bridges and tunnels and opera houses, there is no point in setting up a permanent local office, whereas for recurring "problems" such as auditing, advertising, and legal counselling, local offices may be more cost-efficient than flying the experts in and out from HQ.

The challenge of *coordination* is also different when there are no tangible resources involved, but unless the professionals can work independently with each client, the problems are neither less important nor less complicated than in firms where the equipment or the raw materials force people to be present at the same place (if not the same time). Coordination involves the sharing of information, ideas, problems, methods for problem solving, knowledge about alternative solutions or sources of information, etc. Such information can, with today's technology, be transported world wide without costs, and hence the challenges are more important in terms of the content of information shared, than in terms of the costs of sharing it. On the other hand, there seem to be fundamental problems involved in the coordination of professionals, as the realized effects of seamless exchange of information are substantially smaller than the potential effects (Groth, 1997; 1999). One such problem involves the professional need for autonomy, thereby reducing the willingness to abide by routines and procedures developed by the organization. What is individually rational does not always coincide with what is rational for the firm. The other problem is found at the other extreme: even if professionals want a substantial amount of autonomy, they also need and seek social interaction with peers. Professionals are motivated both by challenging tasks and by experienced and competent colleagues, and unless the firm is able to develop the appropriate learning arena for constructive exchange with other professionals, it risks losing the most competent people. In addition comes the challenges involved in coordination when client demand requires either consistent services at multiple sites or the joint efforts of numerous professionals simultaneously. On the one hand, services may be relatively repetitive and modularizable, such that it is possible to establish common standards to be applied simultaneously at all client sites. Here, the coordination problem involves the development of the best solution, the exchange of this information, and the obedience of the professionals to the standards set. On the other hand, services may be dependent on idiosyncratic inputs of several experts or unusually creative individuals simultaneously, and then the coordination problem may involve getting them all to meet in the same place at the same time, in order to develop a new solution. Whereas the first type of coordination is amenable to globalization, the second is extremely costly to replicate, and I suggest that unless the individual experts who need to travel the globe are motivated by this travelling, they are not likely to accept it. If they are really world class professionals, they are not likely to have any spare time regardless of whether they work locally or in many countries. Similarly, the opportunity cost of their hours worked is likely to be determined by international fees (possibly minus costs of travelling, if that is seen as negative), regardless of whether they work at home or abroad. Hence, for "guru-based" services where the individuals cannot be "cloned" and personally need to be transported, globalization is only possible to the extent that these individuals prefer to travel and work globally.

Professional service firms show very clearly how the development of competitive advantage in a post-industrial context is going to require much more of management than what traditional manufacturing firms (and researchers of them) have been used to (Løwendahl and Revang, 1998; 2000): Competition takes place on two arenas simultaneously – for demanding clients who are willing to pay a premium, and for expert employees who are able to develop the new solutions and sell new services to these demanding clients. The requirements on these two arenas are not always compatible. If globalization involves more subordination to routines and standards than what the best professionals are willing to accept, they will find another employer. Similarly, if globalization involves more individual sacrifices in terms of travelling and staying away from the family than what the best professionals want, again they are likely to leave. And finally, if individual experts are "leveraged" to such an extent that the opportunities to learn more and develop the individual expertise further in collaboration with expert colleagues and demanding clients disappear, the firm is unlikely to be able to keep the best professionals for long, regardless of how much they pay them!

The differences between the manufacturing firm modelled by the value chain and the professional business service firm are fundamental. The professional service firm does not need much capital in order to undertake assignments in new countries, it does not need tangible resources, it does not need to set up an office, and it does not need to worry about the transportation of raw materials, intermediate products and final output from its production site to the customers. The entire value creation process may take place "downstream", in close interaction with the client and at the client's site, and only involves "transportation" of information and knowledge, once the professional experts are on site. Economies of scale do not result primarily from repeating solutions, but rather from "upstream" or back-office modularization of partial solutions and methods for approaching assignments, and from meetingplaces which attract professionals to learning arenas which make the firm attractive to the best "experts" in the industry.

As regards other types of service firms, there are numerous classifications which define typologies and differences. In short, the main dimensions making professional service firms extreme even relative to other service firms is their lack of dependence on tangible equipment, their emphasis on delivering the service to the client site, and their emphasis on idiosyncratic and customized solutions for each individual client. Professional service firms differ, both within and across industries as regards their ability to modularize or reuse solutions from one assignment to another, but by definition they do not just sell one more "package" of a generic solution. In terms of globalization, this means that the professionals have to be physically present and involved in direct interaction with each client to an extreme extent; the firm cannot assign some of the best professionals to an HQ R&D-function and expect them to develop the solutions for the future unless they also transport these professionals to the client sites to see and feel the exact details of the "problems" to be solved.

When it comes to globalization, it is very difficult to judge how global a professional service firm is, especially if we compare across industries. Counting number of offices or looking at the location of the firm's present assignments does not provide a solution. Engineering design firms, for instance, may have worked in every country around the world, without having established more than a single or a small number of offices. In this sense, these firms are very similar to manufacturing firms with ad hoc export contracts, who also rely on local contacts or agents and do not set up offices outside the home-country. Since the tools required are often minimal and carried in the heads of the professionals, maybe with the support of a computer and a cellular phone, operations may be carried out globally without a global infrastructure. And even the percentage of earnings from overseas operations, which is frequently used as an indicator in engineering design, may be a misleading figure in industries where contracts are large and ad hoc, as described in chapter II in terms of the Norwegian engineering design firm Norconsult. Even the term "size" can be misleading, as the norm is to hire a large number of experts on a project by project basis. Hence, the size of the contracting firm often says very little about how large it may be when undertaking mega-projects. In 1990, Norconsult was also among the very best in terms of percentage of revenues gained in international operations, but that was by definition, as the firm was owned by a number of local (Norwegian) engineering consulting firms, and was not allowed to compete with its owners in the domestic market. Today, Norconsult carries out a more typical portfolio of local as well as international projects, but does this shift in portfolio make the firm less global? The example clearly illustrates how difficult it may be to apply the traditional criteria of globalization and global operations to professional service firms, as operations are to a much lesser extent dependent on (permanent) physical location in a given market.

To conclude, then, it is not obvious that global clients require global professional service firms, nor that the increased reputation effect from global operations adds more value than the costs involved in operations. In some cases the globalization adds value; in others, it does not. The most important conclusion regarding the globalization of professional service firms may be that it is important to look carefully at every expected cost and benefit from global operations. Since most professional service firms sell the expertise of their professional employees, these can be more easily transported to the local sites for ad hoc projects, than what is possible with heavy machinery in manufacturing. Hence, short term and temporary offices "on location" are much more common in professional service firms than in manufacturing. The costs of establishing a temporary local office do not need to be prohibitive, whereas the costs of running a permanent local office without a constant stream of new projects may threaten the survival of the entire global firm. On the other hand, for the professional service firm globalization may be profitable not only in terms of "objective" quality and costs, but also in terms of enhanced reputation or improved learning for future quality assurance. Hence, the professional service firm may have fewer reasons to "go global" in terms of a traditional "Porterian" analysis, yet at the same time more options than manufacturing firms, when it comes to access to knowledge creation and the enhanced reputation of services delivered world wide. Maybe it is true that being global is primarily a question of mindset, as the then President Henry Michel of the engineering design firm Parsons Brinckerhoff said in response to my questions in 1990? Here is his description of what being global meant to them:

> "I didn't know we had done anything unusual 'til the surprised messages came back from Hong Kong: did we really promote Hong Kong engineers in the same way as our US colleagues? Of course we did. They were equally good, and working just as hard. They were willing to work on overseas projects in Taiwan, Turkey, and even the United States. They deserved the same treatment as any other highly qualified and hard working loyal employee. After that feedback, we realized that we had turned global. When we imported Hong Kong engineers to an airport project in New York, we finally had the flexibility we had dreamt of, and which most other firms still dream of. Globalization offers great opportunities if we are able to utilize the best people and the best ideas regardless of origin; we can no longer think of globalization as the Marshall Aid and American engineers going

overseas for a short period of time to make a lot of money and revolutionize people who do not know what we are talking about. We cannot simply be carpetbaggers who go in just to rob local populations of their precious items (or best professionals) and then leave. We have to treat them as equal partners and cooperate on an equal basis. If we are able to do so, the man-power available in Asia, for instance, is no threat to us. It is rather a fantastic opportunity!"

If a professional service firm is able to tap into knowledge development all over the world, is able to attract and work with professionals from any country of the world, and is able to undertake projects for clients anywhere in the world, isn't that firm a global firm, even if it only has permanent offices in a few countries? At least as regards engineering design firms, the classification at any one point in time is difficult to make, and hence the firms typically report both where they operate today as well as where they have completed projects over their history. The norm is to go into a country and leave again, even when successful, and project offices set up and closed down after a short period of time are no indicators of operational problems in the local market. The danger of automatically adopting the industrial logic is obvious, and the questions need to be asked before professional service firm managers and owners invest their resources (e.g. time, money, key people, reputation) in local offices in far away locations. Even in the cases where clients do demand global presence, it is not automatically true that they are willing to pay the additional cost involved. Hence, it is extremely important for the professional service firm to pay attention to all the effects – both the costs, the potential benefits, and the risks involved.

VIII. Summary and implications

Competence and creativity in complex organizations

Introduction

In the previous chapters I have argued for an increased emphasis on strategic management in professional service firms, as well as for caution when applying models and frameworks developed for more traditional manufacturing firms. Despite Porter's (1985) strong claims for the universality of his models, the evidence to the contrary is overwhelming. I agree with the professional service firm managers I interviewed before my first study: professional service firms are different. They are different to such an extent that many of the frameworks and models from traditional strategic management theory need to be modified or even replaced in the context of resources with strong opinions and service offerings of extreme heterogeneity.

The differences are so substantial that we may even need to question a large number of our fundamental assumptions about successful firms. We should not, however, reject the principles of strategic management and goal directed activities. It is the content of the strategies, not their existence, that is challenged by extreme firm characteristics. Not only is strategic management crucial to professional service firms, it is even possible that managers in traditional manufacturing firms have more to learn from the practices of professional service firms, than professional service firm managers can learn from their manufacturing colleagues.

In this final chapter, I will briefly summarize key issues that are critical to successful strategic management of professional service firms, with a particular emphasis on the managerial implications. Areas where more research is required will also be highlighted.

The uniqueness of professional service firms

In Chapter II and III the uniqueness and resulting extreme challenges involved in the strategic management of professional service firms were discussed in detail, both in terms of the nature of what the firms produce and deliver and in terms of the characteristics of their strategic resources. When individual judgment and expertise are critical to firm value creation, neither efficiency nor effectiveness can be enhanced through the traditional logic of replication and control. The extreme characteristics of professional service firms may be summarized in terms of five central I's: Intangible inputs and outputs, Interaction, Individual judgment and local solutions, Innovation, and Information Asymmetry. In the following, each of these five dimensions is briefly summarized.

Intangible inputs and outputs. Traditional models for both strategy development and organization design typically focus on the processes involved in the efficient transformation of (tangible) inputs, such as aluminium, into more sophisticated products that are in high demand by firms or consumers, such as drinking cans. In the case of professional services, the inputs are intangibles such as methods, procedures, and the expertise of individual professionals. The outputs are also intangibles such as advertising concepts or new production processes. There is typically no transformation process involved, but rather a process of creativity and new solution development. As a result, it is very difficult to make such delivery processes efficient, and even more difficult to assess quality objectively.

Whereas it is true that in most cases the effects in terms of client firm efficiency and effectiveness can be measured after the delivery of the service, it is generally extremely difficult to isolate the effect of the professional service from other intervening circumstances in the evaluation of results. Ex ante, the evaluation of probable service quality, not to mention the comparison of the service offerings from two (or more) different professional service firms, is even more complex. In most professional service settings, the previous experience of similar client firms as well as the established rapport between professional firm and client firm representatives are critical. Without the direct trust resulting from personal relationships and/or the indirect trust resulting from friends' experience with the firm or the firm's reputation, the client firm has major difficulties assessing ex ante the probable quality of what is to be delivered.

Interaction. Tailormade solutions require close cooperation with each individual client, in order to determine the actual expectations of a given client, to understand the particular circumstances, and to develop solutions that are compatible with the unique quality requirements. As a result, regardless of the basic level of expertise required from the professionals, such as advertising expertise or engineering experience, there is always another critical dimension involved in terms of the management of the interaction process where the client is directly involved. If any one of the subprocesses of service definition, contract negotiations, service delivery, and project closure are inadequately managed, the client may be dissatisfied regardless of the "objective" expert evaluation of the quality of what was actually delivered.

In the case of business services, the management of these interaction processes is even more acute. In many cases, decisions are made by separate individuals to hire a professional firm, define the project content, negotiate price, quality, and time requirements, implement (and often participate in) the actual service delivery process, and, finally, evaluate the outcomes of the project. These individuals may have very different expectations and quality evaluation criteria. As a result, an effective management of the interaction processes is critical to successful project completion, both from the point of view of the service provider and from the point of view of the client.

Individual judgment and local solutions. The professional service firm faces challenges that are extreme because it cannot overcome its dependence on individual professionals who possess both critical expertise and the ability to retain relationships of trust with clients. There are many examples of settings where clients require a contract that not only specifies the number of hours seniors will put in, but also identifies these professionals by name. The higher the degree of interaction (type A) or innovation (type C), the more likely the clients are to require such contract terms.

Some firms (type B) are able to reduce their dependence on individual professionals to a minimum, through their development of a strong firm reputation and a (strategic) emphasis on clients and projects requiring multiple professionals working together on the basis of a common set of concepts and methods. As a result, these firms are less vulnerable to the exit of key individuals. However, whereas some researchers claim that the emphasis on individual experts is exaggerated, for most professional service firms this is not the case. The role of the individual expert may be reduced to a level approaching that of a traditional firm only in cases in which the firm has been able to develop value creation procedures that do not involve specific, named individuals. For most professional service providers, losing one or two of the key (named) professionals may be detrimental.

Innovation. Adding to the complexity of professional service delivery is also the idiosyncrasy of the services delivered to each client. Altruistic and professional service provision means that to a large extent the firm will have to create new solutions for each new client, such that R&D and innovation become integral parts of operations. The higher the degree of tailoring to each client's unique requirements, the more extreme the firm will be in terms of its inability to replicate and routinize its solutions. As a result, the challenges resulting from an inability to preplan and formalize activities are extreme, and the traditional frameworks for strategic planning and control are definitely not appropriate.

In terms of the types of generic strategies of Chapter V, firms of type C are extreme in their search for advanced and unique solutions to new client problems, whereas firms of type A are extremely flexible, yet generally not as advanced. Relationships allow the type A firm and its representative(s) to deliver a satisfactory solution, but it is always possible that a more sophisticated expert firm (type C) could have delivered a more advanced solution (for each specific problem). Type A professionals are typically more generalist, and hence less likely to possess unique expertise in each new area where a given client may request their services. Type B firms are, by definition, less innovative and more like traditional manufacturing firms in terms of their ability to replicate previous solutions.

Information Asymmetry. Finally, professional service firms are unique because their value added results from superior knowledge. They are hired because they possess experience and/or expertise beyond what is available in the client firm. Three particularly salient challenges result from this characteristic: the firm must develop its competence faster than the client firm, in order to stay one step ahead, it must manage interaction processes pedagogically, depending on the level of expertise of the clients, and it must be keenly aware of the danger of clients who want to internalize the expertise by head-hunting the best professionals.

First, the firm must keep learning and developing its knowledge base in order to have valuable expertise to sell to clients who are educated in the process. In some cases, such as in many management consulting contracts, a major part of the project involves the transfer of knowledge such that the client firm possesses an adequate level of expertise after project completion and can continue in a new mode of operations without referring to the professional firm representatives. The transfer of expertise, for instance in terms of the implementation of new and advanced IT solutions, typically requires a great deal more interactive involvement on the part of the consultants and is both more time consuming and more costly than simply being asked as an expert to solve the problem. In extreme cases, the transfer of knowledge is so complete that it may make the professional firm redundant, at least in relationship to that specific client. For the professional firm in this situation, it is important to continue learning rapidly enough to remain one step ahead of its clients, or to move out of a particular niche of expertise as soon as the clients are sufficiently well educated.

Numerous examples of such processes may be cited. An interesting example is offered by the early history of the IKO Group. This management consulting firm in Norway was founded in 1945 on the basis of two obvious needs in the market, namely business accounting and time motion studies. At the time of the foundation, the consultants employed were people who had gone abroad, in particular to German and US graduate schools, in order to learn about the new principles. These consultants played a vital role in terms of enhancing the value creation of the Norwegian industrial firms at that time. Parallel to this process, however, learning took place both in industry and the major Norwegian graduate schools, such that, particularly in terms of business accounting, the client firms were soon able to employ their own experts and develop their own solutions in house.

This story illustrates a process by which previously outsourced professional services became internalized. As the internalization expanded from large to medium sized and finally relatively small firms, and later we even saw the arrival of inexpensive software and computer technology, this entire consulting niche disappeared. Today, the sophistication of the accounting procedures available to the individual consumer through computer software and handbooks far exceeds the expectations of the client firms fifty years ago.

Secondly, there is the challenge of clients with different levels of expertise. Although some firms try to deliver services to all types of clients, most professional service firms end up (at least implicitly) targetting clients with a specific level of expertise relative to that of their own professionals. Only firms with an extreme level of professional expertise are able to deliver services to the most advanced clients, who often see as the most appropriate alternative to hire a university professor of international renown as a consultant to advise their own experts on a specific problem.

Finally, an important dimension to consider is that of client firm recruiting in response to the information asymmetry gap. Rather than spending time and money on learning processes, client firms may seek out the best experts and hire them into their own ranks. Most professional service firms are concerned about their ability to protect their professionals from being attracted to client firms at the completion of a project, rather than returning to the uncertainty of what will come up next in the professional service firm. The more attractive the expert is to client firm internalization, the more vulnerable the professional service firm may be to his/her exit. Similarly, the longer and more intense the interaction period, the higher the probability that the professional will be tempted to accept an offer from the client firm.

To conclude, then, professional service firms are extreme in a number of dimensions, and as a result, the traditional strategic management frameworks and models cannot be applied without substantial adjustments. In many cases, their standard advice is not only wrong, but even detrimental to firm operations. But not only are professional service firms different from traditional manufacturing firms; they also differ substantially both between and within professional service industries. The following chapter briefly summarizes the key dimensions of this heterogeneity.

The multiple types of professional service firms

No management theory or model can be expected to apply to all firms, regardless of strategy and context. In Chapter IV and V, the flexibility and heterogeneity of professional service firms was discussed at length, illustrating how firms differ even within the relatively limited segment of professional service firms. Firms differ in terms of the well-known dimensions of size, age, and geographical reach, but are also affected by industry characteristics, such as the continuous versus ad hoc nature of the service demand, which leads to different requirements, for instance in auditing relative to management consulting. In addition, firm heterogeneity results from past firm behavior as well as present strategic priorities. Characteristics such as the size and duration of each project and the information asymmetry involved are largely factors that are open to the strategic choice of the firms, as is the type of strategic mode and resource base developed. Professional firms have more flexibility than traditional firms in terms of both choosing their target client type and developing the necessary resource base for service delivery. As a result, the firm may choose to develop more or less replicable solutions and formalized structures (type B), and thereby accept both external ownership and traditional assumptions such as increased profits from growth, market share, and internationalization. Or the firm may choose not to evolve beyond the loosely coordinated set of individual professionals and their relationships to clients (type A), in which case the primary strategic management task may be to resist the pressures for growth, capital investments, formalization, and internationalization. The extreme flexibility of professional service firms offers a large number of opportunities for the firms, but also requires a clear focus in order for the firm to build its intangible resources cumulatively. As a result, a conscious choice of strategic priorities, explicit or at least implicit, is required for the firm to maintain a clear strategic posture over time. Without such priorities, the firm needs a lot of luck if it is to avoid the downsides involved in a people- and opportunity driven growth over time.

Both managers and researchers need to look for solutions that apply in each given context, rather than apply indiscriminately the solutions developed for firms of a different type and era. Not only do we need to be very careful with the application of models and theories from traditional manufacturing firms to the reality of professional service firms. We also need to be cautious when applying concepts from one type of professional service firm to the reality of a different type of firm. In the following, I highlight some of the traditional concepts which should not be used indiscriminately in the management and/or evaluation of professional service firms.

The multidimensional nature of success

Professional service firms, then, are not like the average firm registered on the NYSE or accounted for in the national or international statistics. Professional service firms may have no tangible value, but may still be expected to generate substantial amounts of returns both in the short and long run. The value of these returns depends on both the ability of key professionals to continue winning projects and delivering the expected value to clients, and the ability of the firm to retain these individuals and motivate them to provide additional value to clients within the framework of the firm's strategy. As a result, one of the most common measures of success, namely growth and the resulting size of the firm, does not automatically guarantee quality nor an effective learning environment. The largest and most efficient service providers are not necessarily the most attractive, neither to excellent professionals nor to advanced clients. Similarly, all firms need not grow, and for some firms growth beyond a limited size will force the firm into a different and more formalized mode of operations. However, such desirable "stagnation" (in terms of growth) is likely to require as much or even more managerial attention as a growth strategy.

Another frequently used proxy for firm success, *market share*, is also difficult to apply to most professional service firms. Measures of market share may be relevant for firms like Accenture and Cap Gemini, whereas firms like Pharos should not be concerned at all. In most industries we find different firm types complementing each other, and their competitiveness cannot be determined by measuring a single variable. As a matter of fact there is no reason to believe that Accenture, for example, would want to win the majority of the projects that Pharos professionals target. Such projects are probably too small and result in too much dependence on the individual (senior) professionals. Large firms rely on a "multiplier effect", whereby the average income generated by seniors is increased through their involvement in multiple projects where the juniors do most of the work. Similarly, the value of the juniors is increased through their interaction with seniors who teach as well as supervise, and this competence enhancement is one major reason why large firms are able to attract and retain juniors at relatively moderate salaries. If projects only require senior professional time, the entire pyramidal structure suffers, and the firm risks to be left with a number of non-billable juniors on their pay-roll.

The interesting implications, then, are that growth, internationalization, and an emphasis on increased profits and sales may be options, rather than automatic goals or indicators of success. It seems that the entire Western society is focussing on mechanisms for growth and increased international visibility, whereas in many cases the results of both growth and internationalization are highly dubious in terms of both profitability and the happiness of the key people. Why bother, if it is neither profitable nor fun for the professionals owning the firm? For many firms, an improved understanding of the required processes to remain small and highly focussed both in terms of strategy and the types of expertise offered, may be much more important than all the popular advice on rapid growth and globalization! We clearly need to be very cautious if we apply traditional models and measurement criteria to the complex and heterogeneous reality of professional service firms.

The importance of strategy in profesional service firms

Strategy is critical to the long term efficiency and effectiveness of all firms, and professional service firms represent no exception. For the professional service firm the fact that most of the resource accumulation takes place through daily operations (Itami, 1987) is particularly salient. Every new client or project needs to be seen as a building block for future resource availability, and hence the projects that offer a better potential for competence and reputation enhancement may need to be prioritized above the most profitable ones. The difference in revenues should actually be seen as an investment akin to that of a new machine in the manufacturing firm, and a strategic budget should take into consideration how much the firm can afford to invest in competence development, not only directly but also in terms of revenues forfeited. This is often a complex balancing act, as what is needed in order to enhance short term efficiency and revenues is frequently not compatible with what is required in order to improve competence through learning. For example, when the best project manager is put in charge, the project may be safe but if this procedure is repeated in every project, juniors with managerial potential have no chance to practice and learn. Similarly, if the firm takes on too many projects it may end up overextending the professionals, thus preventing them from keeping an eye on professional developments in their own area of expertise. Paradoxically the result may be that the very success of the firm sets off a negative spiral, as exhausted and frustrated professionals leave the firm for employers who are able to offer more time for personal development.

Strategy in the professional service firm, then, involves *setting priorities*, rather than making plans or developing and maintaining a competitive position. Priorities are required in order for a common direction to result from a large number of independent decisions; i.e. in order for local and autonomous decisions to be consistent. But as tasks and clients are continually changing, exceptions are bound to occur frequently. Strategic priorities in professional service firms involve all the fundamental decisions of what to deliver, to whom, where, when, and how. Priorities also need to be set regarding the boundaries of firm activities, the amount of investments the firm targets for learning and resource accumulation, the role of efficiency and (re)use of the best experts for repeated projects, and strategies to attract new and highly qualified professionals.

When priorities are agreed upon and known throughout the firm, the managers should not abdicate from their strategic role. On the contrary, the more autonomy the professionals enjoy, the more important it will be for each individual to know not only the general priorities of the firm but also where to turn for help if an unexpected decision is needed. Since planning and formalization are difficult to implement in firms where clients and tasks change frequently, a continuous management of the critical processes is required in order for the firm to keep on track. Key success factors are not given and stable factors, but rather *critical processes* that must be monitored and supported. Not despite of, but rather because of, the high degree of individual judgment and autonomous decision making, a continuous monitoring and an ability to intervene is required in situations where decisions are not in line with firm priorities. Monitoring does not mean direct supervision and control, but rather frequent interaction and open communication among all professionals involved. In order to avoid being crippled by internal processes, the firm is totally dependent on mutual trust and a faith in the good will of each professional. Interventions are made when priorities are not clear, and are more often than not initiated by a professional in doubt. An open door policy and a high degree of accessibility is more important for a good manager than a detailed overview of what each individual is doing. In addition, an effective communication of interventions where situations have been unclear or misunderstood automatically sets precedent and reduces the probability of the same mistake being made again.

There are a number of challenges that professional firms must deal with, but which typically are impossible to resolve once and for all. The process of *consensus building* around firm priorities is critical, not only because the firm needs a clear focus for its activities, but also because the professionals are mobile. The professionals who fundamentally disagree may choose to find another firm to invest their talent in, if the strategy of the firm is very different from their own targets and they are unable to influence the strategy in the direction of their own priorities. And that is OK!

Striking the appropriate *balance between individual autonomy and consistent firm behavior* is one of the most critical processes of professional firm strategic management, and there is no optimal answer to what this balancing point should be. Firms of type A find their stable equilibrium by reducing coordination to a minimum and allowing individuals full autonomy, whereas firms of type B find their equilibrium by requiring a high degree of submission to firm standards, while at the same time enhancing the learning and value creation potential of each individual. Firms of type C live in a constant balancing act where both autonomy and consistency have to be attended to simultaneously. Needless to say, the firms in this strategic mode are those that require most managerial attention, as the exceptions and challenges are likely to occur almost every day.

As developed in Chapter IV and V, the professional service firm needs to ask four fundamental questions on a regular basis in order to maintain and further enhance its strategic position:

- Do we have the necessary strategic resources to implement our strategic priorities? Can we attract additional key people?
- Are we able to motivate our professionals adequately to obtain their very best effort, both in terms of energy and quality solutions? Are we able to leverage the competence resources in an optimal way, both in the short run and in the long run, without boring or exhausting our people in the attempt to maximize efficiency?
- Are we able to mobilize our resources in teams and support-structures such that a maximum of synergies is achieved?
- Are we assured that these resources will remain with the firm during

the period in question? Do we have the necessary back-up in a crisis situation?

In short, all these questions concern the management of human resources in an extremely demanding context. Attracting the best professional resources, motivating and mobilizing them, putting them together in an optimal way, and retaining them: these are all issues that fundamentally concern the management and development of people and the relationships between them. Hence, strategic management in professional service firms is really more about management than about tools, models, and plans. The following section summarizes both managerial challenges and some potential solutions.

The importance of management in professional service firms

It is both a paradox and an evident truth that the more complex the operations of a firm delivering non-routine services, the more important is management. The paradox lies in the fact that professionals do not want to be managed, nor do they want to be managers. Despite this paradox, excellent managers make all the difference in the world. The professionals I have interviewed all seem to be fully aware of the importance of having excellent managers. Still, most of them were highly frustrated with their own managers. They were not only frustrated with the others: to the extent that they had managerial responsibilities themselves, they were acutely aware of their own inadequacies as managers. The requirements of a good manager seem to be extreme, and at the same time very few professionals want to and are able to develop into excellent managers. A major risk, especially for those who accept a full-time managerial role, is loosing the professional respect and authority. To be a manager without authority vis à vis the people one is supposed to lead, is neither easy nor fun. What can be done to solve this dilemma?

First of all it is critical for professionals to be allowed to, encouraged to, and sometimes even forced to *"manage themselves"* (Manz & Sims, 1989). As few decisions as possible should be referred to managers, and if the strategic priorities are clear, only exceptions need to be handled by the seniors.

Secondly, managers take on roles that are absolutely critical on behalf of their peers. Hence, they need to be *elected by their peers* and chosen based on criteria that clearly prioritize managers who are trusted and respected by the other professionals.

Similarly, those who are chosen must receive all the *help and support* they need in order to develop into good managers. In traditional organizations where managers supervised and controlled employees in order to avoid their shirking and cheating, many teams and firms developed sophisticated ways of "winning over the boss." Dissatisfaction was typically expressed among employees, behind the back of the manager. Many of these traditional attitudes still exist in managers as well as employees, but if they are carried over into the professional firm, they are truly detrimental to performance. When professionals choose to delegate strategic management responsibilities to one of their colleagues, they also have a responsibility to remain part of the support team and help the manager do a good job. Professionals cannot both criticize their peers for being impossible managers, and at the same time play the old, traditional role of "hide-and-seek" with superiors. Rather, they must ask themselves what they as peers at all levels can do to make managerial tasks more fun and rewarding, and to help one of their peers do a better job on their behalf.

In this process of shared managerial responsibility, it is important to remember that professionals are typically people with extreme quality standards, and very often they have led a successful life. For such people it is very difficult to accept a role where they know that they are unlikely to succeed, as their education never prepared them for such (managerial) tasks. As a result, the peers who are persuaded to take on a managerial role are extremely vulnerable. If this background is further exacerbated by the peers criticizing every effort that is less than perfect, as they too are used to expecting the highest quality standards, managerial roles are not only high risk but also likely to lead to reduced self-esteem and reduced professional status. The only way to get out of this dilemma, is for all professionals to accept a team responsibility for the managerial tasks as well as the support of whoever they choose to wear "the managerial hat" at any given point in time.

Hence, it is important to *"minimize the burden of management"*, while at the same time *increasing the incentives* in every way possible. There are many ways in which the burden of management can be reduced, but the most important one may be that of splitting the managerial role into multiple tasks that can be shared among several professionals. In the professional firm there is no automatic need for the traditional hierarchical division of labor where one person takes on all the roles of recruiting, promoting, handling personnel conflicts, assigning people to projects, looking after the professional development of juniors, etc. A careful analysis of the tasks involved can very often lead to a more appropriate division of labor, where a number of seniors share the tasks. This is not the same as being jointly responsible, which very often means a "pulverization" of responsibilities, meaning that all can abdicate without being criticized. A more creative division of labor involves different seniors taking charge of different tasks, such that everyone knows who to turn to in a given situation.

Another frequently used option is that of temporary management, which is clearly a good alternative to encourage potentially talented professionals to try on one of the managerial "hats" for a limited time. Rotating managerial responsibilities is common in many types of organizations, including academic institutions where department heads are typically elected for a term of two to four years.

As regards incentives, economic compensation for additional burdens is obviously not enough to get the best management talent to take on managerial tasks in professional settings. One frequently used "carrot" in academic institutions, which is also practiced in some professional firms, is that of offering a "sabbatical" after the completion of an exhausting time in management.

What is even more important, however, is to *improve the status of managers,* and this can probably only be done through a process of consensus building on the importance of strategic management for the successful evolution of the firm. The status of the presidents of the two US-based engineering design firms of my dissertation study was extremely high, as their peers all recognized the tremendous impact of their excellent managerial practices on the performance of the firm. If the firm is successful in its choice and development of managerial talent, it may even find one of those unique managers who are not only excellent and respected, as managers, but who also enjoy this new task so much that they accept to take on a new career and bring the firm forward by being catalysts for other talented professionals. At the heart of the successful professional firm, there is a group of highly motivated professionals and professionals commit to people they trust and respect. Without excellent senior people, the professional service firm is likely to disintegrate.

The importance of studying professional service firms

Not only are professional service firms different from traditional manufacturing firms and extremely challenging to manage. The impact of these firms on society is also growing every day: Their share of value creation in terms of GNP as well as employment increases. Their indirect impact on the value creation of other organizations increases, among other things as the result of the downsizing and outsourcing processes going on in a large number of industries. And finally, their impact as examples and even "role models" for the future organization seems to be growing every day, as they are brought forward as illustrations by researchers as well as consultants. These three fundamental trends suggest that students of firms and value creation are well advised to look further into the unique processes of strategic management evolving in these firms, and that we must be very careful in transferring our traditional perspectives directly to the realities of firms in new and different contexts. In the following, each of these three trends is explored in further detail.

First, knowledge intensive firms are becoming more and more pervasive in Western economies, regardless of whether they are service or manufacturing firms. In a post-industrial society, knowledge intensive and professional firms are continuously increasing their role, both as employers and as economic value creators. In the future, it may be that more and more of us end up both working for and receiving services from such firms, rather than from the more traditional efficiency-based "organizational machines." Such a development leads to extreme demands on us, as clients as well as employees. More than ever before, our own level of competence will be critical, both for our ability to buy and determine the quality of such service suppliers, and for our own competitiveness in the market for our own knowledge and experience. Individuals are demanding opportunities for personal development, not only from their employers but also from the government in terms of public education for adults. In Norway, we have even recently seen a strike where the main issue for the labor union of the electricians was to get their employers to commit to guaranteed future education such that their competence would not become redundant. Professional service firms are more experienced than most others when it comes to issues of individual development and competence enhancement. Hence, other firms may learn from their successes as well as their previous mistakes.

Secondly, these firms play an important indirect role through the services they deliver to other sectors, private as well as public. Given the rate of increase today, what will be their role in the competitiveness of other firms a decade or two from now? Through outsourcing, many traditional manufacturing firms find themselves highly dependent on such specialized firms not only in order to be able to deliver but also to enhance and develop their solutions. What will be their role in terms of enhancing the efficiency and effectiveness of the public sector? What may happen if their knowledge transfer is "off the mark"? The more advanced the expertise and innovation of the professional service firm, the more important is a close interaction between the firm and other institutions developing new knowledge, world wide. Close ties with other firms as well as universities and research centers are absolutely critical in order to secure the future quality of their inputs to a large number of firms.

And finally, it has been suggested that professional service firms may represent the "pinnacle" of the information age. If this is true, these firms may provide examples of organizational forms as well as strategic management practices that may well be as important "role models" for the organizations of the future as Alfred P. Sloan's streamlined and multidivisionalized car factories were for the organizations of the industrial age. In the extreme professional service firm, capital has no importance, competence is critical, "economic rents" cannot be identified as the cost of professional employee inputs is equivalent to their share of value creation, and financial profits may offer no clues as to the actual value creation in the firm. Value creation must be assessed by the critical resource owners, i.e. primarily the professional experts. And what is considered value must be assessed in a multidimensional framework, where monetary returns only represent one of the dimensions. Stability is achieved through key people, rather than through a stable hierarchy, technology and production processes, or recurring tasks. And these people also serve as catalysts to value creating processes, thus turning other professionals into a potential source of competitive advantage.

At the core of this logic lies the recognition of the fact that knowledge intensive firms have to compete in two markets simultaneously, namely for the most competent people as well as for the most attractive contracts and clients. In fact, competitiveness in these firms is as much about getting the right people to come and to stay, as it is about getting the right clients to buy the services. For the traditional firm, it may be fruitful to look to the professional firm to learn from their practices, where applicable. Even though the professional service firms may have many flaws, in particular in terms of efficiency and resource utilization, these firms do have substantial experience in terms of how to handle individual resources with strong opinions and an awareness of alternative employers. As competence is becoming an increasingly important strategic resource even in traditional manufacturing firms, many of the challenges that are typical to professional service firms are becoming increasingly prevalent in other types of organizations as well.

In a professional environment, the manager who makes you want to come back tomorrow in order to learn more, makes the firm more competitive as (s)he improves the firm's ability to get more excellent people to work together for the firm. And this competitiveness is as important as the one of selling to clients and bringing in more revenues. Without the right people, the revenues are bound to suffer in the long run, and as a result, the firm must be competitive in both markets simultaneously. If this is the role model, the future sounds promising. That means that we try to extract the best from the professional service firms and extend their practices to other sectors, rather than force-fit the traditional models developed for manufacturing in the knowledge-intensive firms and industries.

Future research directions

Professional service firms are extreme in many of the dimensions which concern researchers and managers in most organizations: knowledge intensity, client responsiveness, individual commitment and creativity, flexibility and dynamism. As a result, more research needs to be conducted on the value creation processes in these firms, in order to both learn from them and hopefully help improve the efficiency of such value creation processes. No optimal organization structure has as yet been developed, and most firms still struggle with their attempts to find efficient ways of allocating responsibilities without destroying the motivation of those who must be managers. Similarly, we still do not have a complete understanding of professional motivation and loyalty, and further research is needed as to how highly educated individuals are attracted to firms, mobilized, and motivated to remain committed to the firm. What is the "glue" that sticks professionals together and tie them to the firm, and how is it developed? Insights from successful professional firms may also help others in more traditional firms develop better procedures for the motivation and retention of their best people.

In addition, we need more research into the actual content of value creation in firms that are not capital intensive, and here the professional service firms serve as excellent examples. Value creation, efficiency, productivity, quality etc. are all concepts which need to be redefined and further developed in the context of firms where intangibles dominate the resource base and where the inputs of each individual are not equivalent either in quantity or quality. Even at the aggregate level of national and international statistics, the terms used in the measurement of international trade, GNP evolution, labor hour productivity etc. are rather misleading when applied to professional services.

Finally, we need a better understanding of the organization of the year 2000 and beyond. We seem to be in the middle of a fundamental paradigm shift which may be as powerful as the one we experienced in the transition from an agricultural to an industrial society. Not only are services taking over the dominant position in Western societies, but the impact of value creation based on capital investments and large corporations is decreasing whereas intelligence and competence based value creation is rapidly increasing. The impacts of this fundamental shift are not distinguishable at this point, yet we are beginning to see some indications, especially in organizations where capital owners and managers have very limited power. Flexible organizations, empowered individuals with substantial responsibilities for the totality of the firm, management as a set of distributed and temporary roles, and constantly changing activities are phenomena that are likely to become much more common over the next two or three decades. Maybe the professional service firm will no longer be an anomaly in the year 2025, but rather the most common type of organization?

Conclusions

This book has explored a number of fascinating, but also difficult, challenges facing managers in professional service firms. As a result of this detailed analysis, I would like to highlight three main conclusions:

1) The challenges involved in professional service firm management are extreme, especially because the firms compete on two dimensions simultaneously: They compete to get the best clients and projects, in which they are able to deliver superior value in comparison with their competitors. And they also compete to get and retain the best "production factors", i.e. the professionals who can deliver such superior value. Competitiveness vis à vis the client requires superior professionals. Competitiveness vis à vis the professionals requires a portfolio of challenging clients or projects, prospects of future learning as well as earnings, a positive and creative environment where the interaction with highly qualified peers enhances personal development, excellent support in terms of systems as well as staff, and, above all, managers who are able to bring out the best in all the people involved.

Firms are excellent at focussing on the needs of clients as well as techniques and procedures to ensure high quality service. In addition, professionals are trained both individually and collectively to emphasize client service above all else. Hence, the issue of quality control and competitiveness vis à vis the client is not the most difficult to handle. Rather, the major challenge lies in balancing the attempts to increase efficiency with the demands of individual professionals for autonomy, creativity, and interpersonal trust. As a result, the managerial challenges are at the core of professional service firm success, and the potential is substantial for improvement as well as disasters when it comes to the management of people!

2) The flexibility of professional service firms in terms of choosing both what to deliver, how, where, and to whom is extreme, and this flexibility may be deceptive. Professional service firm managers may be misled to think that as long as each new project adds value, each new hire is excellent, and all professionals are kept busy with billable activities, all is well. Whereas it seems to be the case that professional service firms can live with substantial amounts of uncertainty and even chaos, their accumulation of intangible resources both in terms of competence and reputation is bound to suffer if the firm is unable to develop and communicate a clear and consistent profile. Not only is the flexibility of the firm dangerous for the development of competitive strength through intangible resources, but the very flexibility and autonomy of individual professionals leads to a situation in which the maintenance of a clear profile requires continuous monitoring and intervention by those in charge of strategic management.

3) The fact that professional service firms are extreme and far from equivalent to the traditional manufacturing firms that serve as the explicit or implicit foundation for most theories and models in strategic management makes it extremely important for professional service firm managers to beware of an automatic adoption of concepts and frameworks that are still dominant in the academic as well as the popular business press. A number of the seemingly inevitable processes affecting firms of all kinds, such as the desire to grow, to establish additional offices, to internationalize, and to increase market share, may be extremely detrimental to professional service firms where flexibility and innovation lies at the core of value creation and where economies of scale are unlikely to exist. As a result, managers must develop and communicate clear priorities, and make conscious efforts to avoid being side-tracked by all the interesting competitive challenges presented to them. It may be very difficult to resist the temptation to compete for yet another contract against the same arch-rival firm, when all the professionals are overextended. And it may be equally difficult to reject an offer for a contract for one of the favorite clients, when the services requested involve the development of intangible assets that fall

outside the scope of the strategic profile. However, for the firm that intends to remain flexible and innovative, restraining growth may be critical to future performance.

Professional service firm management concerns the management of a true "people-business", where the relationships between people are critical to competitiveness both in the market for client contracts and in the market for excellent professionals. As a result, strategic management in professional service firms needs to be upgraded and all the activities involved in the development and maintenance of positive spirals of value creation need to be emphasized as the core activities they really are in such a context. In the extreme, superior strategic management may be the only area in which the professional service firm has the potential for developing a core competence and maintaining a superior position in both the market for professionals and the market for contracts and clients in the long run!

Appendix 1

Current research on professional service firms and related topics

Since I started the work on my dissertation study back in the late 1980-ies, a lot has happened when it comes to research on professional service firms as well as research on alternative theoretical approaches, such as the resource based view, that are highly relevant to managers and students of professional service firms. In this appendix I will try to highlight some of the developments that I think are particularly valuable, but I would like to caution the reader that this is my own personal and surely biased perspective. I am sure there are a lot of interesting things going on in the world without my knowing about it. And if I have left someone out or forgotten some people, please forgive me. I am not trying to write a complete "who's who" of professional service firm research, but rather to give the reader some more places to look for additional readings on the topic.

I have divided this appendix into four sections:

Research on the resource based view and related areas

When it comes to research on strategy and competitive advantage from a resource based perspective, this is no longer a new or peripheral area, but rather more or less main-stream. At the Academy of Management, the largest annual conference for researchers in the entire management area, the Business Policy and Strategy division – which is the largest in the Academy – always presents a large number of papers based in the resource based view of the firm. The same is true for the Strategic Management Society, which also has annual meetings.

The researchers with a strong foundation in this area are so many that it is impossible to remember and name all of them, but these are the names of some of the people who have recently and/or are currently publishing in this field: Jay Barney, Russ Coff, Kathleen Eisenhardt, Nicolai Foss, Connie Helfat, Steven Lippman, Tammy Madsen, Joe Mahoney, Richard Makadok, Jeffrey Martin, Anita McGahan, Rita G. McGrath, Margaret Peteraf, Haridimos Tsukas, Richard Rumelt, Harbir Singh, Gabriel Szulanski, Gordon Walker, Sidney Winter, Maurizio Zollo. Some of these people publish more on other topics, based in other theoretical traditions. Similarly, some of the early "pioneers" of this field are, to the best of my knowledge, not currently doing research within this perspective, but it may still be worthwhile looking up their contributions: Raffi Amit, Kathleen Conner, Robert M. Grant, J.-C. Spender, David Teece, Birger Wernerfelt.

A good starting point for looking into current research on the resource based view of the firm is the October 2003 Special Issue of the Strategic Management Journal, edited by David Hoopes, Tammy Madsen, and Gordon Walker, with the following theme: "Why is there a Resource-based View? Toward a Theory of Competitive Heterogeneity". Many of the above listed researchers were contributors to this special issue. Similarly, two earlier special issues of the same journal also relate to the same topic: "The evolution of firm capabilities", edited by Connie Helfat and published in October 2000, and " Knowledge and the Firm", edited by Robert Grant and J.-C. Spender, published in December 1996.

From my perspective, three important debates have taken place (and are still going on) within this perspective: The first has to do with the importance of dynamic capabilities as opposed to a static assessment of the resources available in the firm. This debate goes back to Teece, Pisano & Shuen, 1989 or 1997, but also has roots all the way back to Edith Penrose's original point (1959) that it is not the resources you have, but rather how you use them, that determines whether or not a firm is able to generate profits or develop sustainable competitive advantage. The other has to do with the importance of owning or controlling firm resources, which is contrasted with a more network oriented perspective on firm competitiveness, where it is not so much the resources that a firm has that determines the value creation, but rather the resources the firm can mobilize (see e.g. Haanes, 1997). The third has to do with whether or not a resource based analysis has to be based in traditional positivistic microeconomic assumptions. First of all, I do not think that microeconomic analyses of phenomena related to firm performance and competitive advantage are such a bad idea, and many of the economics-based researchers who publish within the resource based view are thoughtful and wise scholars, far from the charicatured hard-headed positivists people from other disciplines fear the most. While it is true that a lot of the research conducted within the resource based view has been based in microeconomic theory, this is not true for all the research. And my personal view is that other theoretical perspectives such as knowledge development, organizational learning, and critical organization theory can help inform resource based research in

innovative and exciting ways. The challenge is to bridge different traditions by making different viewpoints complementary, rather than mutually exclusive. I think these debates are healthy and of great interest to
researchers trying to understand the competitiveness of professional service firms, and I am sure many more interesting research contributions
will be published over the years to come.

Research on professional service firms

When it comes to research on professional service firms, I am pleased to
say that the situation is similar to that of the resource based view. While it
is not true that research on professional services has become mainstream,
what is true is that a whole sequence of specialized conferences have been
taking place both at the University of Alberta, headed up by Royston
Greenwood and Bob Hinings, and at Oxford University, where Laura
Empson is in charge. Both of these universities have their own centers for
professional service firm research, and have published a large number of
publications in this area over the years. In addition, a special track at the
European Group for Organization Studies (EGOS) has been established,
attracting about 30 researchers from all over the world every year. This
track is headed by Royston Greenwood and Celeste Wilderom. And at the
Academy of Management, several panels and papers have been presented
to a wider audience over the last few years.

In other words, this stream of research is alive and well, and I find at
least four developments in this area to be particularly encouraging. The
first is the number of doctoral dissertations coming out in this area. That
means that future faculty are interested in devoting (at least parts of) their
careers to these particularly interesting organizations. The second is the
truly international nature of this research, taking place both in Europe,
North America, and Australia. The third is the continued multi-discipli-
nary nature of this stream of research. To me, that is a clear sign of good
health. The final is that the research stream seems to be maturing in the
sense that we move from general studies of one firm or one industry, to
either cross-industry comparisons or much more issue specific studies on
topics such as mergers and acquisitions between professional service firms
(e.g. Greenwood, Hinings, and Brown, 1994; Coff, 1999; Empson, 2000;
2001), the management of human resources (e.g. Coff, 1997), incentives
and compensation (Peter Sherer and Ashley Pinnington, among others),
knowledge and professional organizations (two special issues: Human Re-

lations, 2001, edited by Laura Empson, and Organization Studies, 2003, edited by Bob Hinings and Huseyin Leblebici), critical perspectives on knowledge intensive firms (e.g. Alvesson, numerous articles), and so on. In addition, there is clearly a sense of cumulative knowledge development within the research community, and that is very nice to see!

Research on "strategy as practice" or "organizing and strategizing"

Another interesting development in strategy and organization research is the increased emphasis on understanding what actually goes on when people and firms "make" strategies, or when strategies "emerge". Where do they come from? What makes some of them survive, while others disappear? Who participates in making or shaping or adopting the strategies? Good examples of such streams of research are presented in two special issues: One edited by Johnson, Melin, and Whittington, in Journal of Management Studies, 2001, and the other forthcoming (2005) in Human Relations, edited by Jarzakowski, Balogun, and Seidl. Parts of this stream of research are also anchored in a special track at the annual EGOS-conference, but it has also been presented to a wider audience, e.g. at the Strategic Management Society conferences.

Since most professional service firms are not hierarchical in the same sense as traditional manufacturing firms, studies that take as a starting point that "top management" can respond in a representative way on behalf of "the firm" are not particularly well suited. I therefore find the emergence and wide acceptance of this micro-oriented stream of research very encouraging.

Research on organizations in the knowledge economy

Finally, I also wanted to highlight another trend in strategy and organizational research, which has been going on for quite a number of years, and that has to do with attempting to develop alternative theories and models to the traditional positivistic (largely microeconomics based), industrial, and general theories of the 1970ies and 1980ies. For a while we really believed that there could be general models such as the multidivisional organization (e.g. Chandler, 1962 and later) and the value chain (Porter, 1985), applicable to all kinds of firms in all contexts and at all times. We now know that this is not true, and a large number of researchers are working to figure out how to better support the processes of strategizing and organizing in different kinds of firms. Together with my colleague Øivind Revang, I published an article back in 1998 which discussed challenges from increasingly demanding customers and from increasingly demanding employees. We argued that this reality is facing more and more firms in more and more contexts, but also that professional service firms represent firms and managers that have been struggling with these issues for decades, and that we therefore can learn a lot from studying professional service firms, even when it comes to other types of firm contexts.

Quite a few researchers are concerned with these issues, and again I can particularly recommend a "special issue", this time the inaugural issue of the new journal European Management Review – the journal of the European Academy of Management. It was published in spring 2004, and edited by Pierre Dussauge, with a particular emphasis on the "post-industrial" or "after-modern" context or current challenges to strategy and organization research. Another highly recommended volume is the Handbook of strategy and management, edited by Pettigrew, Thomas, and Whittington (2002). It contains a large number of refreshing and thoughtful discussions about challenges we are facing in strategy and management research, and where we may go from here, as well as thoughtful introductory and concluding chapters trying to set the stage for future and more pluralistic "after modern" research.

Conclusion

Many more areas of research could have been highlighted and discussed here, but somehow there is a need to set a limit. I do not argue that these streams of research are the most important at the moment. Only that these are four streams of research that I personally see as particularly fruitful for professional service firm researchers – and maybe also practitioners.

Appendix 2

Bente R. Løwendahl is a professor at BI Norwegian School of Management in Oslo, Norway. Her education includes a "Siviløkonom" degree (Master of Science in Economics and Business Administration) from the Norwegian School of Economics and Business Administration (NHH) in Bergen, Norway, and a Ph.D. in Strategy from Wharton, University of Pennsylvania, Philadelphia, USA. Her research interests are centered around the strategic management of professional service firms, the motivation and mobilization of knowledge workers regardless of organizational context, and the organizational, strategic and managerial challenges resulting from an increasingly knowledge intensive – as opposed to industrial – economy.

Professor Løwendahl has conducted and chaired a number of studies on professional service firms from a number of different industries (Engineering design, Management consulting, PR and Communication consulting, IT consulting, Law, and Advertising), and is currently supervising two Ph.D. dissertation studies in this area. She is also an active member of the networks of professional service firm researchers, both at EGOS (The European Group on Organization Studies) and at Oxford University/University of Alberta. She is an active member of the Academy of Management, Business Policy and Strategy division (previous executive committee member), Strategic Management Society, interest group on Knowledge and Innovation (representative at large in the governing committee), and the Organizational Knowledge, Learning, and Capabilities network (OKLC).

Bente R. Løwendahl teaches in a number of different programs at BI Norwegian School of Management, with particular emphasis on the MSc, MBA, Executive, and doctoral programs. Selected publications are listed in the reference list at the back of this book.

Index of key terms

Bibliography

Aharoni, Y. (Ed). 1993. Coalitions and Competition: The globalization of professional services. London: Routledge.

Aharoni, Y. & Nachum, L. (Eds.) 2000. The Globalization of services: Some Implications for Theory and Practice, in the Routledge Series: Studies in International Business and the World Economy, Routledge.

Ahrnell, B.-M. & Nicou, M. 1989. Kunnskapsföretagets marknadsföring: Att utveckla förtroande, relationer och kompetens. Liber.

Alvesson, M. 1989. Ledning av kunskapsföretag. Stockholm: Norstedts.

Alvesson, M. 1993. "Organizations as Rhetoric: Knowledge-Intensive Firms and the Struggle with Ambiguity." Journal of Management Studies, 30(6): pp. 997-1015.

Alvesson, M. 1994. "Talking in Organizations: Managing Identity and Impressions in an Advertising Agency." Organization Studies, 15(4): pp. 535-563.

Alvesson, M. 1995. Management of Knowledge Intensive Companies. Berlin/New York: de Gruyter.

Alvesson, M. 2000. "Social Identity and the Problem of Loyalty in Knowledge-Intensive Companies." Journal of Management Studies, 37(8): pp. 1101-1123.

Alvesson, M. 2001. "Knowledge Work: Ambiguity, Image and Identity." Human Relations, 54 (7): pp. 863-886.

Alvesson, M. & Köping, A.S. 1993. Med känslan som ledstjärna – En studie av reklambyråer. Lund: Studentlitteratur.

Amit, R. & Schoemaker, P. 1993. "Strategic Asssets and Organizational Rent", Strategic Management Journal, 14, pp. 33-46.

Ansoff, I. 1967. Corporate strategy, Revised edition, 1987. London, UK: Penguin Books.

Babson College. 1993. Transforming the Global Organization: Integrating the Business, People, and Information Technology at Camp Dresser & McKee Inc. Teaching case developed by R. M. Kesner.

Barney, J. B. 1991. "Firm Resources and sustained competitive advantage." Journal of Management, 17, pp. 99-120.

Barney, J.B. & Hansen, M.H. 1994. Trustworthiness as a Source of Competitive Advantage. Strategic Management Journal, Winter Special Issue, 15: pp. 175-190.

Bartlett, C.A. & Ghoshal, S.1989. Managing Across Borders; The Transnational Solution. Boston, MA: Harvard Business School Press.

Blau, P.M. & Scott, W.R. 1962. Formal organizations: A comparative approach. San Francisco, CA: Chandler.

Black, J.A. & Boal, K.B. 1994. "Strategic resources: Traits, configurations, and paths to sustainable competitive advantage." Strategic Management Journal, 15, pp.134-148.

Blackler, F. 1995. "Knowledge, Knowledge Work and Organizations: An Overview and Interpretation. Organization Studies", 16(6): pp. 1021-1046.

Bobrick, B. 1985. Parsons Brinckerhoff; The First Hundred Years. New York: Van Nostrand Reinhold.

Bower, M. 1966. The will to manage. New York: McGraw Hill.

Bradach, J. L. & R. G. Eccles. 1989. "Price, Authority, and Trust: From Ideal Types to Plural Forms." Annual Review of Sociology: pp. 97-118.

Coff, R. 1997. "Human Assets and Management Dilemmas; Coping with hazards on the road to resouce-based theory". Academy of Management Review, 22 (2), pp. 374-402.

Coff, R. 1999. "How Buyers Cope with Uncertainty when Acquiring Firms in Knowledge-Intensive Industries: Caveat Emptor". Organization Science, 10(2): pp. 144-161.

Coff, R. 1999b. "When competitive advantage doesn't lead to performance: The resource-based view and stakeholder bargaining power.

Cooper, D.J., Hinings, B., Greenwood, R. & Brown, J.T. 1996. "Sedimentation and Transformation in Organizational Change: The Case of Canadian Law Firms." Organization studies, 17 (4): pp. 623-639.

Crossan, M., Lane, H.W. & White, R.E. 1999. "An Organizational Learning Framework: From Intuition to Institution." Academy of Management Review, 24 (3): pp. 522-537.

Czepiel, J.A.; Solomon, M.R.; Surprenant, C. F. 1985. The service encounter: Managing Employee/Customer Interaction in Service Businesses. Lexington Books.

Easterby-Smith, M., Crossan, M. & Nicolini, D. 2000. "Organizational Learning: Debates Past, Present and Future." Journal of Management Studies, 37(6): pp. 783-796.

Eccles, R. G. & Crane, D. B. 1988. Doing Deals; Investment banks at work. Boston, MA: Harvard Business School Press.

Eccles, R. G. & D. B. Crane. 1987. "Managing Through Networks in Investment Banking." California Management Review, Fall, pp. 176-195.

Edvardsson, B. & Gummesson, E. E. 1988. Management i tjänstesam-hället. Stockholm, Sweden: Liber.

Eiglier, P. & Langeard, E. 1987. Servuction: Le marketing des services. Paris, France: McGraw Hill.

Eisenhardt, K.E. & Martin, J.A. 2000. "Dynamic Capabilities: What are They?" Strategic Management Journal, Special Issue on The Evolution of Firm Capabilities, 21: pp. 1105-1121.

Engineering News Record. 1990. "Designers seek the global edge; the top 200 international design firms." Engineering News Record (ENR) August 2, pp. 46-61.

Engineering News Record. 1989. "Foreign design billings drift higher; The top 200 international design firms." Engineering News Record (ENR) August 10, pp. 42-52.

Empson, L. 2000. Mergers Between Professional Service Firms: Exploring an Undirected Process of Integration. *Advances in Mergers and Acquisitions*, 1: pp. 205-237.

Empson, L. 2001. (Ed.) Special issue: Knowledge management in professional service firms. Human Relations. 54(7).

Empson, L. 2001. Fear of Exploitation and Fear of Contamination: Impediments to Knowledge Transfer in Mergers Between Professional Service Firms. *Human Relations*, 54 (7): pp. 839-862.

Etzioni, A. 1961. A comparative analysis of complex organizations. New York: Free Press

Fama, E. F. & M. C. Jensen. 1983. "Separation of Ownership and Control." Journal of Law and Economics 26: pp. 301-325.

Fiol, C.M. 1991. "Managing Culture as a Competitive Resource: An Identity-Based View of Sustainable Competitive Advantage." Journal of Management, 17(1): pp. 191-211.

FORTUNE. 1965. (Guzzardi, W. J.) "The Men Who Came to Dinner." February, pp. 138-141, 236-238.

Fosstenløkken, S.M. forthcoming 2005. Competence development for competitive advantage – a study of four professional service firms (tentative title). BI Norwegian School of Management Ph.D. Dissertation Series. Oslo, Norway.

Fosstenløkken, S.M., Løwendahl, B.R. & Revang, Ø. 2003. "Knowledge development through client interaction: A comparative study." Organization Studies, Special Issue: Knowledge and Professional Organizations. 24(6): pp. 859-879.

Freeman, R. E. 1984. Strategic management: A stakeholder approach. Boston, MA: Pitman.

Gouldner, A. 1957-58. Cosmopolitans and Locals: Towards an analysis of latent social roles I and II, Administrative Science Quarterly, Vol 2, No 3 and 4.

Grant, R.M. 1991. "The Resource Based Theory of Competitive Advantage: Implications for strategy formulation", California Management Review, Spring, 114-135.

Grant, R.M. 1996. "Toward a knowledge-based theory of the firm." Strategic Management Journal, Winter special issue on Knowledge and the Firm, 17, pp. 109-122.

Grant, R.M. & Spender, J.-C. (Eds.) 1996. Strategic Management Journal, Winter special issue on Knowledge and the Firm, 17.

Greenwood, R. & Empson, L. 2003. "The Professional Partnership: Relic or Exemplary Form of Governance?" Organization Studies, 24(6), pp. 909-933.

Greenwood, R.; C. R. Hinings & J. Brown. 1990. "P2-form" strategic management: Corporate practices in professional partnerships." Academy of Management Journal 33:4, pp.725-755.

Greenwood, R., Hinings, C.R. & Brown, J. 1994. Merging Professional Service Firms. *Organization Science*, 5 (2): pp. 239-258.

Greiner, L. E. & Metzger, R. O. 1983. Consulting to Management. Englewood Cliffs, NJ: Prentice Hall.

Groth, L. 1997. Building Organisations with Information Technology – Opportunities and Constraints in the Search for New Organisation Forms. Dr.Oecon. Dissertation, Norwegian School of Economics and Business Administration.

Groth, L. 1999. Organizational Design; The Scope for the IT-based Enterprise. Wiley UK.

Grönroos, C. 1985. Strategic Management and Marketing in the Service Sector. Lund, Sweden: Studentlitteratur.

Haanes, K. Mobilizing Resources.1997. Ph.D. Dissertation, Copenhagen Business School.

Hansen, M., Nohria, N. & Tierney, T. 1999. "What's your strategy for managing knowledge?" Harvard Business Review, March-April, pp. 106-116.

Hall, R. 1992. "The strategic analysis of intangible resources." Strategic Management Journal, 13, pp. 135-144.

Hamel, G. & Heene, A. (Eds) 1994. Competence Based Competition. Chichester: Wiley.

Hedberg, B. 1990. "Exit, Voice, and Loyalty in Knowledge-Intensive Firms." Paper presented at the Panel on the Management and Strategies of Knowledge-Intensive Firms, 10th Annual Conference of the Strategic Management Society, Stockholm, Sweden, September 24-27 1990.

Hedlund, G. & Nonaka, I. 1993. "Models of knowledge management in the West and Japan." In: Lorange, P., Chakhravarthy, B. Roos, J. & Van de Ven, A. (Eds) Implementing strategic processes: Change, learning and cooperation. Oxford: Blackwell. pp. 117-144.

Helfat, C. 2000. (Ed.) Strategic Management Journal, Special Issue on The Evolution of Firm Capabilities, 21(10-11): October-November.

Heskett, J. L. 1986. Managing in the Service Economy. Boston, MA: Harvard Business School Press.

Higdon, H. 1969. The business healers. New York: Random House.

Hinings, C.R.(Bob) & Leblebici, H. (Eds). 2003. Special Issue: Knowledge and Professional Organizations. Organization Studies. 24(6).

Hirsch, S. 1993. "The globalization of services and service-intensive goods industries." In: Aharoni, Y. (Ed). 1993. Coalitions and Competition: The globalization of professional services. London: Routledge, pp. 66-78.

Hitt, M.A., Bierman, L., Shimizu, K. & Kochhar, R. 2001. „Direct and Moderating Effects of Human Capital on Strategy and Performance in Professional Service Firms: A Resource-Based Perspective." Academy of Management journal, 44(1): pp. 13-29.

Hoopes, D.G.; Madsen, T. & Walker, G. (Eds.) 2003. Strategic Management Journal, Special Issue on: Why is there a resource-based view of the firm? Toward a theory of competitive heterogeneity. 24(10), October.

Hughes, E. C. 1958. Men and Their Work. Glencoe, IL: Free Press.

Itami, H. 1987. Mobilizing Invisible Assets. Cambridge, MA: Harvard University Press.

Jarzabkowski, P., Balogun, J. & Seidl, D. (Eds) forthcoming late 2005. Special issue on Strategizing: The challenges of a practice perspective. Human Relations.

Johnson, G., Melin, L. & Whittington, R. (Eds) 2003. Special issue on micro-strategy and strategizing. Journal of Management Studies. 40.

Johnson, G., Melin, L. & Whittington, R. 2003. "Micro-strategy and strategizing: Towards an activity-based-view. Journal of Management Studies. 2001. Special issue on micro-strategy and strategizing. 40: pp. 1-22.

Kogut, B. & Zander, U. 1992. "Knowledge of the firm, combinative capabilities, and the replication of technology". Organization Science, 3, pp. 383-397.

Kogut, B. 1996. "What Firms Do? Coordination, Identity, and Learning." Organization Science, 7 (5): 502-518.

Koppang, H. & Løwendahl, B. R. 1995. "Advise us what to do; decide for us." In: Høivik, H. v. W. & Føllesdal, A. (Eds.) Ethics and consultancy: European Perspectives. London: Kluwer.

Kotler, P. & R. A. Jr. Connor. 1977. "Marketing professional services." Journal of Marketing, January, pp. 71-76.

Kubr, M. (Ed.) 1980/1996. Management consulting: A guide to the profession. Geneva, Switzerland: ILO. 3rd (revised) edition 1996.

Levine, S. & P. E. White. 1961. "Exchange as a conceptual framework for the study of interorganizational relationships." Administrative Science Quarterly, No 5, pp. 583-601.

Levitt, T. 1981. "Marketing intangible products and product intangibles." Harvard Business Review : May-June.

Lippman, S.A. & Rumelt, R.P. 2003. "The payments perspective; Microfoundations of resource analysis." Strategic Management Journal, Special Issue on: Why is there a resource-based view of the firm? Toward a theory of competitive heterogeneity. 24(10): pp. 903-927.

Lovelock, C. H. 1983. "Classifying services to gain strategic marketing insights." Journal of Marketing, 47 (Summer): pp. 9-20.

Lovelock, C. H. Ed. 1988. Managing Services: Marketing, Operations, and Human Resources. London, UK: Prentice Hall Int.

Lowendahl, B.R. 1992. Global strategies for professional business service firms. Unpublished Ph.D. Dissertation. Philadelphia, PA: The Wharton School, University of Pennsylvania.

Lowendahl, B.R. 1993. "Co-operative strategies for professional service firms: unique opportunities and challenges". In Aharoni, Y. (Ed). 1993. Coalitions and Competition: The globalization of professional services. London: Routledge, pp. 161-177.

Løwendahl, B.R. 2000. "The globalization of professional service firms – Fad or genuine source of competitive advantage?." In Aharoni, Y. & Nachum, L. (Eds.), The globalisation of services: Some Implications for Theory and Practice, in the Routledge Series: Studies in International Business and the World Economy, Routledge.

Løwendahl, B. R. & Nordhaug, O. 1994. OL 1994 – Inspirasjonskilde for framtidens næringsliv? Oslo: TANO.

Løwendahl, B.R. & Revang, Ø. 1998. "Challenges to Existing Strategy Theory in a Post Industrial Society." Strategic Management Journal, Vol.19, pp. 755-773.

Løwendahl, B.R. & Revang, Ø. 2000. "On Strategic Assets in a Post-Industrial World: Matching Customers and Competence through Organizational Forms." Global Focus.

Løwendahl, B.R. & Revang, Ø. 2004. "Achieving results in an after-modern context: thoughts on the role of strategizing and organizing." European Management Review,1(1): pp. 49-54.

Løwendahl, B.R.; Revang, Ø. & Fosstenløkken, S.M. 2001. "Knowledge and value creation in PSFs: A Framework for Analysis". Human Relations 54 (7), pp. 911-931.

Maister, D.H. 1982. Balancing the Professional Service Firm. *Sloan Management Review*, 24 (1): 15-29.

Maister, D.H. 1993. Managing the professional service firm. Free Press.

Maister, D.H. 1997. True Professionalism. – The courage to care about your people, your clients, and your career. New York: Simon & Schuster.

Maister, D.H. 2001. Practice what you Preach – What managers must do to create a high achievement culture. New York: Simon & Schuster/ Free Press.

Maister, D.H.; Green, C.H. & Galford, Robert M. 2000. The Trusted AdvisorNew York: Simon & Schuster/Free Press.

Makadok, R. 2001. "Toward a synthesis of the resource-based and the dynamic capability views of rent creation." Strategic Management Journal, 22(5): pp. 387-401.

Makadok, R. 2003. "Doing the right thing and knowing the right thing to do: Why the whole is greater than the sum of its parts. Strategic Management Journal, Special Issue on: Why is there a resource-based view of the firm? Toward a theory of competitive heterogeneity. 24(10): pp. 1043-1055.

Manz, Charles C. & Sims, H.P. 1989. Super-leadership. Leading others to lead themselves. New York: Prentice Hall.

March, J.G. 1991. "Exploration and exploitation in organizational learning." Organization Science, 2: pp. 71-87.

McGrath, R.G., MacMillan, I.C. & Venkataraman, S. 1995. "Defining and Developing Competence: A Strategic Process Paradigm." Strategic Management Journal, 16(4): pp. 251-275.

Miller, D. & Shamsie, J. 1996. "The Resource-based View of the Firm in Two Environments: The Hollywood Film Studios From 1936 to 1965." Academy of Management Journal, 39: pp. 519-543.

Mills, Peter K. 1986. Managing service industries. Cambridge, MA: Ballinger.

Mintzberg, H. 1978. "Patterns in strategy formation." Management Science 24:9, pp. 934-948.

Mintzberg, H. 1983. Structure in fives; Designing effective organizations. Englewood Cliffs, NJ: Prentice Hall.

Mintzberg, H. & A. McHugh. 1985. "Strategy formation in an adhocracy." Administrative Science Quarterly 30: pp. 160-197.

Mintzberg, H. & J. A. Waters. 1985. "Of Strategies, Deliberate and Emergent." Strategic Management Journal 6: pp. 257-272.

Mintzberg, H., Quinn, J. B. & Ghoshal, S. 1995. The strategy process; European Edition. London: Prentice Hall International.

Morgan, G. 1986. Images of Organisation. Beverly Hills, CA: Sage.

Morris, T. & Empson, L. 1998. "Organization and Expertise: An exploration of knowledge bases and the management of accounting and consulting firms". Accounting, Organizations and Society, 23 (5-6), pp. 609-24.

Nelson, R. R. & Winter, S. G. 1982. An evolutionary theory of economic change. Cambridge, MA: Belknap.

Newell, S; Robertson, M; Scarbrough, H & Swan, J. 2002. Managing Knowledge Work. New York: Palgrave.

Nonaka, I. & Takeuchi, H. 1995. The knowledge creating company. New York: Oxford University Press.

Nonaka, I., Toyama, R. & Konno, N. 2000. "SECI, Ba and Leadership: A unified model of dynamic knowledge creation." Long Range Planning, 33(1), pp. 5-34.

Nordhaug, O. 1994. Human Capital in Organizations: Competence, training and learning. Oslo: Scandinavian University Press.

Normann, R. 1983. Service Management: Ledelse og strategi i produksjon av tjenester. Oslo, Norway: Bedriftsøkonomens forlag.

Normann, R. 1984. Service Management. New York: Wiley.

Normann, R. & Ramírez, R. 1993. From Value Chain to Value Constellation: Designing Interactive Strategy. Harvard Business Review, JUL-AUG, pp.65-77.

Ogilvy, D. 1988. Confessions of an Advertising Man, 2nd ed. New York. NY: Atheneum.

Orlikowski, W.J. 2002. "Knowing in Practice: Enacting a Collective Capability in Distributed Organizing." Organization Science, 13(3): pp. 249-273.

Ouchi, W. G. 1980. "Markets, Bureaucracies, and Clans."Administrative Science Quarterly, 25 (March), pp. 129-141.

Palmer, R. E. 1987. "Trends in international management: Toward federations of equals." Business Quarterly 52:1 (Summer).

Penrose, E. T. 1959. The Theory of the Growth of the Firm. New York: Wiley.

Perlmutter, Howard. 1969. "The tortuous evolution of the Multinational Corporation." Columbia Journal of World Business. Vol. 4, pp. 9-18.

Peteraf, M.A. 1993. "The Cornerstones of Competitive Advantage: A Resource-Based View." Strategic Management Journal, 14: pp. 179-191.

Pettigrew, A.; Thomas, H. & Whittington, R. 2002. Handbook of Strategy and Management. London: Sage.

Pfeffer, J. & Salancik, G. R. 1978. The external control of organizations; A resource dependence perspective. New York, NY: Harper & Row.

Porter, M. E. 1980. Competitive Strategy. New York: Free Press.

Porter, M. E. 1985. Competitive Advantage: Creating and Sustaining Superior Performance. New York: Free Press.

Porter, Michael E. 1986. "Competition in Global Industries: A Conceptual Framework In: Porter. M.E. (Ed.) Competition in Global Industries. Cambridge, MA: Harvard Business School Press, pp 15-60.

Prahalad, C. K. & G. Hamel. 1990. "The core competence of the corporation." Harvard Business Review 63:3 (May-Jun) pp. 79-91.

Prahalad, C. K. & G. Hamel. 1994. Competing for the future. Cambridge, MA: Harvard Business School Press.

Quinn, J. B.; Mintzberg, H. & James, R. M. 1988. The strategy process; Concepts, contexts, and cases. Englewood Cliffs, NJ: Prentice Hall.

Quinn, J. B. & Mintzberg, H. 1991. The strategy process; Concepts, contexts, and cases. 2nd ed. Englewood Cliffs, NJ: Prentice Hall.

Raelin, J.A. 1985/1991. The clash of cultures – Managers Managing Professionals. Boston, MA: Harvard Business School Press (Paperback edition).

Ramírez, R. 1999. "Value Co-production: Intellectual Origins and Implications for Practice and Research." Strategic Management Journal, 20: pp. 49-65.

Robertson, M., Scarbrough, H. & Swan, J. 2003. "Knowledge Creation in Professional Service Firms: Institutional Effects." Organization Studies, 24(6): pp. 831-857.

Robertson, M. & Swan, J. 1998. "Modes of Organizing in an Expert Consultancy: A Case Study of Knowledge." Organization, 5(4): pp. 543-564.

Rumelt, R. P. 1984. "Towards a Strategic Theory of the Firm." In: Lamb, R. B. (Ed.) Competitive strategic management, pp. 556-570. Englewood Cliffs, NJ: Prentice-Hall.

Shostack, G. L. 1984. "Breaking free from product marketing." In: Lovelock, C. (Ed.): Services Marketing. pp. 37-47. Englewood Cliffs, NJ: Prentice Hall. Reprinted from Journal of Marketing, 1977. April.

Schön, D. A. 1983. The reflective practitioner; How professionals think in action. New York: Basic Books.

Sibson, R. E. 1971. Managing Professional Services Enterprises – The neglected business frontier. New York, NY: Pitman.

Spender, J.-C. 1996. "Making knowledge the basis of a dynamic theory of the firm". Strategic Management Journal, Winter special issue on Knowledge and the Firm, 17, pp. 45-62.

Stabell, C. & Fjeldstad, Ø. 1998. "Configuring value for competitive advantage: on chains, shops, and networks." Strategic Management Journal., pp.413-437.

Stacey, R. 1993. Strategic Management and Organizational Dynamics. London: Pitman. (or second edition 1996).

Starbuck, W.H. 1983. „Organizations as Action Creators." American Sociological Review, 48: pp. 91-102.

Stevens, M. 1985. The accounting wars. New York: MacMillan.

Stevens, M. 1981. The Big Eight. New York: MacMillan.

Sveiby, K. E. & Risling, A. 1987. Kunnskapsbedriften. Oslo, Norway: Cappelen.

Szulanski, G. 1996. "Exploring Internal Stickiness: Impediments to the Transfer of Best Practice within the Firm." Strategic Management Journal, 17: pp. 27-43.

Teece, D. 1998. "Capturing Value From Knowledge Assets: The New Economy, Markets for Know-how, and Intangible Assets." California Management Review, 40(3): pp. 55-79.

Teece, D. J., Pisano, G. & Shuen, A. 1989. "Firm capabilities, resources and the concept of strategy." Working Paper, University of California at Berkeley, Berkeley, California.

Thomas, D. R. E. 1978. "Strategy is Different in Service Businesses." Harvard Business Review, Jul-Aug. pp. 158-165.

Thompson, J. D. 1967. Organizations in action. New York, NY: Mc Graw-Hill.

Tilles, S. 1961. "Understanding the consultant's role." Harvard Business Review, No 39: pp. 87-99.

Tsoukas, H. 1996. "The firm as a distributed knowledge system: A constructionist approach". Strategic Management Journal, Winter special issue on Knowledge and the Firm, 17, pp. 11-25.

Vollmer, H. M. & Mills, D. L. (Eds). 1966. Professionalization. Englewood Cliffs, NJ: Prentice Hall.

Webber, A. W. 1990. "Consensus, Continuity, and Common Sense: An Interview with Compaq's Rod Canion." Harvard Business Review

68:4, (July-August) pp. 114-123.

Weber, M. 1947. The theory of social and economic organization. Glencoe, IL: Free Press.

Weick, K. E. 1976. "Educational Organizations as Loosely Coupled Systems." Administrative Science Quarterly 21:March. : pp. 1-19.

Wernerfelt, B. 1984. "A Resource-based View of the Firm." Strategic Management Journal 5: pp. 171-180.

Williamson, O. 1975. Markets and Hierarchies. New York, NY: Free Press.

Williamson, O. E. 1985. The economic institutions of capitalism. New York, NY: Free Press.

Winch, G. & Schneider, E. 1993. „Managing The Knowledge-Based Organization: The Case of Architectural Practice." Journal of Management Studies, 30(6): pp. 923-938.

Winter, S.G. 1987. "Knowledge and Competence as Strategic Assets." In Teece, D.J. (Ed.) The competitive challenge. New York: Ballinger, pp. 159-184.

Winter, S.G. "Understanding dynamic capabilities." Strategic Management Journal, Special Issue on: Why is there a resource-based view of the firm? Toward a theory of competitive heterogeneity. 24(10): pp. 991-995.

Zollo, M. & Winter, S.G. 2002. "Deliberate Learning and the Evolution of Dynamic Capabilities." Organization Science, 13(3): pp. 339-351.